GRANTA

5

Editorial Correspondence: Granta, Box 666, King's College, Cambridge CB2 1ST. (0223) 315290.
All manuscripts are welcome but must be accompanied by a stamped, self-addressed envelope or they cannot be returned.

Subscriptions: For individuals, £10.00 for four issues; for institutions, £15.00 for four issues. Single copies and back issues available for £2.50 including postage.

Granta is photoset by the Cambridge University Library.

Limited Edition Reprint September 1989.

Granta gratefully acknowledges the assistance of the Eastern Arts Association.

Granta is represented in the U.K. by the Writers and Readers Publishing Cooperative, 144 Camden High Street, London NW1 0NE; **Granta** is represented in Europe by Anthony Melville, 14 Offard Road, London N1; **Granta** is distributed by MacDonald & Evans, Estover Road, Plymouth, Devon PL6 7EZ.

Cover illustration by Ian Pollock

ISSN 978-0-14-014579-3

Contents

GRANTA

DON BLOCH

THE MODERN COMMON WIND

Leprosy. *Amachere. Obukoma. Imbicho.* The Old Wind. The Big Wind. The Common Modern Wind. The Disease of the Two Bodies. What can we do? This disease catches you running both ways. If you are afraid of it, they say, then it will attack you. But they also say you must keep away from a person who is having it, or you will be the next one. Don't be afraid, and be afraid. Fine advice!

Really, this sickness is too dangerous. You are not supposed to speak the name, or the disease is attracted to you. And if any patient should come to you, or you pass one any place, along the road, by the market, at one of our pools or rivers, it makes no matter where, then you must not be rude. You *must* not. If you let a patient feel somehow ashamed, and leprosy patients, they are easily insulted, why when that patient dies, his *shieno* will be taking revenge. Then you will find how your own body begins rotting with leprosy in a serious way. That is the reason when old Opilo comes to borrow clothes,shirts, and trousers that cannot even fit him, we do not refuse. That one, the Man of a Hundred Rags, he gives the clothes back without washing them first. As if we were fools. As if we did not know to put them on our bodies like that wouldn't be the same as kissing his open wounds.

Still, no one likes to die alone! Every misery loves company. That is human. So when we see the old man cut his nails to drop them in our drinking water, we only smile back. We smile and go thirsty.

For the neighbours of a leprosy family, life is most hard. It is most hard and difficult, there is no denying. The heart is heavy always with hidden thoughts. Don't be afraid, and be afraid. What choice do we have really? Formerly it was better in the country. I am not talking about the English, when they ruled in the Wangas. No, earlier. Before religion came, I mean, the priests on their motor bikes. Those good men with their round faces that turn red in the sun. Or weren't they the first to insist how in the eyes of God every person is alike. A sick person and a healthy person, rich man and poor, both the same. Before them, people followed the ideas of our ancestors. Ignorant people. They would build huts for lepers away from human habitation, somewhere on the shore of a swiftly flowing river. There along the path you could leave some little raw food in baskets on the ground. Africans have never loved the sight of suffering. In those days no one needed to pretend not to be happy when one died. So quickly the leprosy body was just pushed into a shallow hole, turned over with sticks and covered with ashes. No one cut grass. No relatives, no neighbours were wailing. It was not good to open your lips and take in the air. Besides, wasn't such a patient dead in life anyway?

That was how the Bawanga near the town were thinking before the priests came. When such a one died it was a time for rejoicing. We buried a leprosy body so far outside the homestead, heaping up thorns and branches there to mark the spot for all time, so no one could walk there by mistake. Leprosy. It is such an infectious disease it cannot stop with death. Did it stop with the death of Asha Makokha? Tell me, if you think I am wrong.

Emmanuel

Asumani Tiema, that most famous *omufumu* of the Wangas, was having seven wives. Together they were bearing him seventy sons. His eldest wife gave him five sons who lived. Shebani was the first born.

Shebani's brothers have become diviners, too. All of them. He is the number one. He inherited the greatness of his father. People keep coming to see him, arriving from far, even from Uganda and Tanzania. When we are attending to the cows or digging the garden, we may see a man being steered up the path to Shebani's hut, we hear the visitor groaning as others hurry him on in a wheelbarrow. Later, sometimes on the same day, but sometimes on another day, we see the same sick man walking away under his own strength. Or patients come laid across the handlebars of a bicycle. Babies carried in baskets. Cows are brought, too. Why not? Don't cattle have stomachs, the breeding place of worms?

Tiema was selecting Shebani as his successor not merely because of his being the first born. Everyone could see he was having a good intelligence. At those times we were all sharing the same ignorance. If you got a letter, you took it on a stick with a split in one end and carried it about the country to find someone who could read for you. There were few schools. Teachers had to write on the clothes of pupils then. There wasn't much knowledge. Tiema taught Shebani many things.

But he was himself so learned that he knew the boy would need other teachers as well. He sent Shebani to study with doctors in all other parts of Kenya.

Shebani travelled out into the world. Wearing a white jellabah, he walked the roads with only the name of his father to help him win friends. That is how it happened Shebani was acquiring his powers. From each doctor he learned some special way of treatment. From one he heard to cure epilepsy disease by feeding the patient the liver of a dog ground up into fine flour, only telling the patient what he has eaten afterwards. From another – they all took him in, the famous healers of that time, welcoming him as a son – Shebani found out that *indwasi* was caused by jiggers in the stomach, their urine rolling down the legs through the veins so that it thickens the water. He has taught us to be telling the difference between *indwasi* and the swelling of legs that happens to a thief who is trapped through witchcraft. If you put a finger on the leg of an *indwasi* patient, the print stays there a long time. With thieves the finger leaves no mark. And it was long ago, too, that Shebani learned medicines to kill. Our African doctors save who they want to. Some, for a high price, will help you from an enemy, too.

Shebani was not yet a man of twenty and his face had already taken on the look it has now. As if some doctor made Shebani sleep and removed his both eyes to pound in a mortar and purify with fire until they were whole again; then trying to set the eyes back, the doctor found they were somehow a bit smaller and so they came to rest deeper in Shebani's skull. No one who comes to ask Shebani's help can ever forget the way he looks out of his eyes. The rest of his manners, that way of sweeping his arms when talking, the gestures of his fingers, how he repeats his phrases, speaking so slowly, the rest all developed later. The stare was his own when he came back from his studies. Even a person not believing in the power of his magic has still to be afraid of him. That then was finally the most important thing Shebani was learning from so many other doctors: the gift to overshadow, to convince.

When Shebani came back to Lubinu from his years of wandering, returning with what he had learned from so many masters, he was prouder than any man we had ever seen. Prouder than Tiema, even. His eyes flashed at us. His robe was whiter than the day he set out. (Not the same robe, he later told, another like the first, washed and washed and worn in the sun until it reached the brilliance of bone, fine as tissue, hanging to his ankles.) Shebani was fully informed with new understandings about the delicate balance of the body. Hardly more than a boy, the heir to Tiema was high and mighty. The story of his life since then has been one of humiliation. So many diseases Shebani can defeat. We know, we are his witnesses. Only one defeats him. Leprosy. What disease runs in the Tiema family?

Still today Shebani's eyes, they flash at us. No one can doubt that he is a proud man who has done miracles in helping patients recover from so many serious illnesses. At the same time Shebani is humble. He has had to accept defeat. The first time was the day he returned from his travels through the world and learned how things were with Asha Makokha.

Not that anybody told him. Finding out by himself, that increased the shock. It isn't of course the first thing you rush to say to someone who is being welcomed home. Shebani had only one remark from his old mother to warn him. She cautioned him not to return to the former kitchen. He shouldn't be going near there, not for any reason. Tiema, too ill to rise up, lay in the dark of his hut calling his first-born's name. There was joy to see on the old one's face when Shebani kneeled and kissed his hands. Shebani stayed with his father to describe his studies. Slowly Tiema's expression began to disturb his son. Happiness, yes, but something more, too. There was distress, defeat really, which Shebani had never noticed before. At first Shebani made a mistake, one that was easy to make. He was thinking his father, Tiema, was struggling to come to terms with death. That was the son in Shebani committing this error, not the doctor. He should have been knowing better. How could death be any cause for concern to Asumani Tiema? Hadn't he been expecting it, preparing for it? Yes, he had even chosen the very place he wished to be buried.

We all came to see Shebani when he returned. Now he was an important person in our eyes. He asked the names of the new children. Who had married while he was away? He told stories about large trucks carrying beer that he had seen drive off the road and crash in fire on rocks far below. He spoke, too, about vehicles for carrying people through the air. That was before the airplanes came flying over our heads, too, to frighten the children.

There were no special signs, but we could see that Shebani was happy to be back. That first night he went to sit under the trees high above the sloping fields, up where his consulting hut still stands. It is so comforting, true, to see the stars again in the places you remembered them when for so long they have had a different look. The night was cool and all the cattles were left out to feed freely. The sounds they made chewing grass were louder even than the cries of our night birds. Probably Shebani had just closed his eyes, leaned back his head so that finally his thoughts might also reach a stop, when the first notes of weeping from the old kitchen reached his ears. We were not used to them yet, either. Each night for weeks now we had heard Asha Makokha's tears, and already it was as if no night would ever be complete without them.

For long hours Shebani sat up there with open eyes listening to the weeping. It was more whimpering, really, someone weeping from fear of too much silence. During those hours there, paralysed, not moving in his blanket, Shebani grew old. Ever after, we say, he carried Asha Makokha's weeping in his body.

There are differences of opinion about so many things that have to do with Asha Makokha's sickness, but everyone agrees about one fact. She was the first. Poor thing, she was the source.

To arrive at a count of the daughters of Asumani Tiema is difficult. Even though daughters are the ones bringing cows into the family through marriage, they are always being forgotten at the time of counting. Asha Makokha, for example, is one who is always omitted. Not from negligence, however. No. There are such good reasons for keeping silent about Asha Makokha. And no reasons for supposing any Tiema has ever forgotten her, not for a day.

Asha Makokha was born in 1926 or 1934 or maybe 1937. A year when the river came over its banks and there was an explosion at the Namulungu jaggery. She died at the Asembo Leprosy Hospital in 1968. She was married at least once, locally. The first husband still lives, and sometimes leaves his bed to walk out in search of beer. At most Asha was married three times. The stories confuse us. Perhaps the stories are naming Asha Makokha by name. Or else they may merely be describing a certain beautiful Luhya woman, one who was suffering from *amachere*. Then we hope to know who these stories are telling about. Even though we are not forgetting Asha Makokha, it is true that really we know so little about her life. What she was like, where she lived when, how she left the Wangas and died – these are mysteries. Everyone knows, everyone knows everything about Asha Makokha once you ask. Only few people know the same things.

When Asha Makokha took up residence, first in the old kitchen and then in her own round hut on Tiema land and did not go away again, not for a day or any part of a day, at least not until the end, that was when she began to make an important difference to the rest of us. Oh, yes, really. Not the things she was saying or the things people were saying about her. Even what she did, her acts, they were not concerning us either in an important way. Already by that time her disease was limiting her movement. She was *always* at her hut, sitting there outside, under the eaves. Asha Makokha, who once had such beauty that everyone who looked had to look again, she sat by her door and we knew, all of us, that her head was ever full of things. Things she was thinking, yes, and remembering.

In her last years Asha Makokha was having to suffer most terribly indeed. Even some talk was arising then in the neighbourhood about wanting to get rid of her. Days at a time no one would see her. People were always talking then about her death and finding out later, no, she was still alive. Who can blame her if she preferred to stay inside, in the dark. Still, always alone, feeling so much pain, was it natural for a person to go on living like that? We were wondering very much what we could do. Shebani, he was knowing about his sister as much as anyone, and he just went on accepting.

No one is denying that Asha Makokha was the first. Also we are agreeing that Emmanuel, son of Asumani Tiema's brother Wattako, followed her soon after. Even though the two of them were living somehow apart. Asha Makokha was not yet returning from her first husband when Emmanuel was showing the early signs of his disease. No one is suggesting that Emmanuel was catching his leprosy from Makokha. Still, you can't help what people are thinking for themselves. We are so careful always in determining the order.

After learning to tell weeds apart from our good Luhya crops, Emmanuel became a good farmer. He was having many friends, too. That was a natural thing. Such a good dancer as he was, and a maker of songs. At the time he was achieving his maturity, there were always flowers in the ground on all sides of Emmanuel's bachelor hut. As we were passing, it made a very pleasant sight for the eye, the flowers. Bougainvillaea was even growing up over the door on to the grass roof. Emmanuel had his cuttings from the wife of the missionary. Chickens he was having, too, and a dog. Some people are not remembering about the dog, but I do. That dog always looked like it was sleeping or maybe dead except for one ear that stood straight up so you could know he was all the time listening to hear if any wild cat might be coming for a meal of chicken.

If any woman from around here claims that when she was a girl she did not see the inside of Emmanuel's hut, then probably she is wishing she had. Him standing in the doorway, the flowers at his feet, with his good temper and a girl knowing, too, how hard he was always working, of course she had to be curious. If it was a woman approaching, that dog never even lifted its head.

Emmanuel wasn't one to go talking about how he played sex, either. Other boys his age, they were quick to tell. No one remembers Emmanuel having many words about anything, in fact. Even before the time he was meeting Margarita. Laughing, yes, and greeting everyone, but for the rest very private.

Church people are sometimes not very Christian. I am thinking of those who keep saying that what happened to Emmanuel was his own reward. By that they are not meaning his catching the wind. God, after all, decides who will have a disease, who not. No, their remarks concern how his illness developed in such a serious way. For that, they say, Emmanuel can thank only himself. Many people here. According to their thinking, Emmanuel was trying to hide his disease!

Hide leprosy? How can you hide the Disease of the Two Bodies? How, tell me, how could Emmanuel try to be hiding leprosy? Impossible with those Luhya shirts and trousers we poor people are mostly wearing. So full of holes, from far away you see through to the muscles. To my mind, he was having other things to be thinking about then than leprosy. A young man and a bachelor. So many visitors to be entertaining. And his farm – only with so much work could he be making a good crop on that soil. Also with a leprosy that is just showing itself in patches there is no pain. Nothing is alarming at first, only the skin is a different colour – like when you have scratched a bite from an insect. Who is going to notice such? Unless other people, they do first. Who is going to become afraid and go running through the country like a mad person? A woman, maybe, but not a man. Leprosy is not a disease that kills in short days. It is slow.

Emmanuel's condition was changing when the disease developed around his eyes. He was looking then like a cow with large white or brown spots around its dark eyes. About that time, visitors to his hut began to be less. We would see Emmanuel with more spare time to be improving his flowers. They were increasing in their number. Orange and flame-coloured, also low purple flowers, the favourites of bees. That must have been when Shebani came to Emmanuel with the *logongo* to be talking about leprosy, the time they were trying to give Emmanuel their advices in a kind way to go to Camp Lepra in Kakamega Town. Instead they only made him to be running away.

After the day of that visit, Shebani pointing out to the village head the different kinds of flowers, praising the character of Emmanuel, the *logongo*, who is dead now, turning his hat just so, and so, in his hands, Emmanuel changed. Fear changed him, not the leprosy. The disease changed him, too, but not so much as the fear.

He did not know, you see. He wasn't hiding, not at all. Shebani was probably doing his best to be so kind, but at that time he was already so proud. At first not, but later we could be seeing the change in Emmanuel. It was there deep in his eyes ringed around with those patches. Emmanuel! Can't you imagine how his heart was just pounding so loud. 'People in the country have been complaining about your disease. Please, for your own and the benefit of neighbours, you should be going to Camp Lepra.' Can you imagine hearing those words from the visitors you have welcomed? No threat the first time. Only friendly advices. Please, tell me, it is too much to accept, isn't it?

Did you ever see Camp Lepra? So many patients living so close together, hundreds and hundreds. That was the terrible thing. To see them together. Better than the huts on the river, more Christian, but how can we not be knowing fear at the sight of so many? Though really, it was just the same as anywhere else, Camp Lepra. By that I mean people just married and made children, only there was a fence and when you went one time behind the fence you didn't come out again. People there had chickens, too, and dogs, and flowers. Wicked people were saying these chickens, dogs, and flowers were having leprosy, too. I don't believe that.

Shebani and the *logongo*, that one was an old man with a medal from the English for fighting in their army, the two of them came out of Emmanuel's hut then and walked away. They walked quickly, up the hill, not smiling to us or looking to the left or right, not speaking to each other either, each keeping busy with his own thoughts. Emmanuel we didn't see again all that day. In the morning he was ploughing his fields again, walking behind his cattle, working hard. The same as the day before, and the day before that. But that must have been a different Emmanuel already, one with fear inside. When fear is new, then it is the most difficult to be living with. Like fear before a first child is being born, not knowing how it will happen. So we were not surprised when later, after the medicine failed, Emmanuel disappeared. He ran into the bush to live.

The cases that meet with success, those are the ones our African doctors are always for remembering. The patients who get better, they can tell you all their names. Who can blame them for forgetting the others? Even Shebani has some weak points in his memory. Still, before Emmanuel ran away, when Shebani was wanting to cure him and the medicine did not work, he was not the doctor giving treatment himself. No, Shebani has never known the leprosy medicine. Instead he was recommending the doctor.

We do not know if Shebani sent for this doctor or if the doctor was travelling in this part of the country by chance, the way it seemed. He was a man who had a reputation for being such a good one to manage *amachere*. Doctors for leprosy are mostly treating only that single disease. The visitor had come about the middle of that day. He supported himself with a walking stick. (I say it was just the handle of an old umbrella.) He was a short person and so very old the skull bone could be seen pressing out against his skin. Half his teeth were somehow rotten and his tongue was covered in a dark substance which he had been chewing in his mouth during safari for strengthening the body. His eyes had so many threads of blood running through them. To be telling the truth, this doctor had only an ordinary appearance, even shabby. Still Shebani was acting very pleased to see him. They shared an embrace like that of true friends.

Shebani and the visitor, they were talking together a long time. They sat apart in Shebani's hut. Even Shebani's wives were bringing beer to drink up there, as an exception. Shebani was not sharing in it, though. I don't think so. All of the afternoon was spent like that, just the two of them, until Shebani sent for his first-born, Sebastian, to invite Emmanuel to come up to the top of the hill. When Emmanuel came, it was night. He was not willing then to move about just by day. Under the moon which was full, Emmanuel's eyes looked like someone had drawn circles around them with chalk.

The treatment came in two parts that the visiting doctor was giving Emmanuel. First they were taking him to the very farthest edge of Tiema's property, to a place where there was a large ant hill. The one with three towers, the tallest one half broken and in ruins. It stands there still, only another tower has been trying to crumble. Shebani walked holding his friend's arm. There was evidence that the visitor had enjoyed much beer. Emmanuel followed them, walking behind by a few steps. Really he was giving the impression that he wanted to be running in some other direction!

It was all supposed to be happening in secrecy. As we were knowing that a stranger had arrived, however, and what with the moon shining so brightly, well, the secret was a few sizes smaller. If I am to reveal everything, then, that stranger, he was also singing in a loud voice. Songs in the language of the English. Perhaps that was for keeping away harmful spirits, but, honestly, it did not help with the secret.

There at the ant hill Emmanuel was given a hollow bamboo filled with medicine to drink. That medicine, *okhutaba*, is for making a patient begin to vomit and it causes diarrhoea. With leprosy they are doing this to clean the blood, to get rid of the leprosy eggs. Without *okhutaba*, no curing is possible. That is why the modern doctors with their pills have to fail. They can cool the disease down, but not cure it. If you are not believing me, ask Shebani.

At night, even with a moon for seeing things, when you accept drinking medicine, you must know for yourself what you are doing. You must be drinking at least enough that it will do its work, but a little too much can be very fatal. It will just make you keep vomiting and diarrhoeaing until you fall dead. And it is mostly so that African doctors measure with their fingers!

Before Emmanuel was given the bamboo with medicine to drink, seven swallows, first he had to be using the hoe they had him carry to break the ant hill open. The patient had to dig until the ground was open. The hole was so that after swallowing the medicine, there would be a place for burying the waste that would pass out of his body. In the moonlight, you could not see the red colour of the clay, but everything was turning just white or black. Sometimes Emmanuel stood right up so we could see the sweat then that was shining on his face. Most people don't remember how happy he used to be for a chance to work.

The best way to be swallowing *okhutaba* is right away, all at once. Even without breathing, it has such a bitter taste. It is an ash medicine, made by burning the roots of some certain trees and boiling the remains in water.

It is never long before *okhutaba* will begin having its effect. Emmanuel soon started to shiver and then to clutch at his stomach. From where we stood watching he even looked to be doing a dance. He went some steps in one direction and then turned back, his upper body rocking, and then he would bend over and finally be crawling. All the time the short doctor went on singing his songs, waving his umbrella stick in the air.

For the working of the medicine it was most important that the moon was full. If a hen is still laying eggs and you are forcing it to incubate, they will not hatch. The same with leprosy eggs in the body. When the moon is not full, shining like day, the eggs are scattered. When it is full they will heap together and come out. The moon is the same to the disease as a hen to her eggs. That is one reason why we are believing the doctor's arrival was by secret plan – the full moon.

Emmanuel son of Wattako! Sometimes he was climbing off his knees, holding on to a tower of the ant hill, and we could hear a gagging noise. There was vomit on his chin, silver it looked, with no one wiping it away for him. And he was fouling his legs. *Okhutaba* makes you a baby again. You cannot be controlling your own body.

Shebani stood to one side. His face stayed the same except sometimes he appeared to press his lips harder against each other. He had his arms folded across his chest and in the moonlight, with his jellabah, he appeared to be floating even a short distance above the ground. The leprosy eggs in their sac, Shebani was waiting to see them coming out. Or else he was standing there without moving because really he was not believing at all. In his mind, there is always something moving.

When a patient has emptied himself completely, then *okhutaba* will slowly be wearing off. Afterwards the place must be covered over with loose earth and marked with thorny branches so no one can come there by mistake and be infected by the leprosy eggs. Even under the ground they are keeping their power. It was the doctor who buried Emmanuel's waste and put down thorns. Often he was sticking himself, and crying out in excitement.

On the way back Shebani carried the hoe. He would even swing it at bushes he saw. Emmanuel was being helped to walk by the visitor who was not singing any more. Really, I think they were helping each other. Emmanuel passed close to us, no more than an arm away. He looked so young and calm, like a new infant.

For some days afterwards he was just keeping inside his hut. Shebani sent a daughter down to him bringing some porridge and tea. The first time she went back up the hill again without even removing the cloth that was covering her tray. Only the second day was Emmanuel agreeing to sip some tea. Also she gave water to Emmanuel's flowers.

There is no doubt that it would have been better to wait before going any further with the leprosy cure, but Shebani's visitor preferred not to delay. He was impatient to be continuing his safari. That is what Shebani was saying.

At the time the doctor was going to Emmanuel for application of smearing medicine, Emmanuel could still not walk better than a small child. Such medicine is a powder mixed with pounded bananas and fat from a cow. It is rubbed over the body at the places where the skin has been trying to change its colour. Then for two days a leaf from a banana tree is tied tightly to these same places where medicine has been rubbed. Afterwards the skin of the patches just falls away, the way sometimes you see the old skin of a snake hanging from the branch of some low bush. The snake has been there, you can know, and now it is gone. The same with the patch.

After the bad skin falls away, this is leaving the body pink. The meat to the body there is also somehow tender. To be healing the pink spots there is another powder the doctors are using, one which they brush on with a chicken feather. Then slowly by slowly the whole skin becomes brown or black again like the rest of the healthy body.

With Emmanuel there was a special problem when the doctor came for applying his smearing medicine. Namely, Emmanuel's eyes. The round patches there. The smearing medicine is so strong. You cannot use it, for example, on the stomach. It will eat through the muscles there. When the doctor came to Emmanuel's bachelor hut the afternoon was almost ending. The man was drunk and also singing. Always the same. Later Shebani was saying that doctor had not been sober for long years. Ah! he was even fearing that if he became sober he could be forgetting everything he knew about medicines.

The smearing medicine was prepared in a mortar outside Emmanuel's house. We could hear the pounding from our own compound. The small children went to be sitting in the shade where they could have a good sight of everything even as it was happening. Emmanuel sat on the ground. He watched Shebani who was walking first one way, then back again, his arms folded across his chest. Perhaps Emmanuel was wishing Wattako, his father, was still alive or his mother, but we cannot decide who lives and dies, that is God's work.

The doctor was careless in the way he was making the medicine ready. Powder was sometimes just spilling on the ground. This frightened the children from coming too close. For the rest the doctor was not noticing anyone, just pounding. Not the way a woman pounds who saves her strength, no, he was attacking the powder. When the pounding finished, the doctor's face was shining with his perspiration. Then he placed some folded cloth on one hand and piled up a heap of the medicine there. With his other hand he went ahead smearing medicine all around Emmanuel's eyes. He moved his hands so quickly for someone old. Next he was tying a strip of banana leaf over the eyes and sewing it at the back with sisal thread. Emmanuel just sat on the ground not moving. The doctor called for water to be washing his hands, but Shebani's daughter was already there with everything he was needing. The whole time Emmanuel was not saying any word. He was licking his dry lips sometimes, or reaching his hand to chase away some insect from his knee. He could not any longer try to see. The children were excited and whispering to each other but their words were not clear. Sure, Emmanuel's fear must have been rising again from where he had put it away.

That night we were sending the boy soup made from a young hen.

Good soup, strong, but Emmanuel wasn't of a mind to be eating. His land was then only half ploughed. He was not ever working there again in a good way.

When a cure fails, we know it is not right always to blame the doctor. He was only trying to help the patient, wasn't he? In the case of Emmanuel, however, we are finding that the doctor should at least have stayed behind until the time of removing the leaves. Instead Shebani was doing this. When finally after three days of waiting Shebani was releasing the leaf bandage from Emmanuel's eyes, oh God, Emmanuel was by way of being a blind person. And much skin peeled away sticking to the leaves. The air had to be burning Emmanuel's face most painfully. We cannot blame him for crying out then.

All the neighbours were gathering there. Mostly we had come hoping to share in Emmanuel's happiness. 'Aie, aie, aie!' The children were laughing the way they do when something happens they do not understand. A grown man crying out in pain! Then Shebani had his second wife be pulling away so many small pieces of skin that were weaving the eyelashes of Emmanuel together, keeping them shut. The whole time she was being so gentle and talking to Emmanuel like a mother to her child. No, I think you are only catching *amachere* if you are afraid of it.

At last Emmanuel could open his eyelids. He sat without moving in Shebani's arms. Water was leaking out from the corners of his eyes. He could see nothing.

'Of course not,' Shebani said. 'It is too soon.' We could see he was frowning himself, so hard. 'In some days you will come back from the darkness.'

For the next week we were hearing every day that Emmanuel could see nothing yet. Only some grey shapes. Everything was shadows. He walked on his own flowers. He called loud to his dog when the dog was there next to him. Because of God's teachings, we were bringing food for Emmanuel. He sat and ate under a black umbrella. We waited the whole time he was eating. How could we talk to him when he himself was not saying any word?

During those days we were not seeing anything of Shebani. Or if we saw him it was at a distance, on top of the hill, his face turned towards Emmanuel's home, a hand shading the top of his eyes. Shebani was keeping to himself, not at all in a good humour.

Only when Sebastian came running up to his father, bringing the news that Emmanuel was seeing again, did Shebani recover his smile. Sebastian was explaining how it happened that Asha Makokha was coming to sit at the side of Emmanuel. She just sat with him for some time. They were talking together, words no one else was hearing. Then she reached up a hand to touch on Emmanuel's eyes. From her touch, he could see! At first he was like a mad person. He was by way of shouting then and thanking God.

Sure, Emmanuel was a happy person then, with light coming inside his eyes again. He made promises to Asha Makokha to be visiting her each day. It was his mistake not to have been visiting her before. Devils had been misleading him, he said, making him too too afraid. He would even plant food for her. Still, Asha Makokha told Emmanuel, 'No, it is better for people to be leaving me just alone.'

Where the raw wounds were on Emmanuel's face, close to his eyes, the skin gradually grew normal again. It wasn't, however, a complete success. His sight was staying damaged. From a distance he could not see well. Also the colours he could see were somehow different from what he remembered. We were always testing to see how far away we could stand with Emmanuel being able to tell us apart. Like a game. Poor Emmanuel, he was bumping into many things, especially at the beginning, bruising himself. Yet even that was so much better than mere darkness. He was keeping a very good nature about it. Besides Emmanuel was seriously thinking that the leprosy was gone from his body. Even some of us were believing the same thing. Emmanuel was accepting his suffering as the price for his being cured. He renewed his flowers.

We cannot be sure, but I think probably Shebani was also convinced that Emmanuel was cured. At least he was talking so openly about the great skill of his doctor friend. Today that man is still drunk all the time. He has been seen falling into gulleys and almost walking in front of motor cars. He was so old then that I am not even guessing at his age now. It is a pity for old people to be acting so.

Emmanuel was a constant guest in Shebani's home. Shebani was even instructing one of his wives to travel to Kakamega Town for buying a pair of sunglasses from the shops. This was a gift for Emmanuel. These glasses had a silver frame. Many children in our villages took turns wearing them – before Shebani presented them to Emmanuel. Some the dark glass frightened, by the way it changed the world that they were seeing. Others it made more serious. Myself, when I put on the glasses, really, I right away was expecting heavy rain!

Emmanuel and Shebani were having a close friendship. To Emmanuel Shebani was telling his stories of travel and medicine. Everything changed when a new patch came out on Emmanuel's face. Really, like some cloud so thin and slow no one can be noticing it at first, not until it drops down to cover the sun. The patch appeared on the forehead, here, high up, by the hairline. When Shebani was first seeing it there, the evil thing was seeming to spread under his eyes. Himself, Emmanuel learned something was there because the first time Shebani was seeing it, he stopped talking. Even in the middle of his sentence, Shebani stopped. That is something so unusual for him. And such a look came on his face. He was even looking like Tiema at the moment Tiema died.

'What has happened?' Emmanuel asked.

Of a sudden he had to understand that his leprosy disease was not cured. Things were the same as they were before the visit of the doctor – only now Emmanuel no longer had the pleasure of seeing things sharply. And in his body, he was always somehow tired. Otherwise he would have been working as he used to, not spending such long hours visiting Shebani. Emmanuel was not lazy, not like today's patients. Those ones, they receive good medicine but how can they expect it to help them if they do no work? Work makes the blood move through the body so the medicine in the blood can reach every part. There were also new patches appearing on Emmanuel's thigh, but he could only barely feel the raised edges. He could not see the difference of his own skin.

'What is it?'

'What did I say?' Shebani replied him. 'If she had not touched on you, this would not have happened!'

Possibly when afterwards Emmanuel was running into the bush it was to be escaping any new medicines which Shebani might be wishing to give him. Also, by sleeping about in the open country, taking his food like a thief, really, except that people here knew about him and we were leaving some food in baskets where he could be getting it without showing himself, Emmanuel was delaying the day when he would be having to disappear behind the high fence of Camp Lepra. He must have been knowing that day would come, but what man likes to be giving up his freedom – not if there is any helping it. Still, sooner or later, it was a sure thing. They would find him and take him. One of the people out hunting Emmanuel with the others was the *logongo*. Even some were saying he was carrying his rifle with him, the same one from the English war.

It was Sebastian who one day found Emmanuel's sunglasses. They were lying not far from the flat rock where Tiema's ancestors used to bathe themselves, leaving their footprints there. Shebani was so angry when Sebastian brought home the glasses. If Emmanuel went back to search for where he dropped them, he could no longer be finding them. It was late in the dry season, too, so the dust was even like a hot mirror to the sun. People with just normal eyes were having to complain, so what must it have been like for Emmanuel then? Unless, of course, he was sleeping in the day like some animals do.

There is also another possibility. Did Shebani suspect that Emmanuel might have been throwing the sunglasses away? Did Emmanuel wonder if Shebani's gift and not the touch of Asha Makokha was behind the return of his wind? Shebani took the sunglasses from his son Sebastian and put them on to his own face. This was by way of showing he was meaning well with his gift of them. These are the same glasses Shebani is wearing still today. He only removes them now when he wants a closer look at people.

When finally the *askaris*, those brave policemen, went into the bush after Emmanuel, they brought him in wearing iron bracelets. The whole time the police were leading Emmanuel in, Shebani was wearing the dark glasses. He stayed on the hill. First they went into Emmanuel's hut for collecting his personal belongings, a few poor things. Then they were riding him in an army car to Camp Kakamega. All the children watched him go. The sight of the *askaris* and the car which stood the whole time with its motor running, made it for them so like a feast day. They were cheering. In our hearts, we were sorry, but what could we do?

The hair of Emmanuel had grown long from the weeks he was hiding and was filled with bits of leaves and grass. His eyes were so red with weeping, not tears of sorrow, but from simply trying to see. His body was also covered all over with spots then, like a salamander. On one knee Emmanuel was even having an open wound. Flies were coming there to walk and he was feeling their feet in his blood. To be brought like a captive back to his hut, it was ashaming. And for us to be staring so while they accomplished their preparations of going. Emmanuel stood looking so sadly at his neglected, scorched flowers. When the car went away, Emmanuel's dog was having to run after it. It is true that dog never came back. Some people here wanted to kill it.

Camp Lepra

From the main road there was a dirt turn-off leading to Camp Lepra. The place was marked with a sign. Kakamega Leprosarium, Danger. The name, that was in white letters. *Hatari* was in red.

Emmanuel and his escort of police reached there in the hottest part of the afternoon. He was told to sit on the grass in front of a small stone building. There were other arrivals waiting to see the doctor, too, with bundles of belongings just beside them. They shared a nervous way of not looking into each other's faces.

For so many months Emmanuel had been in a state of confusion. At last he felt somehow calm. First he picked all the debris out of his hair and pulled at the knots. It was too hot. Instead of just sitting, he walked back and forth a little bit, surveying. Some things he could make out, in blurred outline. There were small groups of people sitting together in front of mud huts with grass roofs. Like at home, some were making music with different kinds of stringed harps, others were stirring food in charred cooking pots above smoking fires.

'I thought they were having a fence,' Emmanuel said to no one in particular. Some new arrivals looked up at him, nodded, smiled. The fence was so much part of people's idea of Camp Lepra, it was a surprise not to be finding any. There was no barrier. Nothing separating what was in from out.

There were guards, however. They stayed at some distance, under trees. Men in uniform: a kind of medal on their shirt front, high socks to the knee, boots. Also they had rifles. Most of the time the rifles were stood up against tree trunks and the guards sat playing at cards with each other, or trying to repair their radios. Even when there was too much static, the guards had to blame this on the leprosy patients. Emmanuel learned there was even a barber there, cutting the hair of the guards, first one then another. The barber was himself a leprosy patient.

'Your name? Age? Are you married?'

Inside the doctor's office the air was also very bright. The walls were clean and freshly painted. Photographs under glass hung on all the walls. The doctor had a kind voice. He was a frail man from India, with thick eye-glasses. Also he had extremely large hands with fine fingers that he drummed on top of the desk. Emmanuel answered the doctor's questions with good will. He wanted to say answers that the doctor would be pleased to hear.

'Emmanuel, have you ever taken traditional treatment for your disease?'

'No, doctor.'

'That is good. In your family, is there anyone else suffering from this wind?'

'No, doctor.'

'Good.'

Then the doctor was coming out from behind the desk where he had been sitting to record Emmanuel's answers on a large pink card. He led Emmanuel by the arm towards the window. It was not unusual, really, for there to be bars on the window. So many houses in the Wangas were having bars, too, to protect against thieves climbing in.

The Indian's face was so close to Emmanuel's own, he could feel the man's breath warming his cheek. He had to struggle then not to pull back, not to close his eyes, but he could tell the doctor was being especially interested in them.

'How long have you been having the disease?'

This question Emmanuel could not answer with yes or no. He swallowed and remained silent.

'Short days only, or long?'

'Short.'

'Good,' the doctor said. There was sweat Emmanuel could feel running down his body everywhere, even the back. 'Now I want you to hold my wrist with your hand, so, and squeeze as hard as you can. Come, don't be afraid. Harder. Harder. Now with the other hand. Fine.'

Emmanuel could not tell why, but it had pleased him so much to hold the Indian's thin wrist in his grasp and to hear the doctor be pleading for him to squeeze harder. He did not know then that people who had leprosy disease in their hands, they couldn't help from slipping when trying to grip with all their strength.

'If you have any difficulties, please, do not hesitate to come to see me.' It was over, the interview of intake. Already there was a new patient standing in the doorway. For seven years Emmanuel was remaining in Camp Lepra and he never saw that doctor again.

It was not that the Indian doctor left, either. Word of his going would have spread too quickly among the patients. No, all the days of the seven years he was still there at his desk greeting new patients in his kind way. Some sixteen hundred patients were living then in Camp Lepra and he was the only doctor. There was not enough time for everybody.

Emmanuel was directed to a small cement building behind the doctor's reception room. Here the different camp supplies were being kept. Inside he met a short, heavy man whose face was swollen with leprosy nodules. No one could like to look at him.

'Some people in camp will be glad to see you,' the man said. His voice was just ordinary, even coming from such a face. 'I mean the women.' Then the keeper of the stores chose a set of green pyjamas with a black stripe down the trouser leg. He held them against Emmanuel's body to satisfy himself they would be a good fit. Then a small bottle of baby oil was lifted down from the shelf, and a package of soap. Later Emmanuel learned that the animal on the soap package was a kangaroo. Whenever he used that soap on his body, Emmanuel slept so soundly. It had a lovely smell. And it was, after all, from the smell that even veterans of Camp Lepra now and then had to grow nauseous. The first time, the soap was a gift from the government. Other times patients had to pay.

Somehow a little bit self-conscious in his new green clothes,

Emmanuel wandered towards the direction of the huts and the groups of people that were living close together in the centre of the camp. No one had told him what to do or what to expect. What had presented itself as such an ordinary picture from a distance changed slowly as Emmanuel, with his damaged eyes, drew near. Now he began to see the signs of their disease in the people who were sitting, eating, smoking together. One way Emmanuel knew he was in Camp Lepra was from how these people were looking at him. No one tried to hide that he was staring. That was so different from the outside world. They stared, too, but not if they thought you might catch them looking. And on the outside they were staring to find some small sign of the disease. In Camp Lepra people were looking past the disease.

That first walk was making Emmanuel afraid in his heart. Too many sick people, too many poor cripples. Really, he filled with horror at the sight of so many leprosy patients close together, for he had only seen here and there an isolated case before in his life. He began to feel a loathing for himself for the first time, too – wasn't he one of those who belonged here, who could fill other healthy people with horror? For the first time the air of Camp Lepra, in the close damp of the early evening before the rain, struck him full in his senses. Without wishing to appear to run, he quickened his step. If he could reach the edge of the area that was smelling so bad, he thought, he could step outside of the circle and catch his breath, but everywhere he turned the air was the same. That was why some people kept a small fire burning all day and night. They never failed to add new wood in time because sitting close to the coals at least the air had a smoky quality. Really, Emmanuel had never before seen how terribly leprosy could be eating the body. Asha Makokha, she was having only patches to see. His own body was not much damaged either. How could he live here? No! He thought of his hut, of his family that had helped to bring him here. Were these people even having a God?

'Boy, come here. Yes, you.'

A voice arrested Emmanuel in his slow-motion flight. That voice was grave, commanding, but warm. Emmanuel saw a man in a wheel chair, someone unlike other people, beckoning to him. This was Nicodeme Khaeri, his first friend in Camp Lepra. People called him an old man, but that was not his real age but because of what he had suffered from the disease. Nicodeme sat in a wheelchair made from the planks of a packing crate. There were two wheels on each side, the outside one a little bit smaller. The tires were from old bicycles. Nicodeme's legs were both ending just below the knee. When he sat talking, smoking a chain of cigarettes, Nicodeme always crossed and uncrossed these stumps, rubbing their rounded bottoms at times with his free hand. He wore a beret, one that had started out red but which years of sun had bleached to pink. Sunglasses, too, which he sometimes removed to reveal raw, bloodshot eyes. The corners most of the time were oozing white pus. Also Nicodeme's ears were looking like they had been laid on a rock and hammered flat with a stone.

'Here, boy. Yes, that's right.'

There was never a minute of doubt for Emmanuel, however, not from the first moment Nicodeme called to him, that Nicodeme was an important person, worthy of much respect.

'You're new? Any cigarettes? Doesn't matter, they only make me cough. Come, I'll show you around. Pretty horrible place, isn't it? You'll get used to it, sooner than you think.'

It steadied Emmanuel, having Nicodeme to push along the criss-cross footpaths that wound through the camp. He learned a great deal that night, some of which made him laugh and some of which made him grateful that his passenger Nicodeme did not look back and see the fear in Emmanuel's eyes.

'The air? What can we do? It comes from the cuts. And we are so careless, too. At least you must be one who washes himself properly.'

Really, it helped Emmanuel to have someone to talk to. Even a crippled person, one who had to be wheeled helpless from place to place. The poor patients Emmanuel saw everywhere, at least they weren't always trying to get away from you. They weren't pitying you, either, and thinking themselves better.

'Here it is not so bad. Sure, we are the outcasts. We are the rubbish. That makes us strong, you see.'

Soon Emmanuel had a life of his own in Camp Lepra and many friends. Friends are a difficult thing for Africans. Family, we know. And neighbours, too. But many new friends at once, new faces and backgrounds that are new, or not being known? Still, the time of hiding in the bush, living like a hunted creature with envy for others as he peered out at them from behind cover of a thicket, envy because they could walk together, talk, sleep, share their lives – that was the worst time! In Camp Lepra there was always something social to be doing. Emmanuel did not talk too much and people liked him. He was young, strong. Nicodeme always had time for him. That patient knew so much about the country. He was often telling history in the evenings, even describing the first arrival of Wanga who came from Egypt with his walking stick and struck the waters of Lake Victoria with it, saying, 'I am Wanga, open for me.' For the first time Emmanuel was thinking there were more clever people in the country than just Shebani.

Outside visitors to Camp Lepra, they came and went. Relatives of some patients paid regular visits, bringing food and tobacco. Everyone shared everything. What Emmanuel missed most at first was work. To work, that was what he was knowing best, even from childhood. Sex was there in plenty. It replaced work.

For Emmanuel the day was even coming when Camp Lepra became home for him. He began to talk about 'newcomers' and to help others learn the life there.

'Yes, the people are so helpful to each other here,' Nicodeme said. 'It is our natural African socialism. Why? It is because we have no hope.'

Sometimes if Emmanuel was to understand what Nicodeme was trying to teach him, he would have to stop pushing the old man, and walk around to the front of the wheelchair and sit and listen.

'We are merely thrown here. They give us some aspirin kind of tablets and washing with cold water so the body shrinks again to normal condition, but there is no curing. Here we belong together. Without hope, who is going to be rude?'

'*Mzei*, is no one going to get better?'

'Some. With some the wind disappears by itself. Maybe you, maybe not. That is why we can be friendly. Even our African doctors, they cannot manage this disease.'

'Aah!'

'If I told you the sheep I have wasted in payment, even the cattles. Run here, run there. Nothing helps.' Nicodeme coughed. 'So we go on living.'

'Yes.'

The first time Emmanuel noticed Margarita was at a prayer meeting which was held in Camp Lepra by a travelling minister of the Pentecostal faith. She was a girl then of about fourteen years with very regular white teeth and a shy smile. Margarita had a round face and her body was somehow round and full, too, without being heavy. Emmanuel tried to move close to her in the crowd but by the time he reached where he had seen her standing, she was gone. Days of rain and more rain followed. Emmanuel had some headaches and stayed indoors. He remembered the girl he had failed to find, how she was swaying slightly as she recited the words of the leader's prayer. Probably, he decided, she was a relative to some patient and had come to the camp for one day only. After the rain was stopping, and the pain in his head, too, Emmanuel forgot about the round-faced girl completely. There was never a lack of women to keep him company.

Emmanuel shared a hut with four other patients. One day he was just sitting outside the door a bit late in the morning, watching clouds gather from the far opposite sides of the sky, when Margarita was suddenly right there, standing in front of him. She was carrying a tray filled with sesame balls, selling them. Her eyes were like some bird's. Still there was a challenge in them. Emmanuel did not say anything unnecessary. He paid for one sweet and asked the girl to choose it out for him herself. Margarita gave him one, two, three, and ran off without looking back. Through a tear down the back of her plain dress, Emmanuel could glimpse a gleaming, healthy body.

'Is one disease not enough, my friend?' Nicodeme somehow knew. It never surprised Emmanuel, not any more, that Nicodeme saw everything.

'That one, tell me, is she also having the wind?'

'Of course. Here –' Nicodeme pointed – 'on her hip.'

The answer pleased Emmanuel. Nowhere had he made out any open signs of the disease. Now, if the girl did have leprosy, at least he had a chance to be her lover. He was puzzled by this feeling and ashamed, really. Happiness in another's misfortune is not to a person's credit. Still Emmanuel was not denying he was grateful that Margarita, too, was one of those with *amachere*.

In the courtship which followed, brief and to the point, the old man Nicodeme played the *wangera*. In his wheelchair the marriage broker went back and forth. He was praising Emmanuel's character, also his strength. He was making the most of Emmanuel's attachment to an illustrious family. The whole day was taken up by his trips between Emmanuel's hut and the house of Margarita's parents. Her father and mother both were very ill with the disease. As Moslem believers they had entered Camp Lepra but soon afterwards, with many others, they had been agreeing to baptism. The father of Margarita carried the Bible with him everywhere, without any ability to read in it. When he sang hymns he would strike the Bible with a flat hand like some drum. Emmanuel was changing his religion then, trying to learn a new way of prayer.

Also Emmanuel needed to send a letter to Shebani in which he was requesting help with the payment of brideprice. Two chickens. Brideprice was not the usual way of marrying in Camp Lepra. People in love eloped each other. But Emmanuel was a Tiema and wanted his marriage to be different. So Nicodeme arranged for the police to carry Emmanuel's letter home for him.

In less time really than a man would need to travel from Camp Lepra in Kakamega to the land of the Tiemas and then back again, Emmanuel received the two chickens he had written for. Large, speckled birds, one hen, one cock. People in the camp spoke about it then as a small miracle. A few kept silent. They knew how the police themselves had purchased the chickens at the covered market. There was so much friendship in the camp, however, no one would tell.

All this while Margarita, she acted shy, looking down at the ground mostly, silently smiling. She was having to smile at the most unpredictable moments. She said few words. Perhaps she was suspecting that too many words too soon might startle Emmanuel and scare him off. Later she could talk to her heart's content. It was when speaking that she came fully alive. So in the beginning they sat long hours in near silence, listening to the domestic sounds of the camp, filling their lungs with putrid air and emptying them again, feeling hot in their bodies. Emmanuel was easy to please, Margarita learned, and pleasing him gave her pleasure.

Together Emmanuel and Margarita appeared to keep each other in good health. Margarita persuaded him to attend school. A European woman taught classes in the camp for those who wanted to learn to read and to write. There was a distinction among patients who could read the newspaper and those who could not. Margarita wished to correct their own position. She managed this almost without any pressure, for she soon came to understand Emmanuel so well that her slight hints did what was necessary. During his months in school Emmanuel absorbed little. People knew he was going, however, one day in every week, and for them it was his regular attendance that counted. In the end he could say 'a e i o u and sometimes y'.

Then one day Margarita climbed on to a stool inside the hut where she cooked Emmanuel's food and removed the piece of rag soaked in menstrual blood which she had hidden there in the roof among the blades of grass. She took it down so it wouldn't be collecting smoke from the cooking fire any longer. That explains why so soon afterwards she conceived. Her first born was a son. A daughter followed, and then another girl. With the birth of her children, Margarita grew so talkative. A woman with children was someone to listen to, just as a girl, without, was not.

Emmanuel was not really very surprised that his wife had so much to say. He remembered that look of challenge he was seeing in her eyes the first day she came to him selling sesame cakes. Margarita had words about everyone. And she said very clever things, too. How people would act, why. She knew. Emmanuel began to pay careful attention to her. He asked for her opinion about things he was thinking. And still, when she talked she kept her eyes on the ground much of the time; and that smile of hers, so often it flashed and then was gone without anyone knowing why.

Years passed without much season. Oh, there was of course an alternation of rainy weeks and dry weeks, but even rain mattered less to people who did not work on the land. The moon changed in the sky, the stars, too, slowly rotated. So few surprises.

Margarita's parents died, first her mother and then almost directly her father, too. She could not stop the doctors from taking their bodies away for burning. Afterwards Emmanuel and Margarita were praying somehow less. The Bible became lost or stolen. New arrivals entered the camp, distinguishable for a short time by the careful way they drew breath or by glints of fear and anger in their eyes. Camp Lepra soon accommodated them, however. It was too convivial.

'Ah, a pity that. I should think we can do something about it. Certainly worth the try.'

The doctor whose arrival changed things for Emmanuel and

Margarita was fat, especially for a white man. His white jacket was spotted with soup. People were joking it was even blood. The doctor was a European with skin you could see right through to the veins underneath. He had slate-grey eyes. He spoke the Kiswahili language with great concentration.

Emmanuel and Margarita had been sitting in front of their hut. She had her youngest on the breast. Emmanuel was wearing a black leather motorcycle jacket with a broken diagonal zip. Some Finn or Swede had thrown it in a wood box outside his church one Sunday. It had journeyed thousands of miles to end up with Emmanuel.

Grunting, the doctor crouched down in front of Emmanuel. 'No, don't look at me. Look up. Now look down. Left. Right.' The doctor had seized Emmanuel's chin and tipped his head back. There was a moment of hesitation before he did so, followed directly by a display of confidence. Margarita saw that the combination was betraying the doctor's fear. With the ball of his thumb, the doctor gently massaged Emmanuel at the temples. Afterwards he removed a small notebook with red cover from his pocket, looked around him for some identifying landmark, and wrote down hasty notations. Before he left he looked at all the children. He tried so hard to amuse them, imitating many wild animals, even crawling. Margarita and Emmanuel had to laugh, but the children looked the whole time about to cry.

Only Margarita understood right away that the doctor was planning to operate Emmanuel's eyes. Towards the evening Nicodeme arrived. The man who was pushing the old man's chair on wheels had no nose, only a flap of cloth that hung down to conceal the hole in the middle of his face.

'So!' Nicodeme was slightly breathless, somehow exhilarated. 'He has sniffed you out, Emmanuel. He has, he has. *Oyenga*, the hyena.'

'Why is he called that?'

'Why?' When the patient behind Nicodeme spoke, his voice sounded like it came from very far away and the hanging flap had to move as if blown by a wind. 'It is because Oyenga feeds off living flesh!'

Emmanuel had few memories of his operation. In a government vehicle they were transporting him to the provincial hospital not at all far away. His face was washed completely with a strong liquid soap that burned when it entered his eyes. Then he was led into a room and made to lie on a long, narrow table covered with slippery white paper.

There were some nurses wearing masks and cloth hats they tied under the chin. Emmanuel could recognize the hyena by his high white forehead. Often the nurses were laughing at things the doctor was saying. A number of lamps were then lowered on ropes from the ceiling and Emmanuel received some injections. Afterwards he had to sleep. That is, part of him. Part was staying awake even the whole time. He could feel liquids flowing down his cheeks. Separate streams that parted direction below his eyes. What the liquid was, water or blood, hot or cold, Emmanuel had no idea. Nor in his waking sleep did it worry him. During the operation someone kept whistling, not very well. Still it was comforting for Emmanuel to listen.

The week after the operation Emmanuel had to spend with his eyes wrapped in bandages. They only told him this was necessary after he was back in Camp Lepra with Margarita. At first, such darkness again was making him too afraid for blindness. He was like a person about to be mad, just shaking and shivering in his body. This time, however, he had Margarita, she could see for him, and also, she could talk to him. Inside her woman's voice were the high sweet tones of a bird. These she knew to use at times to ease Emmanuel in his heart. Other patients, too, they came to greet Emmanuel and shake his hand so that at least he was not alone, not as the last time. Emmanuel was telling Margarita then about Asha Makokha's visit to him, about her gentle fingers touching his eyes and about Shebani's gift of sunglasses. Whatever he said to Margarita, it is true that there was never a time she was liking Shebani, not in any true way.

Removal of the bandages from Emmanuel's eyes took place inside his hut. Quite some people had gathered when the doctor arrived, whistling, a satchel filled with instruments in one hand. That day the ground was very muddy. The doctor was putting his feet down carefully each time but still you thought soon he would slip and fall.

'And how's the patient today? Worried, eh? Can't say I blame you. What if I get rid of all those bandages for you, would you like that? Don't tell me I forgot the bloody – no, there they are.' The doctor held up a pair of gleaming scissors. He opened and closed them close to Emmanuel's ear. 'Now what kind of animal makes that kind of noise?' Margarita laughed.

Slowly, turn by turn, the doctor began to unwind Emmanuel's bandage. When the doctor's whistling stopped, Emmanuel's heart was pounding so he thought the whole neighbourhood could hear.

'Double or nothing,' the doctor was muttering. He reached out his large hands and removed the two final gauze compresses that had been laid directly over the patient's eyes. 'On the first day, the Lord said, Let there be light!'

A cry of pleasure broke from Emmanuel's lips. Then he resumed silence. At such times we Africans are thinking it so much better not to show our feelings, more dignified. The world was indeed much sharper in outline. Emmanuel's children, they looked like strangers. Their features, their thin bodies – everything was nearly like it once had been, oh so long ago. They were in good health, he could see. And Margarita?

The doctor slapped Emmanuel on the back, chucked all the children he could reach under the chin, and strolled off again, mud oozing beneath his feet.

It was not altogether a successful operation, however. The doctor's technique was to blame. Later people said he was himself needing glasses but wasn't liking to wear them. Be that as it may, Emmanuel's eyes were better. He could no longer close them, however, not completely.

And Margarita? How did she look to her husband with his restored sight? Now for the first he could see copper-coloured patches, vague in outline, diffused over her body. And her skin no longer seemed to fit her, not as tightly as he had imagined. Margarita picked up the skein of bandage that the doctor had unwound from Emmanuel's eyes. She was also retrieving the two cotton compresses thrown away in the dirt. Emmanuel followed her movements with his eyes. Then she sat, hands and bandages on her lap. She knew Emmanuel was looking so carefully at her, and she let him look.

Margarita

Margarita and Emmanuel son of Wattako returned to the land of the Tiemas by night. No one saw them arrive. In the morning, there they were. In front of Emmanuel's hut they sat finishing the rest of the food they had taken with them on their journey. No one acted surprised to see them, not at all. But we were, very.

When the government decided to close down Camp Lepra, old patients were seen spreading out everywhere in the country. But when days passed, then weeks and months without Emmanuel and Margarita's turning up, we grew tired of expecting them. And who can blame us if we preferred to hope they would not come? Perhaps they were too ashamed of their disease to return?

Ashamed? No. Margarita she looked everyone in the eye. Both of them, they were looking in such good health, so full of confidence. If we had not known their history, it would have been easy to be deceived.

There was no mistaking that Emmanuel was happy to be home. With Margarita it was difficult to say. We welcomed them with a friendly reception, mostly for Emmanuel's sake. He took his wife to meet people. He boasted about her, saying she was clever, but she would just stare at the ground then, and sometimes smile. But slowly by slowly we came to realize that what Emmanuel told us was so true. When Margarita learned that we had decided to be friendly towards her, she was losing her own reserve. We were having good relations, the kind of small-harmony people are always looking to find. At times we were even almost forgetting the wind in Margarita's body.

That wind of *amachere* though, loves to play tricks. Margarita was not long in Lubina, before she was in danger for her life. Emmanuel did as she told him and brought her away to the new hospital at Asembo. She took the youngest of her children with her, the one on the breast.

After Margarita was there in Asembo she could see for herself what a difference there was with Camp Lepra. There was no comparing, really. Asembo, that was a modern hospital. It had permanent buildings with windows of glass, beds in rows, each with a partition in between. Only some few patients were having mattresses on the floor because of so much crowding. At Asembo there were staff people working to keep the buildings clean, washing the cement floors and washing the windows, too. They began to clean every morning and worked the whole day and the next morning they started again, just the same, spilling out the soapy water from their buckets. Some patients who were not in such a bad condition had to be working for the hospital to keep the grass cut around the buildings. The place was looking very smart. There were many trees and gardens, too. Also in Asembo Hospital, Margarita was learning for the first in her life to wash herself with water from a tap and to use a toilet.

Upon arrival, Margarita was in a serious way so she was given a bed in Ward E. The government was in the process of installing bathtubs for the patients in Ward E so there was noise all the time. What with the building in progress and the constant cleaning, some patients were not getting good rest. Almost three weeks had to pass before Margarita discovered that the patient Asha Makokha was also then in Ward E.

By that time Asha was having no legs below the knee. To walk she was using pads and poles. Her hands were masses of bone like they were melted in fire. With the cooperation of the nurse in charge Margarita arranged for a transfer from her bed to the one right next to Asha Makokha. Not that they were talking much from bed. It was a comfort, however, to wake up, look over and see a friend so close.

No, the place where the two women talked most was in the bathroom after the construction was getting finished. The white tiles on the walls and floors were giving words a special sound. For an hour every day Margarita would wash Asha in the bath. She used a special powder soap which gave bubbles and a strong sweet smell. Sometimes the baby would be joining Makokha in the tub, but usually it fought and cried whenever Margarita lowered it towards the water.

In many places of her body Asha was showing scars from wounds that were never healing, not completely. Still the disease had not marked her face. Only somehow her eyes. They were having that different kind of beauty people sometimes speak about in a leprosy patient.

'You are so beautiful,' Margarita exclaimed. 'What they say is true.' Asha grew warm in her face. She had not heard a compliment in some years. One of the first things that she was wanting to know from Margarita was how it happened that Margarita, too, was needing to come to Asembo Hospital.

'You were having such a good health?'

'It was not bad.' Margarita laughed. 'Sister, can it be that you are coming from that place, too, and still do not know about the secret feelings people there are having in their hearts?'

At that Asha grew so quiet.

'And you, how did you get this way?' Those were the words Margarita used for inquiring into the matter of Asha Mokokha's pregnancy, for Asha would soon bear a child. But Makokha was too shy to give out the name of the man and Margarita was not one to force her.

At Asembo one of the white doctors was coming from Holland. This man was very clever. He could take a bent limb and make it straight and he could give a blind person new eyes again. He lived with his wife in a long low caravan of aluminium. The doctor was a big person, but his wife was even bigger. She wore wooden shoes and was practising a piano in the caravan every day for exactly one hour. Sometimes this surgical doctor was having to work at the special leprosy hospital in Uganda, too. They had no doctor of their own to do similar operations.

From the back of Ward E you could look right into Uganda. At that time there were even troubles between Kenya and this neighbour state. Not the peoples, but the governments. In Uganda no one could secure so many things necessary to daily life, like salt and also sugar. Even the medical was having troubles. The leprosy hospital at Baluba, it was suffering a serious shortage of supplies. So it happened that one morning Asha and Margarita were both invited to make a safari to Baluba Hospital. They would ride there in one of the Asembo Land Rovers. Also a man was being asked to go who was in a very bad way. He was even having sores on his face and almost no nose, just a hole you could see right into all the way to the back of the mouth.

The three patients invited to make the journey came early to the hospital office. There they were asked to wait while nurses loaded the Asembo vehicle with bags of salt and sugar and many other things besides. Spare parts for automobiles, medicines, too. The Dutch doctor was watching carefully, biting on the stem of his pipe. He held a list on which he made a mark whenever something else was stowed inside the Land Rover. Jerry cans filled with petrol were locked to the fenders in special racks. Finally some old blankets were thrown down to cover the goods. The doctor's wife fussed with the blankets a long time until you couldn't see anything that might be sticking out beneath. Then Asha, Margarita with her baby and the man patient were all assisted to take places on top of the blankets.

The doctor was the one driving. He wore a pair of special leather gloves with many tiny holes and tinted wrap-around sunglasses. His wife sat next to him. Although she was knowing the way without having to look, not even one time, she had a map spread out on her knees. Only very few minutes were needed for arriving at the border. Certain boards with long spikes sticking up and a barbed wire fence were blocking the road into Uganda. When the Land Rover stopped, two guards came slowly up to different sides of the car. Each of them had a rifle and was wearing an ammunition belt across the chest. The doctor greeted the guards in a cheerful tone of voice and let them see some legal papers he was carrying with him.

'Where are you going, *masungu*? And what are you taking with you?'

'Some treasures of ivory, *bwana*.' First the doctor was joking but when the soldiers were not appearing to like what he said, the doctor's wife told them that they should be able to answer their questions by just looking at the door of the vehicle. The Land Rover was namely a gift from the people of Switzerland and was having the name of Asembo Hospital written on the outside.

'Baluba Hospital is where we are visiting and our cargo is only some dangerous leprosy patients,' the doctor's wife continued. One guard had stuck his head inside the Land Rover but when Asha, Margarita, and the other patient smiled at him he took it out again in a great hurry. 'Maybe you would like some cake?' The doctor's wife began to fumble with a package of cake wrapped in silver foil but the guards preferred to wave the car through directly.

Soon after crossing the border, Asha Makokha began saying how she thought Uganda looked very beautiful. So much green. Many gardens with banana trees, and swamps. Not so many houses. Villages here were less close together. Asha had always wished to travel into Uganda, ever since she was a girl. She was happy to be making the trip at last.

From time to time, the doctor's wife called out over her shoulder to the patients in the back. She used very correct Swahili phrases. 'Are you comfortable? Did you see the lizard cross the road quickly?' Wind coming in through the window was making her blond hair fly about.

Margarita's baby would reach out to touch the ends of the hair without the doctor's wife feeling it.

In fact for the most part the journey was just continuing in silence. It was a lonely road and few people were seen. Sometimes people ahead were walking down the middle of the road and when they heard a vehicle approaching they would scatter and run for safety in all different directions. Out of the passengers, only the man patient was feeling poorly and breathing a bit loud.

At Baluba the people were acting very happy at their coming. Asha and Margarita did not see the vehicle unloaded. They were escorted right away to a quiet room for sleep and also a meal of light porridge. Soon after their arrival it was pitch dark. Many patients from the wards were crowding in to see them. There was a lamp on the table made from the seeds of the castor-oil tree, several on a piece of wire like so many white beads. That was the only poor fuel they were having. It gave a clear light, though. With everyone talking, they all were wanting to know only one thing. This was the same subject so popular in Asembo. What was the true cause of leprosy disease? Like always, no one could be saying how it came. Many suggestions, but no certainty. Then one young girl with her arm in plaster up to the elbow tried to ask if everybody at Asembo Hospital was in such a bad way. For herself Margarita laughed.

'Really they were not choosing patients for this trip who were showing a good condition. Rather the opposite.' Then Asha told how they were being used, the three of them, for the purpose of smuggling, to be frightening the guards at the border. 'Even some left behind at the hospital were feeling too jealous. They began saying that perhaps we patients going to Uganda were the ones who would be thrown away and forgotten there.'

On the next day when the visitors from Asembo were returning to go aboard the Land Rover, they found that everything, even the old blankets, had been removed. Now it was not so comfortable as it was before. They were having to ride on the metal itself.

Now it was the turn of the doctor's wife to be driving. You could see from the back of her neck and shoulders how she was not feeling relaxed. The doctor slept, his head thrown back on to the top of the front seat, his mouth a slight bit open. He had operated all night. So many bad cases had been waiting for him.

At one point the doctor's wife swerved to avoid a large rock that had fallen from a cliff on to the road. 'Sorry,' she called back. 'Excuse me.' The doctor only opened one eye and let his head roll to the other side. Then the man with no nose said suddenly to Asha and to Margarita, 'I would rather have this wind than be a mad person.' By way of answer, the others kept still. Each was having private thoughts.

'It is a friendly place, Uganda,' Margarita finally was telling Asha Makokha. The baby was asleep, bound tightly to Margarita's back. The Land Rover was passing through shining hills and now and again there would be a river winding below, water catching the sun. 'Here there is not so much crowding as with us.' Leaving Camp Lepra, Margarita and Emmanuel had first gone to Uganda to live. Somehow Asha Makokha understood at once that Margarita was going to answer the question now that Makokha had asked her when they were meeting in Asembo. How had it happened that someone who had recovered and was as healthy as Margarita was so suddenly becoming ill again. To show her understanding and also her willingness to listen, Asha laid her head down on Margarita's lap. That way she could be seeing only little of the countryside going by outside the window, the tips of the trees against the sky, but she could see her friend's face so completely. Margarita kept one hand with the fingers open resting lightly on Asha's belly. The foetus inside was sometimes these days already moving hands and feet. For the women it was a happy time despite their suffering. In addition to her own pain each was feeling pain for the other.

'Sister, I will tell you now what I have never before been telling to any living soul, not one. You are the one I am telling because you have asked it of me. But first let me say there is no anger when I repeat these things. Anger is also a disease.' At that Asha looked up into her friend's eyes and the story began.

'As you yourself know, at the time I was coming back from Kakamega I was just in a normal way again. Really, to look at I was just a healthy person, my skin was a healthy skin. And I was joining people in the country, drinking and eating with them. Yes, they laughed as if welcoming me but they played tricks to make the disease grow worse. That was my mistake, to be trusting their good show of friendliness. Yes, we shared the same food and there was no one saying how I had to be the last to wash my hands before the meal or the final one to stop eating. Tiema's people, they welcomed me to their homes and even came to visit me. I was thinking they were not such bad people.

'But for them it was not enough to come by day. They visited me also in the middle of the night. They came when I lay asleep. They stood outside the door and threw those *things* over the roof.'

'How do you know?' The male patient, he was straining to hear, too. Without eyebrows, his eyes looked like they could belong to dried fish. 'How do you know what those people were doing if you were asleep?'

'You are asking a proper question. I would find their ant's nests crushed on the ground behind the house the next day. And one night they were having a quarrel who should throw the nest. Inside I was listening. Even I caught them leaving the bones of isebu fish in my bathing place. So suddenly I was having a very serious case of open ulcers. My disease, it was never of that serious kind before. It was the disease of patches only I was having, not the one of cuts. That only happened to me on the land of the Tiemas. Without fearing, I visited my neighbours and they gave me food cooked in a pot where they had prepared goat's meat or some other food that is too bad for a leprosy body. When I went home at night is when I could feel much pain and realize I had been eating from the wrong pot.' It was as if only now, riding in the Land Rover, Margarita was discovering the whole truth, or rather fully and deliberately weighing it for the first time. 'And truly they want me to die here, but that is for God to decide.'

'You are right,' Asha commented.

Something in the road grated against the oil sump so that a loud *clank* woke the doctor. He and his wife briefly quarrelled whether he should take over the driving. There were corrugations in the road which made the vehicle in its empty condition shudder. The passengers even felt such shaking in their teeth. Only if a car went very very fast, then you wouldn't have to feel the washboard effect, but the doctor's wife wasn't a person liking high speed.

'But why was it not making Emmanuel get the disease in a bad way, too, the yellow balls and other tricks of those good people?'

'Asha Makokha, I am only speaking about what was practised on my body. They were just aiming for me. They would watch for me, wait until I went to the well alone, drop things on the path then, or in the water. Even before I came to the hospital here, at the time I was leaving, people removed a pole from the house and they tore some grass from the roof to throw into the road so that I might die.'

Asha Makokha sighed. 'Yes, those are the things people do.'

The doctor had fallen asleep again and was snoring. His wife drove on back towards the border with her husband's special gloves on her hands. Asha Makokha sang softly to the baby whose curious eyes were peering down at her from behind Margarita's shoulder.

'I have been hearing the words you say,' the male patient informed Asha and Margarita. Whenever people listened to him they looked away because of the hole in the middle of his face. He didn't like that. It made him wish to close his eyes when he talked, but what could he do? 'I, too, when I was still living at my home place, used to be hearing so many useless things that people were trying to practise against me so that the disease should grow worse. People were bringing me their different stories like expensive gifts. But me, I used not to follow or to believe them. Otherwise I would have to be fighting this one and that one.' The driver honked the horn, but the patients could see nothing on the road ahead. 'I did not want to quarrel. After a little while the stories were stopping.'

'Or people told them to each other,' Margarita said, 'instead of to you.'

'Anyway, for myself, I just believe this wind to be decided by God to come to me, whatever people say.'

When Asha Makokha's child was born, a boy, it was an easy birth. The baby was just healthy and for some months all was going well. Juma they called him, in honour of Asha Makokha's grandfather. When Asha's own breasts went dry after some weeks, Margarita even nursed the new baby along with her own child. The two infants, they were favourites in Ward E. It was a happy time, despite the hospital surroundings and even with Asha's poor body torn and damaged as never before.

As for Margarita, her old wounds had almost healed. Then, without warning, she suffered her very first lucio attack. Overnight there came sudden swellings to cover her entire body, lumps and cones. Her nerves were enlarged and tender. No position offered any comfort, there was always a sore place rubbing raw against the mattress. Asha Makokha could not assist her friend physically. She could only do her best to keep up Margarita's courage. And, when Asha could no longer stand Margarita's pain, she would scream for the nurse. Those screams were loud ones, terrible for the other patients to hear. For herself Margarita was stubborn, not giving way to pain. It was her habit always to be thinking that worse pain was coming and so for now she had better hold out as best she could. Even then during the attacks which gave her a feeling of being at war with her own body, she kept a command over her secret smile. Why, asleep, that smile might convince people she was a newborn child.

And all the time Margarita was having to wonder where the new seriousness of her leprosy could be coming from. Did she have an enemy in the hospital? We know of stories, too, where people from outside bribe the nurses to be putting poison in a patient's food. Bed is not always such a safe place! But Margarita was suspecting that the blame this time, truly it had to be nobody else's but her own. Why? – for telling Asha Makokha the story of how people in Lubinu had played their tricks on her. There must have been spirits listening. Or perhaps her mistake had been to take Asha Makokha's baby on her breast? No, for her friend she would do that again, gladly. Often when not awake, but not asleep either, Margarita was undecided what to think. Her mind drifted and was ever changing. With such a wind who can ever say how or why it is coming?

Doctors, they were gathering now several times in the day to see Margarita. They would stand not far from her bed, talk with each other in serious low voices. Then maybe one would leave the group, come closer to feel Margarita's pulse or to see if she could bend her leg. With flat sticks they would collect pus from the whorls erupting everywhere from her flesh. These doctors tried new medicines and combinations of medicines. Injections, but also pills with stripes and red pills and sweet liquids and rubbing ointments with such strong smells that other women in the ward had to complain. Some medicines worked, some did not. There were even short periods when all Margarita's distress would clear. Then she was weak but coherent. At these times the Dutch doctor's wife was her special companion, bringing thermoses filled with weak pale tea, caring for Margarita's baby and Asha Makokha's, too. She was clumsy, large and generous the way a woman is who has no children of her own.

Asha Makokha's health was going down, too. She had stayed at home without treatment too long so that now her bones were infected in a way no one could stop. Also the roof of her mouth was collapsing, her eyes, her lungs. The doctors had thought that pregnancy and birth would be dangerous for her. Her condition upon arrival had been so poor there were even voices against admitting her. A death was never good for the name of the hospital.

For three weeks Margarita wife of Emmanuel hung between life and death, her breath by times too weak to disturb even a mosquito alighting on her lips. A priest was coming to pray for her at bedside. The other patients, they heard him but about Margarita no one could be certain.

'You must learn to obey God who is merciful and the only ruler. You must learn to face the highest court. Your blood, your meat, your bones will remain here. They will rot. Now you are facing up to what you have done. What you are going to be asked for is your soul.'

For three weeks a great many notes and photographs were taken. Doctors no one had ever seen before came to look at Margarita, to give their opinion and then to disappear again for good. A group of medical students in training were given a lecture while the doctor pointed with his pencil at different signs of Margarita's suffering. Some of them were becoming weak in the knees. The other patients went on with weaving mats and exercising their hands, opening and closing their fingers in time to a definite count. You could not tell what they were thinking. Death is a subject they preferred to avoid, until it happened.

Finally, smiling, Margarita emerged from her long crisis. It was over, just like that, her first ordeal. And a few days before, less than five, Asha Makokha had died. Her death was a quiet affair, of hardly any medical interest. She had held out as long as possible. She had not wanted to die without knowing if Margarita was going to recover.

The heat was such that it was necessary to remove a leprosy body right away. One of the nurses told Margarita that her friend had been buried in the hospital grounds. Patients from the hospital had washed the corpse, wrapped it properly and dug the grave. The government paid them a small wage for doing these duties. Until Margarita was better enough in her health to explain that she was a relative to Asha Makokha and to name the name of the Tiemas, there had been no way to know what family to inform about the deceased. On arrival Asha herself had not spoken about her home. She was feeling so ashamed of her neglected condition.

The doctor's wife had been caring for both Margarita's and Asha's sons. She had made a place for them in her caravan, side by side in the corner next to the piano and across from the rabbit cage. Now as Margarita continued to regain strength, a cot for the children was set up right beside her. Usually she left her own child lying there, but took Asha's new baby to sleep on the mattress with her.

A time came when Margarita inquired into the place where Asha Makokha lay buried. By then her own body was beginning to feel a little bit all right. Even the doctors were acting pleased with her.

The day was clear. For Margarita things which were themselves bright looked brighter still. For weeks and weeks she had not been setting foot out of the ward. She had grown so used to the semi-dark and to sounds of muffled suffering. The rest of life had just faded, like some far-away stream, one you could hear only occasionally, the water passing over stone. For so long now Margarita's world had been a mere landscape of beds and bandaged patients, carts on wheels with bottles and labels, impatient nurses, white linen growing foul and stained and then renewed to white again. So much white, and black and grey.

Now the trees, the lawn, thickets with berries, bursts of flowers, the freshness, the colour were a celebration. Air rushed into Margarita's lungs, welcoming her. She was even lifting up her hands as if she might touch the insubstantial, feel the world. Most beautiful of all was a view of the distance, the Tororo hills in Uganda. As she looked, Margarita could feel her smile changing on her face until it was wider than it had been in so long, like a wound that has been given stitches but stretches in the healing. Really, to ask for anything more than one day at a time, that would be too ungrateful.

Margarita had already begun to practise walking inside the ward, testing her legs to carry her some short distance. Outside, after few steps, she knew to go further she would need help. Leaning against a support of the portico roof, Margarita was considering whether to return to her bed when an old man in a wheelchair called to her. Someone with a pair of sunglasses and a beret of a faded red colour. 'Come,' he said. 'We two, we are both children.' By holding on to the handles of the man's wheelchair, Margarita could more easily keep her balance. And other people thought it was she who was being so helpful! Without hurry the man took her all the way to the quiet plot near the far edge of the hospital grounds where Asha Makokha's body lay newly interred.

Especially when the man in the chair would speak, choosing his words carefully and well, Margarita had to smile. She recognized the voice. She knew it was Nicodeme from Camp Lepra. Still she did not want to tell him she was his old friend. She did and she didn't. He looked very much the same except now his hands were swollen and some fingers were gone, too. Also his wheelchair was a fancy modern model made of gleaming metal. Isn't it true that more than almost anything else people would rather believe that their old friends are not suffering any more?

'You see, *she* has been cured,' Nicodeme said. 'Finally.'

'God must have loved her very much,' was Margarita's answer. That was what the wife of the Dutch doctor had been telling her, '– to let her suffer so.' Only now, the end of the woman's message of Christian consolation, that Margarita was keeping to herself.

Next to the old man in his wheelchair, Margarita on the ground sat still some minutes in a kind of peace. The sight of the soil and footprints of an animal across the grave, they began to fill her with feelings of loneliness. Then, as in a dream, Margarita said, '*Mzei*, you and I, we are knowing each other many years already now. We were even friends in Camp Lepra. I am the wife of that Emmanuel son of Wattako whose eyes were always shedding much water.' When Nicodeme failed to reply, Margarita looked up. He was sleeping, his head back, his dark cracked lips so slightly open. She could see now how badly his sunglasses were needing cleaning, but to try to remove them would risk waking the old man.

The Return

We are not remembering when Margarita was returning to Lubinu from Asembo Hospital, not exactly. At present it is as if she never was away. But then? No one, I think, was missing her, not really. After she was back, when we became used to her, she belonged. That is all. What is, is.

Shebani probably can name the day Margarita returned. He has reasons, we must be thinking, for keeping an accurate memory of Margarita's homecoming. Days here, though, they are so much the same. What difference is it making on which one Margarita's new life began?

Of course Margarita sent no word on ahead. The day of her discharge she was merely accepting bus fare from the administrative director of Asembo and leaving there. A few friends, some serious cripples, waited with Margarita for the bus to come. No one said goodbye. All the way home Margarita wore a little smile. She set out for Lubinu without expectation or dread. Illness had cured her from the habit of wondering about the future. Ask nothing from tomorrow, then how can it disappoint?

Even though the parcel of properties which Margarita carried was not heavy, she frequently stopped to rest during the foot journey which followed the bus ride. Despite all the years, it did not seem such a long time that she had been away. It was almost as if Margarita took many rests to keep herself from hurrying. She did not want to appear eager.

Those people on the bus, so many going places, they were expected, welcomed on their safe arrival. They were wrestling packages in and out of the racks overhead or shouting loudly for attendants to climb on to the roof of the bus to lower down a bale or suitcase. Really, so much to notice. In Asembo Hospital life had become predictable, comfortable even, and very private. On the bus Margarita had changed her seat several times. Then she always looked back to where she had just moved away from, as if she had hope of seeing herself sitting there still, one cheek pressed against the window, staring out into the countryside. Few patients discharged from Asembo Hospital choose to send word ahead. They are not thinking to surprise, but why not let a sleeping dog lie?

One of Margarita's stops for resting was at a footbridge over the narrow nameless river where, in a previous life it seemed, she had come so often early in the morning to bathe. It was her custom then to wash before sunrise, enjoying how the dark lifted and how first sunlight made the parts of her body under water visible. There were young women down there now, splashing each other, rubbing sponges across each other's backs and breasts, laughing and singing through their teeth. Colourful clothing lay scattered on the far bank, together with clay water-jars and calabashes the bathers had carried with them. When Margarita went to Asembo, these women had been shy girls, children who kept silent and at a little distance when women went to bathe.

As Margarita continued on her way, she chewed a new thought. Some of the bathers who looked up at her, staring into her face, surely they must have recognized her. But no one showed it. To Margarita it did not occur that in the years she had been kept under care of the doctors, the months when she had balanced on the edge between life and death, the moments of pain so bad that only by deceiving herself that this pain belonged to someone else could she keep from giving a scream that might never have ended, no, it did not dawn on Margarita wife of Emmanuel, returning to the only place she ever had called home, a place peopled with enemies who she believed had conspired to bring about her death, that perhaps she herself had changed so much in her appearance, that with the sun shining down from behind her, none of the bathing women with water on their eye-lashes, with cold stones under their feet, would know, would even guess, who she was.

Perhaps one of them did. At least less than a minute after Margarita had stopped smiling and walked ahead, this particular woman waded silently to the bank and sat there with her head forward, resting on her knees.

Almost before she knew it, there in the distance Margarita could see the roof of her hut, the thatch gone grey with age and exposure. She rounded a towering clump of bamboo and the whole scene grew familiar. Now, with every forward step, she went on repeating to herself the resolution she had formed in the hospital. A promise she was making when the doctors advised her that she was being released, one she had told no one about. How people looked at her, what they did or said – she would not let it matter. Friendly, not friendly. *This time she would keep to herself.* Yes, for a hundred per cent. The last time, after Camp Lepra, she, the wife of a young man, had believed in the welcome people gave. She had gone visiting. She had laughed when they laughed. And she had thought of herself as healthy. Now, she accepted the truth that leprosy disease was never going to leave her body. *Amachere*, it did not let go. The doctor at Asembo had told

Margarita to go to the health centre for an examination immediately after reaching home. She should go on with receiving proper medicine at a tree clinic near where she lived. On and on. Margarita shifted her pack, mostly belongings of the late Asha Makokha, and she thought, 'Well, let us see how long it lasts this time.'

By now the fields along the path were filling with curious children. Children are always the first ones to see that a visitor is coming.They rush out to stare, for them it is allowed. As Margarita walked past they whispered to each other, crouching down among young maize stalks, their dark eyes at a level with the pale green tassels. Most of these children, when Margarita had left Lubinu, had not yet been born. She had no names for them, no stories to match with their faces. Her own children? They would be returned to her. Oh, yes. This time – she would keep to herself, and her children.

'Hello! Hello!'

These children did not react to Margarita as if she were a stranger. Why? Was there something in her walk, some way she took the surroundings in with her eyes that told them she, too, belonged there?

'*Nya!*' Margarita swiped an insect from her forehead. Of course people might think Margarita had to know how changed she was in her appearance. Couldn't she feel the difference of her skin? Ah, they might think so, but then they would be wrong. Her leprosy fingers had no normal feeling left in them and so the skin of her face was still somehow smooth to touch. And as for the sight of scabs, the spider wrinkles on her arms, across her trunk and over all her legs – Margarita still thought of her body as a young body. From the inside, it was not feeling so different now from when before the lucio attacks had begun. In fact Margarita was having a photograph of herself with Emmanuel that was taken in a shop in Kakamega soon after they met. They had even to sneak past the guards at Camp Lepra into the town for visiting the photographer. To pose Margarita was given a special dress to put on. Nicodeme had arranged for Emmanuel to have a white shirt. Ten shillings it cost, the expense was a bit extra for leprosy patients. Margarita always thought of herself as looking the way she looked in that happy photo. Who can blame her?

The house Margarita returned to was just derelict. More of the walls had crumbled away than still stood. The grass of the roof was thinned and disarranged by wind and rain. The door hung crooked. Margarita had expected to find some work that would have to be done, reclaying at least. What met her eyes, however, that was so bad she had to smile. Then and there she decided not to move back into those ruins, never. Look, the front post still lay in the dust a few yards away. The roof support someone came by night to pull out from under the eaves, in a magical gesture to kill her. No one had removed it. For the Luhya to see a house like that is a sign that the person living there has died. But Margarita only shook her head and walked a short distance away. She had learned not to listen to the shriekings of memory. The past, it could only touch her if she let it.

Emmanuel was nowhere to be seen. Margarita could not help looking for the son of Wattako even though she knew he would be away. Even she was preferring a time by herself for growing accustomed again to the world. Anything other than utter loneliness, anything more, would take getting used to. Since Asha Makokha's death, there had been no one, really. Emmanuel was in the town now. He had work there, Margarita knew, as night watchman. A relative of Nicodeme had hired him. And also Emmanuel had inherited a wife. A woman old enough to be his mother, they said, a leprosy patient. She had a prayer mat and would sit on it to worship outside the mosque in the town on Friday, touching the ground with her forehead. The patients coming to Asembo, they had much news to share. Something for everybody.

Margarita looked down and watched a file of ants disappearing into a black hole in the ground. What she had to do now was stay put. Life would re-form by itself. Left alone, weeds will grow. Others, without her asking, had already gone to find Emmanuel, she knew, to argue with him to come back to her.

Back straight up against one of the young eucalyptus trees which she had urged Emmanuel to be planting when they first came to the land of the Tiemas, trees grown so tall now, just the way she had described, Margarita sat with her face out of the sun, legs extended their full length in front of her. She wore the blue dress of the hospital with its small round frayed white collar. So through the next years she sat. Her posture, the dress, the same. Mostly her face was like an old mask, but sometimes for visitors the mask broke into a warm human face. And after Emmanuel did return and they had brought more healthy children into the world, Margarita slowly by slowly allowed herself more freedom. She wandered to the next homestead. She stood chatting to the women there – Tiema's relations by marriage. But never further. And never did she accept an invitation to sit down. Really, we just invited, she refused.

As long as she remembered nothing, only felt the sun and shade making their claims on her body, watched Emmanuel walking about in the rags he wore so well, busied herself with the children, then she stayed shy, peaceful. Only when one certain memory separated out from all the rest, only if slowly Asha Makokha's face, defiant with beauty, rose again into view, then Margarita had to grow angry.

That first hot day of Margarita's return to us, worn out from her walk, from the hours of jolting along in the full bus, too, Margarita had all but fallen asleep directly when finally she sat on the earth near the remains of her hut. Her eyes, they closed – but not completely. It was as if she sat waiting for some person to keep an appointment. She was a trifle early, that was all, but whether by an hour, a day, or a year was not certain. Our children spread the news. A woman with such a flat nose had come to sit near the house of Emmanuel. Then they had hurried back to sit in rows at the edge of the fields where Emmanuel had raised millet in the past. Cassava was planted there now. Cassava is a lazy man's crop. Drought does not kill it. Margarita knew that after Camp Lepra Emmanuel was not working so hard any more.

At first through her half-closed eyelids, breathing so silently, Margarita thought she was seeing a cloud come floating down the hill. Every so often the cloud would stop and then she saw dark arms rise out of its sides and then draw back in again. Days of such harsh illness, careening within easy reach of death and then, to her endless surprise, cheating death despite her own lack of any strength for making an effort – such days had made Margarita used to visions. She no longer tried in a great hurry to put them out of her mind, no longer opened her eyes wide as if in that way she could chase them. Rather she learned to welcome them, to inhale them deeply as her privilege. Besides, she knew at once in her heart what it was, who it was. Shebani in his jellabah.

'Margarita wife of Emmanuel, greetings. But you did not send word?'

Margarita grinned. This was not the smile the children loved. It was a grin to confuse the doctor, a grin you could burn your eyes on. The doctors, they were always after her to tell about her pain. To give it words she knew could only make it worse. So she grinned instead and they could not reach her.

'No.' Margarita was having to decide how much kindness there was to hear in Shebani's voice. With him, that was never easy. In seven years he had not aged. Not a hair was different. Or maybe he aged from morning to night, every day the same and then, asleep, was renewed like the moon. One day perhaps the moon would drop out of the sky but until then it would appear splendid as ever. Margarita ran her fingers through the dry soil, truly smiling now, eyes on her lap.

'He has gone for a funeral, Emmanuel.'

Without interrupting the meaningless drift of her fingers, still with her eyes down, Margarita did something no one outside the Tiema family had ever done before. She contradicted Shebani.

'Oh, brother, no, he has not.'

'He has not,' Shebani agreed. Those few words, they were so important.

The children began to giggle despite themselves because of their not understanding. They were clasping hands over each other's mouths. Shebani looked hard at them but they were not minding. Very carefully he adjusted his jellabah before speaking again.

'Did you travel well, Margarita?'

'Sure.'

'And now, how are you feeling in your body?'

'A little bit all right.'

Shebani cocked his head to one side, studying Margarita's bundle of properties. She could not be sure whether he was recognizing his dead sister's *khanga*, the one Margarita was using to wrap her few poor possessions in. It was to be kind that Shebani had come, she decided. To try. That was not easy for such a man. He was better at being proud.

'Thank you,' Margarita said. Strangers would have to wonder very much at these words of hers, the way they seemed to fly out of the air, so without any reference at all. Still, Margarita spoke them slowly, with emphasis. And she repeated what she said with her eyes. It seems that was what Shebani had come for. His shoulders dropped very slightly. Lines relaxed at the corners of his mouth. Then after she said Thank you and nodded, Margarita leaned her head back against the eucalyptus trunk and closed her eyes completely. Like that she fell asleep in no time.

Shebani returned up the hill, covering the ground with long strides. The words had come sooner than he even had hoped. He felt for Emmanuel's sunglasses in the pocket of his jellabah. Margarita wasn't afraid, how exceptional. Or was that what the modern common wind had taught her – how to conceal fear? If so, then Margarita was close to the root of his magic.

Russell Hoban

Mnemosyne, Teen Taals, and Tottenham Court Road

All India Radio broadcasts to Europe and the United Kingdom daily from 1745 to 2230 GMT on a frequency of 11,620 kHz. I listen to it almost everyday and I record as much music as I can. Sometimes reception is beautifully clear, and the chromatic splendours of the classical Karnatak style build palaces of sound all round me in my Fulham work-room. Swaying painted elephants and iridescent peacocks, chanting priests, multitudes of worshippers, solitary mystics and astronomers, saffron-veiled beauties and dancers with ankle bells glisten in the misty drizzle of the London night outside my window, all India vivid with my ignorance. Great wild eastern dawns and screaming birds rise where the red and green lights of the District Line wink to the passing of the golden windows rumbling townwards, rumbling homewards. Distant passengers, perhaps seen every day, perhaps never to be seen again, pass in the passing windows among the painted elephants and the clash of ankle bells, the marble and the filigrees. At other times the ionosphere is unfavouring: Shiva as Destroyer, Kali with her necklace of skulls, garish polychrome demons dance in my short wave receiver, roaring and crackling and filling the room with chaos which is, after all, to be expected; I accept it without complaint.

On the night of January 18th on 11,620 kHz there came across the more than four thousand miles of night air between Delhi and London in the General Overseas Service of All India Radio an illustrated talk devised, written, and presented by V. Petanjali: *The Concept of Time in Indian Music*. Having been pondering that very matter for the last year or so I wanted to hear what Mr Petanjali had to say but I was able to hear only a little; most of his talk was lost in the crackle and roar of the deities and demons of the air. Of the intelligible remainder much disappeared into the abyss between a dinner guest and my remembering to put a fresh tape cassette into the recorder. Some of his words, however, were not lost: while my wife and I and our friend ate sweet-and-sour spare ribs and drank red wine my Yaesu FRG-7000 communications receiver listened to Delhi and my Uher CR240 listened to the FRG-7000. The next morning when I played back the tape I had Mr Petanjali's opening words. Here they are:

> To talk about the time concept in Indian music I have to begin at the very beginning: in the rotation of planets, in the cycle of time, in the very cosmic design the ancient

> Indians discerned a fascinating rhythmic pattern. They felt proud about their knowledge, and in great reverence placed a drum, called *damaru*, in the hands of Lord Shiva, a god of their trinity.

There followed music and the beginning of Mr Petanjali's detailed exposition, which was soon lost in the roar and the crackle. I contented myself with Shiva's drum; that alone was enough for me; the idea of it, conveyed from a four thousand miles-distant mind by radio waves reflected from the ionosphere, immediately began to exist everywhere in my mind, my mind that recognizes its own action as emanating from the beat of that cosmic drum.

Heinrich Zimmer in his book *Myths and Symbols in Indian Art and Civilization* describes South Indian bronzes of Shiva-Natarāja dating from the tenth and twelfth centuries A.D. This is Shiva as Lord of the Dance, gesturing conventionally with his double arms as he dances in a ring of flame upon the prostrate body of a dwarfish demon:

> The upper right hand, it will be observed, carries a little drum, shaped like an hour-glass, for the beating of the rhythm. This connotes Sound, the vehicle of speech, the conveyor of revelation, tradition, incantation, magic, and divine truth. Furthermore, Sound is associated in India with Ether, the first of the five elements. Ether is the primary and most subtly pervasive manifestation of the divine Substance. Out of it unfold, in the evolution of the universe, all the other elements, Air, Fire, Water, and Earth. Together, therefore, Sound and Ether signify the first, the truth-pregnant moment of creation, the productive energy of the Absolute, in its pristine, cosmogenetic strength.

Shiva's drum beats time and creates sound which is the vehicle of speech and the conveyor of revelation, tradition, incantation, magic, and divine truth – all of which rely on or collaborate with memory. With the gyroscope of memory we navigate our forward course both mental and physical, whether from bathroom to kitchen, Tchaikovsky to Bach, or ten leagues beyond the wide world's end. Through memory we refer, we connect, we recall, we retain, we bring back, we hold on to.

Mnemosyne is Memory and she is the mother of the nine muses because all of our arts and sciences – all of what we are and where we are – comes from the womb of memory spiralled in the double helix of human genetics and the collective conscious and unconscious experience of the human race.

The etymology of such a word as *memory* is bound to be worth looking into; there will always be surprises. *Memory* comes, by way of Middle French, from the Latin *memoria* – *memor* meaning mindful. It is akin the Old English *gemimor* meaning well-known; *mimorian* to remember; the Middle Dutch *mimeren* to muse, brood; the Latin *mora* delay; the old Irish *airmert* prohibition; the Greek trouble *mermēra*; and the Sanskrit *smarati* he remembers.

Delay, prohibition, trouble! *Mora, airmert, mermēra*! Yes, indeed – how often memory delays and is delayed, prohibits and is prohibited, troubles and makes trouble!

And returning to Heinrich Zimmer and Shiva-Natarāja, what do we find in his description of the prostrate dwarfish demon on whom Shiva dances? Zimmer says:

> This is Apasmāra Purusha, 'The Man or Demon (*purusa*) called Forgetfulness or Heedlessness (*apasmāra*)'. It is symbolical of life's blindness, man's ignorance. Conquest of this demon lies in the attainment of true wisdom. Therein is release from the bondages of the world.

So Shiva's prostrate demon, the demon that must be conquered, is forgetfulness. And yet we remember, we do not forget, that the word *memory* in its rolling ramble on the roads of speech and time has picked up and gathered to itself *mora, airmert,* and *mermēra*: delay; prohibition; trouble.

Memory is the natural and necessary partner of music. Music is a puissant recaller of time past; music is memory's sister and for its very life relies on memory to hold in our minds the passage of sounds through time.

Shiva's drum beats time, makes sound for music to live in, music that lives by memory, or at least in our usage it *seems* to live by memory. Certainly when we listen back inside our heads for Mario Cavaradossi pacing the battlements of the Castel Sant'Angelo and singing '*E lucevan le stelle*', we are invoking memory, or when we listen back for a Chopin mazurka or even a Bach cantata. When we come to such as Bach's *The Art of Fugue*, however, something else enters into it: we find ourselves not so much retracing a track of note-by-note sound as experiencing a mode of being to which sound is a rite of passage and a way of the spirit to a place beyond music, a place where memory cannot reach, where every time is now. The music that puts us in that place does not depend on memory; it is without greed, makes no demands; it doesn't ask to be remembered. By such music Apasmāra Purusha – who is Forgetfulness and Heedlessness, who is life's blindness and man's ignorance – is overwhelmed, defeated, crushed beneath our foot at the very outset because there is no need to remember, nothing to remember: there is only being and the flicker of time/no time, dance and stillness.

An exemplary form of the ungreedy, not-asking-to-be-remembered kind of music is the Indian time cycle: the *teen taal*, the *jhap taal*, and other rhythmic patterns. Keep in mind that this is not a scholar's analysis: I am not a scholar nor am I taking in the music in a scholarly way. It comes to me varying in the strength and clarity of its signal according to sun-spots, weather, and interference; its transmission and reception seem a paradigm of the heart's desire in a dark wood full of dangers. Wounded, broken, near dismembered, it arrives sometimes, and always I await it with a lover's hopes and fears. I listen to All India Radio addictively and indiscriminately: ragas; folk songs; song hits from the silver screen; news; commentary; talks on drought, famine, and holy days – anything, even cricket test match resumés. I do it because that music has made all of All India Radio interesting to me. I never know in what form it will turn up, that music that takes me to the place deeper than memory. Most often it's the time cycles but often it happens in the vocal and instrumental ragas and sometimes in folk songs, particularly those of Manipur.

What's happened is that I've come to a time when I don't want much emotion in my music; I don't require either to be uplifted or downput by it. I find myself not listening to my favourite Bach, Haydn, Mozart, Beethoven, Schubert, Chopin. I don't want much emotion; I want the dance in the stone. That's how I think of it: the dance in the stone; not the foam forever fading in the wake of our forward motion. As I write this I'm listening to Haydn's String Quartet Opus 54 No 2 in C; it is lean, muscular, brilliantly brooding; the adagio always breaks my heart. But I find that breaking the heart with music isn't the thrill it once was. What I'm after more and more is on the other side of heartbreak; it's in the stone of things, with bare, spare music that not only doesn't ask to be remembered, it doesn't ask for anything at all, makes no attempt to hold on to the hearer or anything else. It moves to the beat of Shiva's drum, which is after all nothing especially eastern or exotic: it is only that same everyday drum in the heart of the atom, the same in Hammersmith as in Hyderabad, moving to the beat of the stillness in the dance and the dance in the stillness.

Of the Indian time cycles the sparest and barest are those performed on the *tabla*, the two drums often heard in accompaniment of the sitar. In the *teen taal* I most admire, the drums, played by Alla Rakha, are the foreground instruments, providing a constantly varying percussion against the unvarying melodic continuo of unknown wind instruments. The continually varying sameness of the *teen taal* gives us the alternating of stillness and dance that is the audible flicker of what we call time. Hearing this music I remember having molecules and atoms explained for the first time, how the wooden table that looks and feels so solid, so much the very essence of tangible everyday reality, is in fact a phantom table, a table of illusion, the very sketchiest transparency of the ghost of a table in which molecules and atoms glance and ricochet, whizzing silently in the figures of the table dance. I remember my astonishment at leaning my elbows on the table dance, on the transparent ghost of the thing, on the whizzing lightning interplay of particles that agree, by courtesy only and as a favour, to dance in the shape of a table for a while. I remember amazement at the spilling of milk and the spooning up of porridge on that metaphysical accommodation in the shape of a table. All of that is in the flicker of the stillness and the dance that is the *teen taal* that doesn't ask to be remembered, doesn't try to hold on, offers its steady flicker without greed and without assumption.

The Indian time cycle offers a continually unassuming repetition with its modest but seemingly infinite variation and permutation. This continual repetition sets all clocks at nought, defeats all haste and hurry, gives us a place to be. We are not remorselessly and implacably hurried along on a track of mortal tragedy. Because that is after all the mortal tragedy, that the foam is continually fading in the wake, that the moment will not stay.

The moment will not stay. We seek out places where the sorrow will be lessened, places where there is heart's ease in the sorrow, heart's comfort amidst the pain. For good or ill the moment will not stay. How fast the world flees in all directions from us! How can we hold on to just a little more world, only a little. It isn't much to ask.

With hardware, with machines, with steel precision, with nickel-cadmium, with digital readouts and light-emitting diodes we hope to grip the slippery sea-goddess moment that slides so smoothly through our longing, through our lusting, and our lonesome fingers. There are places to which we go for what we need: there is Tottenham Court Road.

Along Tottenham Court Road drift men with hungry faces, hungry eyes, and I among them. Drifting, pausing, looking, hoping, lusting for heart's ease, soul's comfort, all that gleams and flaunts its steely-satin lustre in the shining windows of the shops in Tottenham Court Road. Tottenham Court Road! Street of sin, street of shame! I go there by underground, rumbling beneath the surface, howling through black tunnels. I emerge into the light of those windows of desire gleaming in the winter dusk. Heart's ease! Soul's comfort! Precision, weight, accuracy, professional quality! There is so much I need, so much I want, and all of it is here in my street of love and lust, of audio and video, of high fidelity, of liquid crystal display and digital read-out.

How shall I speak my heart? I want so much, need so much! I need circuitry and calibration and oscillations of quartz: I need synthesizers and equalizers; I need whatever is the very latest development, because whatever I have is not quite the very latest development, not quite the state-of-the-art thing, not truly the reference model.

I need a quartz digital watch with a liquid crystal display in a steel case weighing five pounds, bound together with quarter-inch thick steel rivets and secured to my wrist with half-inch thick steel links. It must have a stop-watch function, a lap timer, and an alarm function. It must of course tell the day and the month and the time in principal cities all over the world. It must withstand pressures of five thousand pounds to the inch, must operate underwater to a depth of a mile and a half, and be perfectly resistant to the suckers of giant squids. It must not lose more than a tenth of a second per year. The watch I have now is useless: it loses three tenths of a second per year and it won't tell me the time in Kuala Lumpur.

I need, I need, I am faint with need and with desire. The calculator I have now won't do anything but add, subtract, multiply, and divide. I need one with a digital clock on it, and of course the clock must have the alarm function and the principal cities capability. I need a square root and a round root function. I need both logarithms and plankarithms. I need in my calculator a memory that will retain not only the square roots, the round roots, the logarithms, and the plankarithms but also my passport number, mortgage number, life assurance number, car insurance number, car registration number, driver number, AA membership number, credit card numbers, current account number, cheque-card number, National Health Service number, telephone number, name, and address. Also it must tell me when and where the sales meeting is and who is selling what to whom. This calculator must be as thin as one side of a very thin sheet of paper or I can't use it. If it weighs more than a postage stamp it's no good to me. Very thick watches and very thin calculators are what I need.

High fidelity. Never have I had fidelity of sufficient height, and I crave it. I require the fidelity of hundreds, of many, many symphony orchestras, all of them faithful from twenty to twenty thousand hertz and with watts enough to do it to my neighbour louder than he can do it to me. I need speakers as big as vans. What I'm after is that the reproduced sound be more original than the original. The original came and went like everything else; it was no more than a fleeting murmur in a doubting ear. I need professional quality pre-amplifiers and amplifiers and graphic equalizers; I need massive woofers and ultrasonic tweeters because I want nothing less than a sound that will extend rearward in time to replace the sound of which it is a recording, so that nothing whatever is lost. What's the use of holding back any longer? I want to duplicate the world. I want to have in reserve a second world that does not pass away. I want in sound and image the equivalent of that map that Jorge Luis Borges tells of, that map that was the same size as the country it was a map of.

Now you know, and I needn't go into all the rest of it; I needn't tell of the short wave receiver that will pick up broadcasts from the South Pole or indeed from Jupiter if Jupiter is broadcasting. I needn't tell of the tape recorder that will listen to and record the receiver that will listen to Jupiter. I needn't tell of the filters and the antenna tuners and the trembling blue-lit needles of signal-strength meters and the tiny red and green and yellow glow of light-emitting diodes cosy in the night. I needn't tell of the teleprinter that plugs into the short wave receiver and prints out the news on paper as it comes in. There's retention for you; there's world and passing moment held if you like. Ah! So much else I needn't tell of – the video-recorders and the cameras, the 800mm telephoto lenses and the infra-red capability for seeing in the dark and recording what is seen in the dark – the owl's hunting and the mouse's death recorded with the price of gold, the fall of nations.

I've told you now and I feel better for the telling of it, so much better. There it is: one may control the habit but one doesn't change. I know what I am; I keep within decent limits – no more than one new major piece of equipment every six months and no more than three of the same thing, but I know I shall always be an equipment freak. I offer myself and my aberration for study so that others may come to understand this affliction that consumes me.

It isn't quite so bad as it was; if I live long enough I may possibly change. There may be other, more developed states of being. Possibly the only keeping is a constant letting go.

Possibly the only keeping is a constant letting go. If I speak now the name of something, how much will be in it for the hearer? If I say: the black-and-white bull of Evangelistrias. As I hear the words there seems to be world in them. Mule bells on the wind through the olive trees. The calling of the hooded crows and the sight of the sea through a notch in the mountains. World of the seen, world of the unseen.

The monastery chapel faced east. West of the altar down a steep and stony path was a spring of clear, cold mountain water like some paradigm of virtue. A crucifix in red was painted on the blue-shadowed rock; there were Greek words on a white stone tablet let into the rock from which the shining water gurgled sparkling over brown leaves, singing through its stone trough in the shade.

West of the altar was the spring. North was the sea, seen misty blue through the wooded mountains forested in recessive tones of green from the warmer foreground to the cooler distance. The most distant slope was the sparsest, the barest, the bluest before the sea. The sea seen from a mountain through a notch in mountains under the calling of hooded crows and the sighing of the wind is more world than can be taken in; one can only offer oneself to it.

East of the altar was the stable. Tethered near it were a young brown-and-white she-goat and a black mule with a tinkling bell. Some cows grazed nearby. Inside the stable in the breathy darkness was a black-and-white bull. He was lying on the straw with his back to me but when he became aware of me looking in through the window he scrambled to his feet, blowing out his warm breath, and turned to face me. He was chained to a stake with a chain that went round his horns. That black-and-white bull in the breathy darkness with a chain round his horns, that bull east of the altar in his stable on the shoulder of the mountain, that bull to be reached only by the steep ascent of a winding road, that bull seemed strong in significance, powerful in his references.

That monastery bull was the heart of the place for me and he became at once a place of the heart for me. His person became the heart of the place by virtue of his personal power and his ritual aspect. His mountain, his monastery, and his stable were on the island of Skiathos, a place between whose heart and mine nothing had happened up to that time. The bull was an epiphany that changed that. I felt privileged, awed, respectful.

I knew at once that the bull thus manifesting himself – horns and chain, breath and bollocks and pizzle in the breathy darkness – had entered me, had taken up a being at my centre, offering there his salutary magic and his unimpeachable power. I knew that nothing could be added to him or taken from him.

I must back up now and approach the bull again by way of the monastery. The Monastery of Evangelistrias on its mountain shoulder at the end of a rough and winding ascent is a manifestation of power. Whether you pray to other gods or to no gods you know it when you see it: the white walls and the cypresses, the pantiles and the slated roofs like tumuli – like breasts – the buildings of the complex holding themselves in steady converse with stone and tree and sky.

It was at the Monastery of Evangelistrias that the Greek flag was first flown in 1807, and it was with that flag that the oath was made to liberate Greece from Turkish domination. That mountain shoulder has the air of a stronghold that has defended itself; it has the look of a place that has paid its dues. The monastery has the presence of what people worship. It makes its claim upon the most casual visitor; it is serious, not to be trifled with. It makes unfaith and disbelief seem silly.

My attainment of the monastery/bull place of the heart was in three stages. On the first day that I saw Evangelistrias my family and I had driven up that rough and dusty road to find the monastery locked up. Its place was there, its place on which to stand; its spring was there, cold and clear; its bull was there, dark and patient; the monastery itself was closed. We tried the locked doors east and west, knocked, and got no answer. We walked all round it; we looked up at a dovecote rising from a ruined annex. We admired the cypresses and the olive trees; we drank from the spring. Having only two exposures left in the camera I photographed an olive tree before finding the stable and the bull. That was the first stage.

The next day I came back alone with the camera, two rolls of film, and a tape recorder; I am after all, both by instinct and profession, a hunting-gathering animal. The equipment was modest; the camera was one I'd just given my wife for her birthday. It is not a professional instrument; she prefers something undemanding and simple to use. For the last ten years I have avoided buying myself a proper camera; I haven't wanted to over-excite myself. The tape recorder was the little cassette machine I use for a notebook.

Using my forty-eight exposures carefully I covered the subject reasonably well. First I photographed the approach on the tawny road that wound through olive trees with glimpses of the tiled and slated roofs of Evangelistrias behind the cypresses. Having arrived I photographed the front and the entrance, then went through the now unlocked door into the courtyard with its carefully placed trees growing out of square apertures in the flagstones, their trunks whitewashed to wainscot height. The trees grew up out of the stones and the stones rose up among the trees in compact stairs and arches, in white walls with dishes ornamentally let into them and slanting roofs of tile or breast-shaped slated roofs.

In one of the white walls of the courtyard was a shallow arched alcove in which there was a small arched niche painted red. In the niche was a tile with a Madonna and Child pictured in blue and white; the tile's white margin made it look like a large postage stamp. Just below the tile was a large square marble inlay which enclosed, with a black and white and red circular border, a black Greek cross with red rays on a white ground. The effect was like a compass rose. White arabesques on black filled out the corners of the square. Out of the centre of the black cross grew an iron water tap. There was a brown-painted cement trough under the tap, green plants on either side of it – one in a red pot and one in a large red tin can; a yellow melon by the red tin can. In front of the trough a yellow-handled mop stood in an olive-coloured plastic bucket as if confessing to the iron tap. Little trees on either side, not orange trees, arched towards each other in front of the arched alcove. There was a grape arbour as well, and as I backed up to photograph the red-painted niche I took into my field of view a low-hanging tendril of the vine swaying its green leaves in front of the face of the Virgin on the blue-and-white tile.

Seeing is not a simple thing, neither present sight nor sight recalled. I have been looking at my photographs as I write this: at the same time they give me what I didn't see and they take away what I did see. They take away the seeing of it; they present me with facts I cannot arrive at. Even if I put all fifty of them up on the wall in two rows of twenty-five or in five rows of ten or ten rows of five, I cannot take in all of them at once: moving my eyes from one to the next I lose the image as I go. If they lie in a stack on my desk, only the one on top is visible. If I have slides made, they'll be in a box waiting to be shown; if they're shown, they'll have only their brief moment of illumination. Why did I take the photographs? I wanted a world in reserve, nothing lost, everything stored for retrieval. I photographed all the buildings in the monastery compound so that I have the visual equivalent of a walk round the inside of the place. I photographed the chapel, its ikons, its candelabra, the vaulting of the ceiling. I went outside again and photographed the ruined annex and the dovecote. I photographed the top of the mountain where the hooded crows were calling. I photographed the notch in the mountains and the misty blue where the sea was.

I thought: should I photograph the bull or shouldn't I? The bull was already both himself and the image of himself, I knew that. There was already in me a total recognition of that bull east of the altar, a total reception of his significance. It had already occurred to me that there is such a thing as conservation of significance. I knew, as I have written earlier, that nothing could be added to him or taken away from him. And yet . . . and yet I thought: why not be dead sure? (As I write this the thought comes to me that Othello will strangle Desdemona every time because he has simply got to have a dead certainty.) The lens and film I had were not fast enough to get a picture of the bull with the light available in the stable. I thought: shall I use flash? How can I possibly intrude on the privacy of that bull with flash? And if I do, what shall I get? It can only be a blank and wondering bull, diminished and robbed of his strong darkness by a silly flash of light.

I photographed the bull once without flash; that's why I don't actually have fifty prints from the fifty monastery exposures, only forty-nine. Then I photographed the bull once with flash. I have the print before me now as I write. There is the bull rendered flat on a piece of paper three and a half by five and an eighth inches, a tiny blank and wondering bull, diminished and robbed of his strong darkness by a silly flash of light. The causing of that diminished image of the bull to be stored on film for development later into tiny flatness constituted the second stage of my attainment of the monastery/bull place of the heart. Having done that I stood in front of the monastery looking towards the notch in the mountains and speaking my thoughts into the tape recorder.

I told myself that I'd done the bull no harm by photographing him; I hadn't taken anything away from him; if significance truly is conserved then I had lessened neither his nor mine. Yet I did something wrong, I know that. I interfered with something that doesn't want to be interfered with. That's the third stage: my knowing that my action with the monastery/bull place of the heart was incorrect.

Is it really necessary to bother this much about that place, that bull, and whether or not I acted correctly? I think it is. I think that all our capabilities were meant to be used, and I think that we are still evolving through the evolving use of our capabilities. We are the hunting and seeking animal; we are the sorting and pondering animal; we are the perceiver of the perceptible and the pursuer of the imperceptible, and our perceptions change us. It is in us to be continually more fine-tuned than we are, and the fine-tuning wants to happen.

I said that I had interfered with something that doesn't want to be interfered with. I sense that what I interfered with was the moving on of being; not the moving on of the being of the mountain or the monastery or the bull. No: it was the moving on of my own being that I interfered with when I tried to stop and hold and keep the present moment.

Just now while writing this I've misplaced my Evangelistrias photographs somewhere in the clutter on my desk; there's a flash of fear as my fingers scrabble for them. Once you've tried to stop and record the speeding moment with machines then you're lumbered with things that can be lost: bits of celluloid and paper; reels of tape. Once they're lost you feel as if you've lost some of the substance of those moments. And indeed you have lost it – you've lost it in the very act of trying to keep it. Oh, there's something dreadfully wrong here!

There's something at the back of my mind that wants to come in here. I don't know whether I can find the connection but let it come. Here it is, a recurrent male fantasy – one sees it in film after film: the man is hard and strong; his eyes are cold; he's not a man you'd trifle with. He's in a hotel, a motel, a flat, a farm-house, a warehouse. With two fingers he parts the slats of a venetian blind or he delicately moves aside a curtain or he looks through a broken place in a dusty window. Having looked out he goes to the black attaché case. He opens the case and exposes the gun. Religiously, almost. Not almost. He does it religiously: he exposes the gun. There it is, its disassembled parts all cleverly recessed in foam rubber or sometimes in red velvet: stock, breech, bolt, barrel, magazine, and telescopic sight. Lean, precise, black, sharp, clean, no doubts and no fears, it is power; it is control; it can stop the fleeting moment that beats in heart and brain. The cold-eyed man takes the clean, lean, sharp, black parts in his hands. With clicks and snaps and sharp metallic noises he assembles his lethal member. He runs his hand along the shining barrel of it. He is ready. I believe that such guns exist because I see them all the time on television. Somewhere those guns are being made and each time one is made some lesser cold-eyed man steps forward to buy it for the cold-eyed man who will use it. He never has to buy that gun for himself, the man who stands at the window; somebody always buys it for him because they need him; he doesn't need them. Everybody wants him because he is so hard, so effective, so utterly reliable.

There it is, a fragment of a fantasy you've seen many times, a fantasy you know well. I don't quite know why I've brought it in here. I can't make a rational connection. I don't think I'll try. Maybe I'm a little crazy, that could well be. But the more I see in my mind the gleaming seductions of Tottenham Court Road the more I see that cold-eyed man looking out of the window and putting his gun together.

Before I let that fantasy come in I was talking about the moving-on of being and how I had interfered with it. I did it out of fear, fear of that onward motion that leads to extinction. In moving on towards death we lose moment by moment our lives. In trying not to move on, in trying to hold on to the present moment we lose our lives moment by moment just the same and we feel the loss even more. We want at the same time to hold on and to let go.

Earlier I quoted from Dr Heinrich Zimmer's description of Shiva-Natarāja. You will remember that the upper right hand held the little hour-glass-shaped drum called *damaru.* Here is more of that description:

> The opposite hand, the upper left, with a half-moon posture of the fingers (*ardhacandra-mudrā*), bears on its palm a tongue of flame. Fire is the element of the destruction of the world. At the close of the Kali Yuga, Fire will annihilate the body of creation, to be itself then quenched by the ocean of the void. Here, then, in the balance of the hands, is illustrated a counterpoise of creation and destruction in the play of the cosmic dance. As a ruthlessness of opposites, the Transcendental shows through the mask of the enigmatic Master: ceaselessness of production against an insatiate appetite of extermination, Sound against Flame. And the field of the terrible interplay is the Dancing Ground of the Universe, brilliant and horrific with the dance of the god.
>
> The 'fear not' gesture (*abhaya-mudrā*), bestowing protection and peace, is displayed by the second right hand, while the remaining left lifted across the chest, points downward to the uplifted left foot. This foot signifies Release and is the refuge and salvation of the devotee. It is to be worshipped for the attainment of union with the Absolute. The hand pointing to it is held in a pose imitative of the outstretched trunk or 'hand' of the elephant (*gaja-hasta-mudrā*) reminding us of Ganesha, Shiva's son, the Remover of Obstacles.

'Fear not,' says the uplifted hand. The uplifted foot signifies Release and is the refuge and salvation of the devotee. Release. Letting go.

I'm thinking now about the shapes of holding and of letting go.

Earlier, speaking of the sea seen through a notch in the mountains, I said that it was more world than could be taken in; one could only offer oneself to it. Now as I write I'm looking at photographs in books to which I have been led by a craving both obscure and exacting. I first became aware of it in the treasury of Durham Cathedral, noticing the columns and the vaulting, how they were in essence trees of stone with arching branches. Pondering that, I looked again at the crypt in Canterbury Cathedral; I looked at the doors and the tympani; I looked at the interior and exterior shapes of Barfreston Church in Kent and Kilpeck Church in Herefordshire; in books I looked at photographs of crypts in French cathedrals; I looked at photographs of the sculptures of Gislebertus in the Cathedral of St Lazarus at Autun. Moving eastward through the bookshops of Great Russell Street and Charing Cross Road, I found myself possessed of large thick books full of wondrous photographs. Here is the Church of the Holy Virgin in Sanahin in Armenia; here is the College Mosque of Sultan Hassan in Cairo; here is the Church of Christ of the Chora in Constantinople. In the churches in my mind and the churches in my books are the domes and arches, the crypts and cloisters of the shapes of holding and letting go. Up and around and returning go the arches, always open. Open domes let in the light. The churches – whether domed or spired, round or pointed – hold and focus the God-receiver, the self held receptive to that which cannot be held at all. Even when ruined, empty, and abandoned those ardent, patient stones retain a consecration and a concentration intensified only by the absence of the flesh that is grass.

If the human mind is still evolving, as I believe it is, if our mind/soul capability is still developing, then the pattern of our mental intake and sorting and storing is not static but changing. It may well be that we shall learn to let go rather than hold on, that we shall become capable of being with the world rather than attempting to consume it. I went to Kilpeck Church without a camera and without a tape recorder, so the being with it was not interfered with; it's still in me happening as it will.

On February 10th Mr Petanjali's talk on the concept of time in Indian music was broadcast again by the General Overseas Service of All India Radio – twice, completely intelligible both times, and I recorded it both times. I couldn't take it in; time and being had moved me on beyond explication. The music is in me; the time of the music is in me; there is no space for an explanation of the concept of time in the music.

Reason is not sufficient; I know what I cannot explain. I know that we must outgrow the control fantasy of the man at the window with the high-fidelity gun and I know that we must find in ourselves the shapes of letting go where the bull is our dark brother and we offer ourselves to the sea beyond the notch in the mountains. We must find in ourselves the shapes of letting go because we're not free to become what we're going to be next until we let go of what we are now. We need to stop putting our seeing and our hearing of the world between us and it. We need to stop putting our perceptions between us and the thing perceived. We need to stop putting our retention ahead of the thing to be retained which cannot be retained, which must be let go of so that we can move with the Sound and Ether that spread in circles from Shiva's drum in the continuance of creation.

It's a matter of learning what cannot be taught. If I were a teacher... but of course I *am* a teacher; every mother and every father is a teacher. How can I bring my children to this being-with that doesn't hold on, this offering of the self that is a constant letting-go? Is it possible that they're born with it? Is it possible that the best I can do as a teacher is not to hammer it out of them? I think that may well be the case. I think I must let go, must fear not, must be quiet so that my children can hear the Sound of Creation and dance the dance that is in them.

GRANTA

SUSAN SONTAG

ELIAS CANETTI

> I cannot become modest; too many things burn in me; the old solutions are falling apart; nothing has been done yet with the new ones. So I begin, everywhere at once, as if I had a century ahead of me.
>
> Canetti, 1943

The speech that Elias Canetti delivered in Vienna on the occasion of Hermann Broch's fiftieth birthday, in November 1936, intrepidly sets out some of Canetti's characteristic themes and is one of the handsomest tributes one writer has ever paid to another. Such a tribute creates the terms of a succession. When Canetti finds in Broch the necessary attributes of a great writer – he is original; he sums up his age; he opposes his age – he is delineating the standards to which he has pledged himself. When he hails Broch for reaching fifty (Canetti was then thirty-one) and calls this just half of what a human life should be, he avows that hatred of death and yearning for longevity that is the signature of his work. When he extols Broch's intellectual insatiability, evoking his vision of some unfettered state of the mind, Canetti attests to equally fervent appetites of his own. And by the magnanimity of his homage Canetti adds one more element to this portrait of the writer at his age's noble adversary: the writer as noble admirer.

His praise of Broch discloses much about the purity of moral position and intransigence Canetti aspires to, and his desire for strong, even overpowering models. Writing in 1965, Canetti evokes the paroxysms of admiration he felt for Karl Kraus in the twenties while a student in Vienna, in order to defend the value for a serious writer of being, at least for a while, in thrall to another's authority: the essay on Kraus is really about the ethics of admiration. He welcomes being challenged by worthy enemies (Canetti counts some 'enemies' – Hobbes and Maistre – among his favourite writers); being strengthened by an unattainable, humbling standard. About Kafka, the most insistent of his admirations, he observes: 'One turns good when reading him but without being proud of it.'

So wholehearted is Canetti's relation to the duty and pleasure of admiring others, so fastidious is his sense of the writer's vocation, that humility – and pride – make him extremely self-involved in a characteristically impersonal way. He is preoccupied with being someone *he* can admire. This is a leading concern in *The Human*

Province, Canetti's selection from the notebooks he kept between 1942 and 1972, during most of which time he was preparing and writing his great book *Crowds and Power*. In these jottings Canetti is constantly prodding himself with the example of the great dead, identifying the intellectual necessity of what he undertakes, checking his mental temperature, shuddering with terror as the calendar sheds its leaves.

Other traits go with being a self-confident, generous admirer: fear of not being involved or ambitious enough, impatience with the merely personal (one sign of a strong personality, as Canetti says, is the love of the impersonal), and aversion to self-pity. In the first volume of his autobiography, *The Tongue Set Free*, what Canetti chooses to tell about his life features those whom he admired, whom he has learned from. Canetti relates with ardour how things worked for, not against, him; his is the story of a liberation: a mind – a language – a tongue 'set free' to roam the world.

That world has a complex mental geography. Born in 1905 into a far-flung Sephardic family then quartered in Bulgaria (his father and his paternal grandparents came from Turkey), Canetti had a childhood rich in displacements. Vienna, where both his parents had gone to school, was the mental capital of all the other places, which included England, where his family moved when Canetti was six; Lausanne and Zurich, where he had some of his schooling; and sojourns in Berlin in the late twenties. It was to Vienna that his mother brought Canetti and his two younger brothers after his father died in Manchester in 1912, and from there that Canetti emigrated in 1938, spending a year in Paris and then moving to London, where he has lived ever since. Only in exile, he has noted, does one realize how much 'the world has always been a world of exiles' – a characteristic observation, in that it deprives his plight of some of its particularity.

He has, almost by birthright, the exile writer's easily generalized relation to place: a place is a language. And knowing many languages is a way of claiming many places as one's territory. Family example (his paternal grandfather boasted of knowing seventeen languages), the local medley (in the Danube port city where he was born, Canetti says, one could hear seven or eight languages spoken every day), and the velocity of his childhood all facilitated an avid relation to language. To live was to acquire languages – his were Ladino, Bulgarian, German (the language his parents spoke to each other),

English, French – and be 'everywhere'.

That German became the language of his mind confirms Canetti's placelessness. Pious tributes to Goethe's inspiration written in his notebook while the Luftwaffe's bombs fell on London ('If, despite everything, I should survive, then I owe it to Goethe') attest to that loyalty to German culture which would keep him always a foreigner in England – where he has now spent well over half his life – and which Canetti has the privilege and the burden of understanding, Jew that he is, as the higher cosmopolitanism. He will continue to write in German – 'because I am Jewish,' he noted in 1944. With this decision, not the one made by most Jewish intellectuals who were refugees from Hitler, Canetti chose to remain unsullied by hatred, a grateful son of German culture who wants to help make it what one can continue to admire. And he has.

Canetti is reputed to be the model for the philosopher figure in several of Iris Murdoch's early novels, such as Mischa Fox in *The Flight from the Enchanter* (dedicated to Canetti), a figure whose audacity and effortless superiority are an enigma to his intimated friends.* Drawn from the outside, this portrait suggests how exotic Canetti must seem to his English admirers. The artist who is also a polymath (or vice versa), and whose vocation is wisdom, is not a tradition which has a home in English, for all the numbers of bookish exiles from this century's more implacable tyrannies who have lugged their peerless learning, their unabashed projects of greatness, to the more modestly nourished English-speaking islands, large and small, off-shore of the European catastrophe.

Portraits drawn from the inside, with or without the poignant inflections of exile, have made familiar the model itinerant intellectual. He (for the type is male, of course) is a Jew, or like a Jew;

---

*'What's odd about him?' he asked.

'Oh, I don't know,' said Annette. 'He's so–er–'

'I don't find him odd,' said Rainborough, after waiting in vain for the epithet. 'There's only one thing that's exceptional about Mischa, apart from his eyes, and that's his patience. He always had a hundred schemes on hand, and he's the only man I know who will wait literally for years for even a trivial plan to mature.' Rainborough looked at Annette with hostility.

'Is it true that he cries over things he reads in the newspapers?' asked Annette.

'I should think it's most improbable!' said Rainborough. Annette's eyes were very wide.... *The Flight from the Enchanter* poly-cultural, restless, misogynistic; a collector; dedicated to self-transcendence, despising the instincts; weighed down by books and buoyed up by the euphoria of knowledge. His real task is not to exercise his talent for explanation but, by being witness to the age, to set the largest, most *edifying* standards of despair. As a reclusive eccentric, he is one of the great achievements in life and letters of the twentieth century's imagination, a genuine hero, in the guise of a martyr. Although portraits of this figure have appeared in every European literature, some of the German ones have notable authority – *Steppenwolf*, certain essays by Walter Benjamin; or a notable bleakness – Canetti's one novel, *Auto-da-Fé*, and, recently, the novels of Thomas Bernhard, *Korrektur (Correction)* and *Der Weltverbesserer (The World Improver)*.

Auto-da-Fé – the title in German is *Die Blendung (The Blinding)* – depicts the recluse as a book-besotted naïf who must undergo an epic of humiliation. The tranquilly celibate Professor Kien, a renowned Sinologist, is ensconced in his top-floor apartment with his twenty-five thousand books – books on all subjects, feeding a mind of unrelenting avidity. He does not know how horrible life is; will not know until he is separated from his books. Philistinism and mendacity appear in the form of a woman, ever the principle of anti-mind in this mythology of the intellectual: the reclusive scholar in the sky marries his housekeeper, a character as monstrous as any in the paintings of George Grosz or Otto Dix – and is pitched from the world.

Canetti relates that he first conceived *Auto-da-Fé* – he was twenty-four – as one of eight books, the main character of each to be a monomaniac and the whole cycle to be called 'The Human Comedy of Madmen'. But only the novel about 'the bookman' (as Kien was called in early drafts), and not, say, the novels about the religious fanatic, the collector, or the technological visionary, got written. In the guise of a book about a lunatic – that is, as hyperbole – *Auto-da-Fé* purveys familiar clichés about unworldly, easily duped intellectuals and is animated by an exceptionally inventive hatred for women. It is impossible not to regard Kien's derangement as variations on his author's most cherished exaggerations. 'The limitation to a particular, as though it were everything, is too despicable,' Canetti noted – *The Human Province* is full of such Kien-like avowals. The author of the condescending remarks about women preserved in these notebooks might have enjoyed fabulating the details of Kien's delirious misogyny. And one can't help supposing that some of Canetti's work practices are evoked in the novel's account of a prodigious scholar plying his obsessional trade, afloat in a sea of manias and schemes of orderliness. Indeed, one would be surprised to learn that Canetti doesn't have a large, scholarly, but unspecialized library with the range of Kien's. This sort of library building has nothing to do with the book collecting that Benjamin memorably described, which is a passion for books as material objects (rare books, first editions). It is, rather, the materialization of an obsession whose ideal is to put the books inside one's head; the real library is only a mnemonic system. Thus Canetti has Kien sitting at his desk and composing a learned article without turning a single page of his books, except in his head.

Auto-da-Fé depicts the stages of Kien's madness as three relations of 'head' and 'world' – Kien secluded with his books as 'a head without a world'; adrift in the bestial city, 'a world without a head'; driven to suicide by 'the world in the head'. And this was not language suitable only for the mad bookman; Canetti later used it in his notebooks to describe himself, as when he called his life nothing but a desperate attempt to think about everything 'so that it comes together in a head and thus becomes one again,' affirming the very fantasy he had pilloried in *Auto-da-Fé*.

The heroic avidity thus described in his notebooks is the same goal Canetti had proclaimed at sixteen –'to learn everything' – for which, he relates in *The Tongue Set Free*, his mother denounced him as selfish and irresponsible. To covet, to thirst, to long for – these are passionate but also acquisitive relations to knowledge and truth; Canetti recalls a time when, never without scruples, he 'even invented elaborate excuses and rationales for having books.' The more immature the avidity, the more radical the fantasies of throwing off the burden of books and learning. *Auto-da-Fé*, which ends with the bookman immolating himself with his books, is the earliest and crudest of these fantasies. Canetti's later writings project more wistful, prudent fantasies of disburdenment. A note from 1951: 'His dream: to know everything he knows and yet not know it.'

Published in 1935 to praise from Broch, Thomas Mann, and others, *Auto-da-Fé* was Canetti's first book (if one does not count a play he wrote in 1932) and only novel, the product of an enduring taste for hyperbole and a fascination with the grotesque that became in later works more static, considerably less apocalyptic. *Earwitness*, published in 1974, is like an abstract distillation of the novel-cycle about lunatics Canetti conceived when he was in his twenties. This short book consists of rapid sketches of fifty forms of monomania, of 'characters' such as the Corpse-Skulker, the Fun Runner, the Narrow-Smeller, the Misspeaker, the Woe Administrator; fifty characters and no plot. The ungainly names suggest an inordinate degree of self-consciousness about literary invention – for Canetti is a writer who endlessly questions, from the vantage of the moralist, the very possibility of making art. 'If one knows a lot of people,' he had noted years earlier, 'it seems almost blasphemous to invent more.'

A year after publication of *Auto-da-Fé*, in his homage to Broch, Canetti cites Broch's stern formula: 'Literature is always an impatience on the part of knowledge.' But Broch's gifts for patience were rich enough to produce those great, patient novels *The Death of Virgil* and *The Sleepwalkers*, and to inform a grandly speculative intelligence. Canetti worried about what could be done with the novel, which indicates the quality of his own impatience. For Canetti, to think is to insist; he is always offering himself choices, asserting and reasserting his *right* to do what he does. He chose to embark on what he calls a 'life work', and disappeared for twenty-five years to hatch that work, publishing nothing after 1938, when he left Vienna (except for a second play), until 1960, when *Crowds and Power* appeared. 'Everything,' he says, went into this book.

Canetti's ideals of patience and his irrepressible feeling for the grotesque are united in his impressions of a trip to Morocco, *The Voices of Marrakesh* (1967). The book's vignettes of minimal survival present the grotesque as a form of heroism: a pathetic skeletal donkey with a huge erection; and the most wretched of beggars, blind children begging and, atrocious to imagine, a brown bundle emitting a single sound (*e-e-e-e-e-e*) which is brought every day to a square in Marrakesh to collect alms and to which Canetti pays a moving, characteristic tribute: 'I was proud of the bundle because it was alive.'

Humility is the theme of another work of this period, 'Kafka's Other Trial', written in 1969, which treats Kafka's life as an exemplary fiction and offers a commentary on it. Canetti relates the drawn out calamity of Kafka's engagement to Felice Bauer (Kafka's letters to Felice had just been published) as a parable about the secret victory of the one who chooses failure, who 'withdraws from power in whatever form it might appear.' He notes with admiration that Kafka often identifies with weak small animals, finding in Kafka his own feelings about the renunciation of power. In fact, in the force of his testimony to the ethical imperative of siding with the humiliated and the powerless, he seems closer to Simone Weil, another great expert on power, whom he never mentions. Canetti's identification with the powerless lies outside history, however; the epitome of powerlessness for Canetti is not, say, oppressed people but animals. Canetti, who is not a Christian, does not conceive of any intervention or active partisanship. Neither is he resigned. Incapable of insipidity or satiety, Canetti advances the model of a mind always reacting, registering shocks and trying to outwit them.

The aphoristic writing of his notebooks is fast knowledge – in contrast to the slow knowledge distilled in *Crowds and Power*. 'My task,' he wrote in 1949, a year after he began writing it, 'is to show how complex selfishness is.' For such a long book, it is very tense. His rapidity wars with his tenacity. The somewhat laborious, assertive writer who set out to write a tome that will 'grab this century by the throat' interferes with, and is interfered with by, a concise writer who is more playful, more insolent, more puzzled, more scornful.

The notebook is the perfect literary form for an eternal student, someone who has no subject or, rather, whose subject is 'everything'. It allows entries of all lengths and shapes and degrees of impatience and roughness, but its ideal entry is the aphorism. Most of Canetti's entries take up the aphorist's traditional themes: the hypocrisies of society, the vanity of human wishes, the sham of love, the ironies of death, the pleasure and necessity of solitude, and the intricacies of one's own thought processes. Most of the great aphorists have been pessimists, purveyors of scorn for human folly. ('The great writers of aphorisms read as if they had all known each other well,' Canetti has noted.) Aphoristic thinking is informal, unsociable, adversarial, proudly selfish. 'One needs friends mainly in order to become impudent – that is, more oneself,' Canetti writes: there is the authentic tone of the aphorist. The notebook holds that ideally impudent, efficient self that one constructs to deal with the world. By the disjunction of ideas and observations, by the brevity of their expression, by the absence of helpful illustration, the notebook makes of thinking something light.

Despite having much of the aphorist's temperament, Canetti is anything but an intellectual dandy. (He is the opposite of, say, Gottfried Benn.) Indeed, the great limit of Canetti's sensibility is the absence of the slightest trace of the aesthete. Canetti shows no love of art as such. He has his roster of Great Writers, but no painting, theatre, film, dance, or other familiars of humanist culture figure in his work. Canetti appears to stand rather grandly above the impacted ideas of 'culture' or 'art'. He does not love anything the mind fabricates for its own sake. His writing, therefore, has little irony. No one touched by the aesthetic sensibility would have noted, severely, 'What often bothers me about Montaigne is the fat on the quotations.' There is nothing in Canetti's temperament that could respond to Surrealism, to speak only of the most persuasive modern option for the aesthete. Nor, it would seem, was he ever touched by the temptation of the left.

A dedicated enlightener, he describes the object of his struggle as the one faith left intact by the Enlightenment, 'the most preposterous of all, the religion of power.' Here is the side of Canetti that reminds one of Karl Kraus, for whom the ethical vocation is endless protest. But no writer is less a journalist than Canetti. To protest against power, power as such; to protest against death (he is one of the great death-haters of literature) – these are broad targets, rather invincible enemies. Canetti describes Kafka's work as a 'refutation' of power, and this is Canetti's aim in *Crowds and Power*. All of his work, however, aims at a refutation of death. A refutation seems to mean for Canetti an inordinate insisting. Canetti insists that death is really unacceptable; unassimilable, because it is what is outside life; unjust, because it limits ambition and insults it. He refuses to understand death, as Hegel suggested, as something within life – as the *consciousness* of death, finitude, mortality. In matters of death Canetti is an unregenerate, appalled materialist, and unrelentingly quixotic. 'I still haven't succeeded in doing anything against death,' he wrote in 1960.

In *The Tongue Set Free* Canetti is eager to do justice to each of his admirations, which is a way of keeping someone alive. Typically, Canetti also means this literally. Displaying his usual unwillingness to be reconciled to extinction, Canetti recalls a teacher in boarding school and concludes: 'In case he is still in the world today, at ninety or one hundred, I would like him to know I bow to him.'

The first volume of his autobiography is dominated by the history of a profound admiration: that of Canetti for his mother. It is the portrait of one of the great teacher-parents, a zealot of European high culture self-confidently at work before the time that turned such a parent into a selfish tyrant and such a child into an 'overachiever', to use the philistine label which conveys the contemporary disdain for precocity and intellectual ardour.

'Mother, whose highest veneration was for great writers,' was the primal admirer; and a passionate, merciless promoter of her admirations. Canetti's education consisted of immersion in books and their amplification in talk. There were evening readings aloud, tempestuous conversations about everything they read, about the writers they agreed to revere. Many discoveries were made separately, but they had to admire in unison, and a divergence was fought out in lacerating debates until one or the other yielded. His mother's policies of admiration created a tense world, defined by loyalties and betrayals. Each new admiration could throw one's life into question. Canetti describes his mother being distracted and exalted for a week after hearing the *St Matthew Passion*, finally weeping because she fears that Bach has made her want only to listen to music and that 'it's all over with books.' Canetti, age thirteen, comforts her and reassures her that she *will* still want to read.

Witnessing his mother's leaps and raging contradictions of character 'with amazement and admiration', Canetti does not underestimate her cruelty. Ominously enough, her favourite modern writer for a long time was Strindberg; in another generation it would probably have been D. H. Lawrence. Her emphasis on 'character building' often led this fiercest of readers to berate her studious child for pursuing 'dead knowledge', avoiding 'hard' reality, letting books and conversation make him 'unmanly'. (She despised women, Canetti reports.) Canetti relates how annihilated by her he sometimes felt and then turns this into a liberation. As he affirmed in himself his mother's capacity for passionate commitment, he chose to revolt against the febrility of her enthusiasms, the over-exclusiveness of her avidity. Patience ('monumental patience'), steadfastness, and universality of concern became his goals. His mother's world has no animals – only great men; Canetti will have both. She cares only about literature and hates science; starting in 1924 he will study chemistry at the University of Vienna, taking his Ph.D. in 1929. She scoffs at his interest in primitive peoples; Canetti will avow, as he prepares to write *Crowds and Power*: 'It is a serious goal of my life to get to know all myths of all peoples.'

Canetti refuses the victim's part. There is much chivalry in his portrait of his mother. It also reflects something like a policy of triumphalism – a steadfast refusal of tragedy, of irremediable suffering, that seems related to his refusal of finitude, of death, and from which comes much of Canetti's energy: his staunchless capacity for admiration and enthusiasm, and his civilized contempt for complaining.

Canetti's mother was undemonstrative – the slightest caress was an event. But her talk – debating, hectoring, musing, recounting her life – was lavish, torrential. Language was the medium of their passion: words and more words. With language Canetti made his 'first independent move' from his mother: learning Swiss German (she hated 'vulgar' dialects) when he went away to boarding school at fourteen. And with language he remained connected to her: writing a five-act verse tragedy in Latin (with an inter-linear German translation for her benefit, it filled 121 pages), which he dedicated to her and sent, requesting from her a detailed commentary.

Canetti seems eager to enumerate the many skills which he owes to his mother's example and teaching – including those which he developed to oppose her, also generously counted as her gifts: obstinacy, intellectual independence, rapidity of thought. He also speculates that the liveliness of Ladino, which he'd spoken as a child, helped him to think fast. (For the precocious, thinking is a kind of speed.) Canetti gives a complex account of that extraordinary process which learning is for an intellectually precocious child – fuller and more instructive than the accounts in, say, Mill's *Autobiography* or Sartre's *The Words*. For Canetti's capacities as an admirer reflect tireless skills as a learner; the first cannot be deep without the second. As an exceptional learner, Canetti has an irrepressible loyalty to teachers, to what they do well even (or especially when) they do it inadvertently. The teacher at his boarding school to whom he now 'bows' won his fealty by being brutal during a class visit to a slaughterhouse. Forced by him to confront a particularly gruesome sight, Canetti learned that the murder of animals was something 'I wasn't meant to get over.' His mother, even when she was brutal, was always feeding his flagrant alertness with her words. Canetti says proudly, 'I find mute knowledge dangerous.'

Canetti claims to be a 'hear-er' rather than a 'see-er'. In *Auto-da-Fé*, Kien practises being blind, for he has discovered that 'blindness is a weapon against time and space; our being is one vast blindness.' Particularly in his work since *Crowds and Power* – such as the didactically titled *The Voices of Marrakesh, Earwitness, The Tongue Set Free* – Canetti stresses the moralist's organ, the ear, and slights the eye (continuing to ring changes on the theme of blindness). Hearing, speaking, and breathing are praised whenever something important is at stake, if only in the form of ear, mouth (or tongue), and throat metaphors. When Canetti observes that 'the *loudest* passage in Kafka's work tells of this guilt with respect to the animals,' the adjective is itself a form of insistence.

What is heard is voices – in which the ear is a witness. (Canetti does not talk about music, nor indeed about any art that is non-verbal.) The ear is the attentive sense, humbler, more passive, more immediate, less discriminating than the eye. Canetti's disavowal of the eye is an aspect of his remoteness from the aesthete's sensibility, which typically affirms the pleasures and the wisdom of the visual; that is, of surfaces. To give sovereignty to the ear is an obtrusive, consciously archaizing theme in Canetti's later work. Implicitly he is restating the archaic gap between Hebrew as opposed to Greek culture, ear culture as opposed to eye culture, and the moral versus the aesthetic.

Canetti equates knowing with hearing, and hearing with hearing everything and still being able to respond. The exotic impressions garnered during his stay in Marrakesh are unified by the quality of attentiveness to 'voices' that Canetti tries to summon in himself. Attentiveness is the formal subject of the book. Encountering poverty, misery, and deformity, Canetti undertakes to hear, that is, really to pay attention to words, cries, and inarticulate sounds 'on the edge of the living.' His essay on Kraus portrays somone whom Canetti considers ideal both as hearer and as voice. Canetti says that Kraus was haunted by voices; that his ear was constantly open; that 'the real

Karl Kraus was the *speaker.*' Describing a writer as a voice has become such a cliché that it is possible to miss the force – and the characteristic literalness – of what Canetti means. The voice for Canetti stands for irrefutable presence. To treat someone as a voice is to grant authority to that person; to affirm that one hears means that one hears what must be heard.

Like a scholar in a Borges story that mixes real and imaginary erudition, Canetti has a taste for fanciful blends of knowledge, eccentric classifications, and spirited shifts of tone. Thus *Crowds and Power* – in German, *Masse und Macht* – offers analogies from physiology and zoology to explain command and obedience; and is perhaps most original when it extends the notion of the crowd to include collective units, not composed of human beings, which 'recall' the crowd, are 'felt to be a crowd', which 'stand as a symbol for it in myth, dream, speech, and song'. (Among such units – in Canetti's ingenious catalogue – are fire, rain, the fingers of the hand, the bee swarm, teeth, the forest, the snakes of delirium tremens.) Much of *Crowds and Power* depends on latent or inadvertent science-fiction imagery of things, or parts of things, that become eerily autonomous; of unpredictable movements, tempos, volumes. Canetti turns time (history) into space, in which a weird array of biomorphic entities – the various forms of the Great Beast, the Crowd – disport themselves. The crowd moves, emits, grows, expands, contracts. Its options come in pairs: crowds are said by Canetti to be quick and slow, rhythmic and stagnant, closed and open. The pack (another version of the crowd) laments, it preys, it is tranquil, it is outward or inward.

As an account of the psychology and structure of authority, *Crowds and Power* harks back to nineteenth-century talk about crowds and masses in order to expound its poetics of political nightmare. Condemnation of the French Revolution, and later of the Commune, was the message of the nineteenth-century books on crowds (they were as common then as they are unfashionable now), from Charles Mackay's *Extraordinary Popular Delusions and the Madness of Crowds* (1841) to Le Bon's *The Crowd* (1895), a book Freud admired, and *The Psychology of Revolution* (1912). But whereas earlier writers had been content to assert the crowd's pathology and moralize about it, Canetti means to explain, explain exhaustively, for example, the crowd's destructiveness ('often mentioned as its most conspicuous quality,' he says) with his biomorphic paradigms. And unlike Le Bon, who was making a case against revolution and for the status quo (considered by Le Bon the less oppressive dictatorship), Canetti offers a brief against power itself.

To understand power by considering the crowd, to the detriment of notions like 'class' or 'nation', is precisely to insist on an ahistorical understanding. Hegel and Marx are not mentioned, not because Canetti is so self-confident that he won't deign to drop the usual names, but because the implications of Canetti's argument are sharply anti-Hegelian and anti-Marxist. His ahistorical method and conservative political temper bring Canetti rather close to Freud – though he is in no sense a Freudian. Canetti is what Freud might have been were he *not* a psychologist: using many sources that were important to Freud – the autobiography of the psychotic Judge Schreber, material on anthropology and the history of ancient religions, Le Bon's crowd theory – he comes to quite different conclusions about group psychology and the shaping of the ego. Like Freud, Canetti tends to find the prototype of crowd (that is, irrational) behaviour in religion, and much of *Crowds and Power* is really a rationalist's discourse about religion. For example, what Canetti calls the lamenting pack is just another name for religions of lament, of which he gives a dazzling analysis, contrasting the slow tempos of Catholic piety and ritual (expressing the Church's perennial fear of the open crowd) with the frenzied mourning in the Shi'ite branch of Islam.

Like Freud, too, Canetti dissolves politics into pathology, treating society as a mental activity – a barbaric one, of course – that must be decoded. Thus he moves, without breaking stride, from the notion of the crowd to the 'crowd symbol', and analyses social grouping and the forms of community as transactions of crowd symbols. Some final turn of the crowd argument seems to have been reached when Canetti puts the French Revolution in its place, finding the Revolution less interesting as an eruption of the destructive than as a 'national crowd symbol' for the French.

For Hegel and his successors, the historical (the home of irony) and the natural are two radically different processes. In *Crowds and Power*, history is 'natural'. Canetti argues to history, not from it. First comes the account of the crowd; then, as illustration, the section called 'The Crowd in History'. History is used only to furnish examples – a rapid use. Canetti is partial to the evidence of historyless (in the Hegelian sense) peoples, treating anthropological anecdotes as having the same illustrative value as an event taking place in an advanced historical society.

Crowds and Power is an eccentric book – made literally eccentric by its ideal of 'universality', which leads Canetti to avoid making the obvious reference: Hitler. He appears indirectly, in the central importance Canetti gives to the case of Judge Schreber. (Here is Canetti's only reference to Freud – in one discreet footnote, where Canetti says that had Freud lived a bit longer he might have seen Schreber's paranoid delusions in a more pertinent way: as a prototype of the political, specifically Nazi, mentality.) But Canetti is genuinely not Eurocentric – one of his large achievements as a mind. Conversant with Chinese as well as European thought, with Buddhism and Islam as well as Christianity, Canetti enjoys a remarkable freedom from reductive habits of thinking. He seems incapable of using psychological knowledge in a reductive way; the author of the homage to Broch could not have been thinking about anything as ordinary as personal motives. And he fights that more plausible reduction to the historical. 'I would give a great deal to get rid of my habit of seeing the world historically,' he wrote in 1950, two years after he started writing *Crowds and Power*.

His protest against seeing historically is directed not just against that most plausible of reductionisms. It is also a protest against death. To think about history is to think about the dead; and to be incessantly reminded that one is mortal. Canetti's thought is conservative in the most literal sense. It – he – does not want to die.

'I want to feel everything in me before I think it,' Canetti wrote in 1943, and for this, he says, he needs a long life. To die prematurely means having not fully engorged himself and, therefore, having not used his mind as he could. It is almost as if Canetti had to keep his consciousness in a permanent state of avidity, to remain unreconciled to death. 'It is wonderful that nothing is lost in a mind,' he also wrote in his notebook, in what must have been a not infrequent moment of euphoria, 'and would not this alone be reason enough to live very long or even forever?' Recurrent images of needing to feel everything inside himself, of unifying everything in one head, illustrate Canetti's attempts through magical thinking and moral clamourousness to 'refute' death.

Canetti offers to strike a bargain with death. 'A century? A paltry hundred years! Is that too much for an earnest intention!' But why one hundred years? Why not three hundred? – like the 337-year-old heroine of Karel Čapek's *The Makropulos Affair* (1922). In the play, one character (a socialist 'progressive') describes the disadvantages of a normal life span.

> What can a man do during his sixty years of life? What enjoyment has he? What can he learn? You don't live to get the fruit of the tree you have planted; you'll never learn all the things that mankind has discovered before you; you won't complete your work or leave your example behind you; you'll die without having even lived. A life of three hundred years on the other hand would allow fifty years to be a child and a pupil; fifty years to get to know the world and see all that exists in it; one hundred years to work for the benefit of all; and then, when he has achieved all human experience, another hundred years to live in wisdom, to rule, to teach, and to set an example. Oh, how valuable human life would be if it lasted three hundred years.

He sounds like Canetti – except that Canetti does not justify his yearning for longevity with any appeal to its greater scope for good works. So large is the value of the mind that it alone is used to oppose death. Because the mind is so real to him Canetti dares to challenge death, and because the body is so unreal he perceives nothing dismaying about extreme longevity. Canetti is more than willing to live as a centenarian; he does not, while he is fantasizing, ask for what Faust demanded, the return of youth, or for what Emilia Makropulos was given by her alchemist father, its magical prolongation. Youth has no part in Canetti's fantasy of immortality. It is pure longevity, the longevity of the mind. It is simply assumed that character has the same stake as mind in longevity: Canetti thought 'the brevity of life makes us bad.' Emilia Makropulos suggests its longevity would make us worse:

> You cannot go on loving for three hundred years. And you cannot go on hoping, creating, gazing at things for three hundred years. You can't stand it. Everything becomes boring. It's boring to be good and boring to be bad.... And then you realize that nothing actually exists.... You

> are so close to everything. You can see some point in everything. For you everything has some value because those few years of yours won't be enough to satisfy your enjoyment.... It's disgusting to think how happy you are. And it's simply due to the ridiculous coincidence that you're going to die soon. You take an ape-like interest in everything....

But this plausible doom is just what Canetti cannot admit. He is unperturbed by the possibility of the flagging of appetite, the satiation of desire, the devaluation of passion. Canetti gives no thought to the decomposition of the feelings any more than of the body, only to the persistence of the mind. Rarely has anyone been so at home in the mind, with so little ambivalence.

Canetti is someone who has felt in a profound way the responsibility of words, and much of his work makes the effort to communicate something of what he has learned about how to pay attention to the world. There is no doctrine, but there is a great deal of scorn, urgency, grief, and euphoria. The message of the mind's passions is passion. 'I try to imagine someone saying to Shakespeare, "Relax!"' says Canetti. His work eloquently defends tension, exertion, moral and amoral seriousness.

But Canetti is not just another hero of the will. Hence the unexpected last attribute of a great writer that he finds in Broch: such a writer, he says, teaches us how to breathe. Canetti commends Broch's writings for their 'rich store of breathing experience.' It was Canetti's deepest, oddest compliment, and therefore one he also paid to Goethe (the most predictable of his admirations): Canetti also reads Goethe as saying, 'Breathe!' Breathing may be the most radical of occupations, when construed as a liberation from other needs such as having a career, building a reputation, accumulating knowledge. What Canetti says at the end of this progress of admiration, his homage to Broch, suggests what there is most to admire. The last achievement of the serious admirer is to stop immediately putting to work the energies aroused by, filling up the space opened by, what is admired. Thereby talented admirers give themselves permission to breathe, to breathe more deeply. But for that it is necessary to go beyond avidity; to identify with something beyond achievement, beyond the gathering of power.

GRANTA

T. Coraghessan Boyle

Mungo Among the Moors

The Soft White Underbelly of Mungo Park

At an age when most young Scotsmen were lifting skirts, ploughing furrows and spreading seed, Mungo Park was displaying his bare buttocks to al-haff Ali Ibn Fatoudi, Emir of Ludamar. The year was 1795. George III was dabbing the walls of Windsor Castle with his own spittle, the *Notables* were botching things in France, Goya was deaf, De Quincey a depraved preadolescent. George Bryan 'Beau' Brummell was smoothing down his first starched collar, young Ludwig van Beethoven, beetle-browed and twenty-four, was wowing them in Vienna with his Piano Concerto Number 2, and Ned Rise was drinking Strip-Me-Naked with Nan Punt and Sally Sebum at the Pig & Pox Tavern in Maiden Lane.

Ali was a Moor. He sat cross-legged on a damask pillow and scrutinized the pale puckered nates with the air of an epicure examining a fly in his vichyssoise. His voice was like sand. 'Turn over,' he said. Mungo was a Scotsman. He knelt on a reed mat, trousers around his knees, and glanced over his shoulder at Ali. He was looking for the Niger River. 'Turn over,' Ali repeated.

While the explorer was congenial and quick-to-please, his Arabic was somewhat sketchy. When he failed to respond a second time, Dassoud – Ali's henchman and human jackal – stepped forward with a lash composed of the caudal appendages of a half dozen wildebeests. The tufted tails cut the air, beating on high like the wings of angels. The temperature outside Ali's tent was 127° Fahrenheit. The tent was a warp-and-woof affair, constructed of thread spun from the hair of goats. Inside it was 112°. The lash fell. Mungo turned over.

Here too he was white: white as sheets and blizzards. Ali and his circle were astonished all over again. 'His mother dipped him in milk,' someone said. 'Count his fingers and his toes!' shouted another. Women and children crowded the tent's entrance, goats bleated, camels coughed and coupled, someone was hawking figs. A hundred voices intertwined like a congries of foot-paths, walks, low-roads and high-roads – which one to take? – and all in Arabic, mystifying, rapid, harsh, the language of the Prophet. 'La-la-la-la-la!' a woman shrieked. The others took it up, an excoriating falsetto. 'La-la-la-la-la!' Mungo's penis, also white, shrank into his body.

Beyond the blank wall of the tent was the camp at Benowm, Ali's winter residence. Three hundred parched and blistered miles beyond that lay the north bank of the River Niger, a river no European had ever laid eyes upon. Not that Europeans weren't interested. Herodotus was exercised about its course five centuries Before Christ. Big, he concluded. But tributary to the Nile. Al-Idrisi populated its banks with strange and mythical creatures – the vermicular Strapfeet, who crawled rather than walked and spoke the language of serpents; the sphinx and the harpy; the manticore with its lion's torso and scorpion's tail and its nasty predilection for human flesh. Pliny the Elder painted the Niger gold and christened it black, and Alexander's scouts inflamed him with tales of the river of rivers where lords and ladies sat in gardens of lotus and drank from cups of hammered gold. And now, at the end of the Age of Enlightenment and the beginning of the Age of Imbursement, France wanted the Niger, Britain wanted it, Holland, Portugal and Denmark. According to the most recent and reliable information – Ptolemy's *Geography* – the Niger lay between Nigritia, land of the blacks, and the Great Desert. As it turned out, Ptolemy was right on target. But no one had yet been able to survive the sere blast of the Sahara or the rank fever belt of the Gambia to bear him out.

Then, in 1788, a group of distinguished geographers, botanists, philanderers, and other seekers after the truth, met at the St Alban's Tavern, Pall Mall, to form the African Association. Their purpose was to open up Africa to exploration. North Africa was a piece of cake. They had it staked out, mapped, labelled, dissected, and distributed by 1790. But West Africa remained a mystery. At the heart of the mystery was the Niger. In its inaugural year the Association commissioned an expedition headed by John Ledyard. He was to begin in Egypt, traverse the Sahara, and discover the course of the Niger. Ledyard was an American. He played the violin and suffered from strabismus. He'd been across the Pacific with Cook, into the Andes, through Siberia to Yakutsk on foot. I've tramped the world under my feet, he said, laughed at fear, derided danger. Through hordes of savages, over parching deserts, the freezing north, the everlasting ice and stormy seas have I passed without harm. How good is my God! Two weeks after landing at Cairo he died of dysentery. Simon Lucas, Oriental interpreter for the Court of St James's, was next. He landed at Tripoli, hiked a hundred miles into the desert, developed blisters, thirst, and anxiety, and returned without accomplishing anything other than the expenditure of £1,250. And then there was Major Daniel Houghton. He was an Irishman, bankrupt, fifty-two years of age. He knew nothing of Africa whatever, but he came cheap. I'll do it for three hunnert pund, he said. And a case o' Scots whisky. Houghton sallied up the Gambia in a dugout canoe, drank from fetid puddles, and ate monkey meat, and through sheer grit and the force of intoxication survived typhus, malaria, loiasis, leprosy, and spotted fever. Unfortunately, the Moors of Ludamar stripped him naked and staked him out on the crest of a dune. Where he died.

Mungo stood to hitch up his pants. Dassoud knocked him down. The ululations of the women were fanning the crowd to a frenzy. 'Eat pig, Christian,' they shouted. 'Eat pig.' Mungo didn't like their attitude. Nor did he like exposing his prat in mixed company. But there was nothing to be done about it: they'd cut his throat and bleach his bones at the least show of resistance.

Suddenly Dassoud had a dirk in his hand: narrow as an ice pick, dark as blood. 'Infidel dog!' he shrieked, veins tessellating his throat. Ali watched from behind the folds of his burnoose, dark and impassive. The temperature inside the tent rose to 120°. The crowd held its breath. Then Dassoud levelled the blade at the explorer, gibbering all the while, like some rabid anatomist lecturing on the eccentricities of the human form. The point of the blade drew closer. Ali spat in the sand, Dassoud exhorted the crowd, Mungo froze. Then the blade pricked him – ever so lightly – down below, where he was softest, and whitest. Dassoud laughed like a brook gone dry. The crowd whistled and shrieked. It was then that a grizzled *Bushreen* with straw in his beard and an empty eyesocket burst through the press to push Dassoud aside. 'The eyes!' he howled. 'Look at the devil's eyes!'

Dassoud looked. The sadistic gloat gave way to a look of horror and indignation. 'The eyes of a cat,' he hissed. 'We must put them out.'

The Fall of Ned Rise

Ned Rise wakes with a head-ache. He has been drinking gin – a.k.a. Strip-Me-Naked, Blue Ruin, the Curse – enfeebler and ennervator of the lower-classes, clear as a souse's urine and tart as the juice of juniper. He has been drinking gin, and he is not quite sure where he is. Though he is reasonably certain that he recognizes the soleless half-boots, hairy knuckles, and cinnamon-red cape that are among the first things to present themselves to his eye. Yes: that cape, those knuckles and boots, the tear in the trousers: they are familiar. Intimate, even. Yes, he concludes, they belong to Ned Rise, and thus the splintered head and staved-in eyes which perceive these phenomena, however imperfectly, must in some way be connected to them.

He sits up, and after a long pause, rises. It seems that he's been lying in a heap of discoloured straw. On his hat. He bends to retrieve it, lurches forward, then regains his balance with an assertive belch. The hat is a ruin. He stands there a moment, assuming a meditative pose, something drumming in the back of his head. Then he scans the room through half-closed lids, feeling a bit like an explorer setting foot on a new continent.

He is in a cellar, no question about it. There's the dirt floor, mop in a bucket, walls of rough stone. Against the back wall, a double row of sealed casks: Madeira, port, Lisbon, claret, hock. In the corner, a shovel or two of coal. Could these be the nether regions of the Pig & Pox Tavern? At this point Ned discovers that he is not alone. Other forms, possibly human, occupy patches of straw scattered over the floor. There is the sound of snoring, a moan, and gargle like rain in the gutter. The concurrent odours of urine and vomit hang heavy in the air.

'So ye're up then, are ye?' A balding crone, her face a memento mori, is addressing him from behind a plank set across a pair of hogsheads. A gold ring rides her lower lip like a bubble of sputum. 'Well. Good mornin' to ye sir,' she says. 'Ha-haaa! and 'ow was yer sleep and will ye 'ave a dram to start the day off proper?' Two pewter measures the size of egg-cups and a terra-cotta jug stand atop the plank in still-life. A sow lies on her side beneath the makeshift bar, the swell of her jaw obscured by an overturned chamberpot. Ned wonders what happened last night.

Suddenly the beldam shrieks as if she's been stuck with a dagger, a long rasping insuck of breath: 'Eeeeeeeee!' The drumming in Ned's brain becomes a series of paradiddles, thunder rolls, the booming of a big bass drum. But wait. The crone isn't suffering a stroke after all: she's laughing. Coughing now, hacking, and pounding the plank until a long yellow taper of phlegm appears at the corner of her mouth and makes its resilient way to the countertop. 'Cat . . .' she chokes, 'Cat got your tongue, peach fuzz?'

A sign hangs on the wall behind her, its characters scrawled in a clonic hand:

DRUNK FOR A PENNY
DEAD DRUNK FOR TUPPENCE
CLEAN STRAW, FREE

Ned bites his thumb at her. 'Screw you and your mother and your hagborn dropsical brood, you scrofulous tit-sore slut!' he shouts, already beginning to feel better.

'Eeeeeeeeeeeee!' she screeches. 'Ye've no taste for Mother Geneva's 'lixir, eh? Taste enough ye had for it last night . . . . 'Ere, give Mother a look at yer manhood then – she'll find a cure for ye,' lifting her skirts with a leer, the spindle legs and yellowed bush like the denouement of a gothic tale.

Off to the left a flight of ramshackle stairs leads up to an outer door, through the chinks of which Ned can discern the chill light of dawn. He curses himself for wasting breath on the crazed hag – there's business to tend to this afternoon – and starts up the reeling stairs to the door.

'Eeeeee!' shrieks the old woman, 'Mind yer gown now, fairy quean!'

Ned draws the cinnamon robe tight, and swings back the door on Maiden Lane and the light of day. Behind him, from the depths, a broken shriek like a viola gone sour: 'Beware, beware, beware the hangman's cravat!'

Ere Half My Days

The machine for extinguishing sight consists of two strips of brass, and looks something like an inverted chastity belt. One strip circles the head at eye level, the other fits snugly over the crown. There are two screws involved: each has a convex disk attached to the working end. The device was originally fabricated in the ninth century for al-kaid Hassan Ibn Mohammed, the blind Bashaw of Tripoli. Insecure about his infirmity, the Bashaw decreed that all who desired to come into his presence must first submit to having their eyes put out. He was a very lonely man.

The machine operates on the same principle as a vice. The screws are twisted until they meet the surface of the eye, and are then tightened, crank by crank, until the cornea bursts. Simple, inexorable, final.

A hush has fallen over the crowd. A moment earlier they'd been on the brink of hysteria, razzing and gibbering like the hoi polloi at a bull-baiting or a freak show. But now: silence. Flies saw away at the hot, still air, and the sound of a goat or camel making water in the sand is like the boom of a cataract. Sandals shuffle, a man scratches his beard. Many have drawn rags over their faces, as if to escape the contamination of the explorer's gaze. Dassoud and the one-eyed interloper stare down at him, arms akimbo, faces solemn.

Mungo has had difficulty grasping the gist of the proceedings. He is reasonably certain that he has pinned down one word at least – the word for eye, *unya* – which he recalls from *Ouzel's Arabic Grammar* ('We lift up our *unyas* to heaven wherein Allah resides'). But why on earth would they be nattering about eyes? And the sudden hush – he wonders about that too. But it is hot, beastly hot, and he can hardly keep his mind on anything at all. So hot in fact that it surpasses anything in his experience, with the possible exception of the Swedish Baths off Grosvenor Square. Sir Joseph Banks, Treasurer and Director of the African Association, had taken him to the baths one afternoon to iron out some of the details of Mungo's drive for the Niger. There they had been subjected to the emanations of baked stones, stones that glowed like molten lava – or so it seemed. An attendant thrashed them with birch switches and buffeted their kidneys and backbones with the sharp heels of his hands. Sir Joseph seemed to find the whole operation invigorating. The explorer nearly lost consciousness. He is beginning to experience the same sort of light-headedness at the moment, in fact. And small wonder, when you consider that not only must he contend with the sun, sand fleas, dysentery and fever, but the inanition as well. The Moors have confiscated his supplies, appropriated his horse and interpreter, and apparently decided to put him on a stringent diet. Too stringent, by his way of thinking: he hasn't seen a scrap of food in two days.

And so, despite the critical situation and the ring of strange hostile faces, Mungo begins to feel giddy – almost as if he'd drunk too much claret or gill-ale. He glances round at the furtive eyes and knitted brows, at the beards and burnooses, the prophets' robes and pilgrims' sandals, and suddenly all those hard minatory faces begin to melt, lose their contours, droop into vagueness like figures of wax. The whole thing is a masquerade, is what it is. Dassoud and One-Eye are tumblers or fire-eaters,and Old Ali is only Grimaldi – Grimaldi the clown. But now they seem to be fitting something over his head . . . a helmet? Do they expect him to go to battle for them? Or have they finally come to their senses and decided to measure him for a crown?

The explorer grins stupidly beneath his brazen cap. His eyes are grey. Grey as the tentative fingers of ice that reach out over the deep pools of the yarrow on a frosty morning. Gloucester's eyes, they say, were grey. Oedipus' were black as olives. And Milton's – Milton's were like blue-jays scrabbling in the snow. Dassoud knows nothing of Shakespeare, Sophocles, or Milton. His rough fingers twist the screws. The explorer grins. Obvious. The onlookers, horrified at his mad composure, turn away in panic. He can hear them rushing off, the slap of their sandals on the baked earth . . . but what's this? – he seems to have something caught in his eye. . . .

Corrective Surgery

'Stop!'

Mungo can't see a thing (the cap seems to have a visor, and every time he goes to lift it a hand seizes his wrist), but he recognizes the voice instantly. It is Johnson. Jolly old Johnson, his guide and interpreter, come to the rescue.

'Stop!' the voice of Johnson repeats, before pitching headlong into the spillway of Arabic glottals and fricatives. Dassoud answers him, then One-Eye harmonizes with a concatenation of grunts and emphatics, his voice pitched high. Johnson rebuts. And then Ali's voice sounds from the corner, harsh and grainy. There is the sound of a blow, and Johnson tumbles to the mat beside the explorer.

'Mr Park,' Johnson whispers. 'What you got that thing on your head for? Don't you realize what they doin' to you?'

'Johnson, jolly old Johnson. How good to hear your voice.'

'They puttin' out your eyes, Mr Park.'

'How's that?'

'The Chief Jackal here he says you got the eyes of a cat – and apparently that don't go down too good around here, as they is presently engaged in grindin' them out. If it wasn't for my fortuitous intercession I'd lay odds you'd be blind as a beggar this very minute.'

Mungo's head clears like a hazy morning giving way to noon. As it does so he becomes increasingly agitated, until finally he leaps to his feet, tearing at the brazen cap and wailing like a lost calf. Dassoud knocks him down, cracks the wildebeest whip a time or two and then calls out in Arabic for some further instrument of torture. There is the sound of padding feet, the swish of the tent flap, and then close at hand, the cry of a human being in mortal agony. The cry seems to be emanating from Johnson. The explorer is alarmed, and tugs at the cap with renewed vigour, feeling very much like a ten-year-old with his head caught between the bars of an iron railing. 'Johnson,' he gasps. '– what have they done to you?'

'Nothin' yet. But they just sent out for a two-edge bilbo.'

The cap finally releases its grip, heaving up from the explorer's head like the cork from a bottle of spumante. He blinks and looks round him. Ali, Dassoud and One-Eye are crouched in the far corner, jabbering and gesticulating. The mob is gone and the flap of the tent is drawn closed. A massive black man in turban and striped robe blocks the entrance, arms folded across his chest. 'A bilbo? What does that mean?' Mungo whispers.

'Means we goin' to be two monkeys – see no evil, speak none either. They say I got the tongue of a shrike, Mr Park. They goin' to cut it out.'

Johnson

Concerning Johnson. He is a member of the Mandingo tribe. At the age of thirteen Johnson was kidnapped by Foulah herdsmen while celebrating the nubility of a tender young sylph in a corn-field just outside his native village of Dindikoo. The sylph's name was Nealee. The Foulahs didn't ask. Their chieftain, who took a fancy to Nealee's facial tattoos and to other features as well, retained her as his personal concubine. Johnson was sold to a travelling slave merchant who shackled his ankles and drove him, along with sixty-two others, to the coast. Forty-nine made it. There he was sold to an American slaver who chained him in the hold of a schooner bound for South Carolina. The boy beside him had been dead for six days when the ship landed at Charleston.

For twelve years Johnson worked as a field hand on the plantation of Sir Reginald Durfeys, Bart. Then he was promoted to house servant. Three years later Sir Reginald himself visited the Carolinas, took a liking to Johnson, and brought him back to London as his valet. This was in 1771. Slavery was still sanctioned in England, George III was already harbouring the renegade porphyrins that would cost him his sanity, and Napolean was storming the palisades of his playpen.

Johnson, as he was christened by Sir Reginald, began to educate himself in the library at Piltdown, the Durfeys' country estate. He learned Greek and Latin. He read the Ancients. He read the Moderns. He read Smollett, Ben Jonson, Molière, Swift. He spoke of Pope as if he'd known him personally, denigrated the puerility of Richardson, and was so taken with Fielding that he actually attempted a Mandingo translation of *Amelia.*

Durfeys was fascinated with him. Not only with his command of language and literature, but with his recollection of the dark continent as well. It got to the point where the Baronet couldn't drift off at night without a cup of hot milk and garlic, and the soothing basso profundo of Johnson's voice as he narrated a tale of thatched huts, leopards, and hyenas, of volcanoes spewing fire across the sky, of thighs and buttocks glistening with sweat and black as a dream of the womb. Sir Reginald allowed him a liberal salary, and after emancipation in 1772 offered him a handsome pension to stay on as valet. Johnson considered the proposal over a glass of sherry in Sir Reginald's study. Then he grinned, and hit the Baronet for a raise.

When Parliament was in session Sir Reginald moved his establishment to town, accompanied by Johnson and a pair of liveried footmen. London was a ripe tomato. Johnson was a macaroni. He strutted down Bond Street with the best of them, decked out in his top hat, wasp-waisted coat, and silk hose. Soon he was frequenting the coffee-houses, engaging in repartee, learning to turn an epigram with a barb in it. One afternoon a red-faced gentleman with mutton-chop whiskers called him a 'damned Hottentot nigger' and invited him to fight for his life. The following morning, at dawn and in the presence of seconds, Johnson put a bullet through the gentleman's right eye. The gentleman died instantly and Johnson was incarcerated. He was subsequently sentenced to be hanged by the neck until dead. Sir Reginald exerted his influence. The sentence was commuted to transportation.

And so, in January of 1790 Johnson's legs were once again shackled, spoiling the lines of his hosiery. He was out aboard the H.M.S. *Feckless* and deposited at Goree, an island just off the west coast of Africa, where he was to serve as a private in the military. When he stepped ashore an ancient thrill went through him. He was home. Two weeks later, while on late watch, Johnson appropriated a canoe, paddled his way to shore, and melted into the black bank of the jungle. He then made his way back to Dindikoo, where he married Nealee's younger sister and settled in to repopulate the village.

He was forty-seven. His hair was salted with grey. It rained. Crops grew, goats fattened. He lived in a hut, went bare-foot, wrapped a strip of broadcloth round his chest and loins and called it a toga. He gave himself over to sensuality.

Within five years Johnson was providing for three wives and eleven children plus an assortment of dogs, simians, rope squirrels, and skinks. Still, he wasn't exactly working himself to the bone – no, he cashed in instead on his reputation as a man of letters. Villagers would come to him with a calabash of beer or a side of kudu and ask him to scribble off a few words in return. Logos was the supreme charm. The written word could bring wisdom, sexual potency, plenty in times of want. It could restore lost hair, cure cancer, attract women, and kill locusts. Johnson was quick to realize the market potential of his penmanship. He would scribble off a line or two of doggerel in exchange for three pounds of honey or a month's supply of grain. Or he'd quote Pope and purchase a pair of gold anklets for his youngest bride.

Then one afternoon a runner came from Pisania, the British trading colony on the Gambia. He carried a letter from England sealed with the Durfeys' coat-of-arms (a goat ruminant). England – the clubs, the theatre, Covent Garden and Pall Mall, the sweep of the Thames, the texture of the late afternoon light in the library at Piltdown – it all rushed back on him. He tore open the envelope.

Piltdown, 21 May, 1795

My Dear Johnson:

If this missive should reach you, I trust it finds you in good health. I must confess that the news of your elopement from Gorea pleased us all immensely. I rather suspect you've 'gone native' with a few of those honey-complected sirens you were forever rhapsodizing, what?

But to business. This letter is by means of introducing one Mungo Park, the young Scot we've commissioned to penetrate to the interior of your country and discover the course of the Niger. If you will consent to act as guide and interpreter for Mr park, you may name your price.

Yours in Geographical Fervor,

Sir Reginald Durgeys, Bart.
Founding member
African Association

Johnson's price was the complete works of Shakespeare, in quarto volumes, just as they had appeared on the shelves of Sir Reginald's library. He packed a bag, travelled to Pisania on foot, sought out the explorer and drafted an agreement of terms of service. The explorer was twenty-four. His hair was cornsilk. He was six feet tall and walked as if a stick were strapped to his back. He took hold of Johnson's hand in his big buttery fist. 'Johnson,' he said, 'I am truly pleased to make your acquaintance.' Johnson was fifty four and fifteen stone. His hair was a dust mop, his feet were bare, he wore a gold straight pin through his right nostril. 'The pleasure is mine,' he said.

Mungo rode, Johnson walked. They passed through the kingdoms of Wooli and Bondou without incident, but found on entering Kaarta that the king of that country, Tiggitty Sego, was at war with the neighbouring state of Bambarra. The explorer suggested a detour to the north, through Ludamar. Two days after crossing the border they were accosted by thirty Moors on horseback. The Moors looked as if they'd just cooked and eaten their mothers. They carried muskets, dirks, and scimitars – scimitars as cold and cruel as the crescent moon, weapons that hacked rather than thrust: a single blow could remove a limb, separate a shoulder, cleave a head. Their leader, a hooded giant with a hyphenated scar across the bridge of his nose, trotted forward and spat in the sand. 'You will accompany us to the camp of Ali at Benowm,' he said. Johnson tugged at the explorer's gaiters and whispered in his ear. The horses stamped and stuttered. Mungo looked up at the grim faces, smiled, and announced in English that he would be delighted to accept their invitation.

Fatima

A boy bursts into the tent, double-edged bilbo in hand. Dassoud leers, Johnson shudders. Mungo scrambles to his feet, pulls up his trousers and buckles his belt. 'I'd like to know just what crime we've –' he begins. Dassoud knocks him down. At that moment a second boy darts into the tent with a message for Ali. Dassoud turns back to his companions and a frenetic colloquy ensues. Fingers are shaken, arms waves, beards pulled. Through it all the explorer can make out a single word, repeated again and again, as if it were an incantation: Fatima, Fatima, Fatima. Keeping his eyes fixed on the conferees, he snakes out a hand to tug at Johnson's toga. 'Johnson,' he whispers. 'What's up?'

Johnson's eyes are wide. 'Shh!' he says.

A moment later Ali rises. One-Eye takes up the damask pillow, Dassoud flings down the bilbo in disgust, and the three stalk out of the tent. Explorer and guide are left alone with the Nubian sentry. And the sand fleas.

'Pssst. Johnson,' Mungo whispers. 'What's this Fatima business they're jabbering about?'

'Beats the hell out of me. But whatever it is you can bet it's nothin' to lose your senses over.'

Leavening

At the Vole's Head, Ned Rise calls for rashers, mutton chops, wheatcakes, boiled eggs, tongue, ham, toast, pigeon pie, and marmalade – 'and a pint of bitter for lubrication.' Then he sends a boy out to one of the pawnshops across from White's Gaming House to pick him up a suit of clothes, 'as what a gentleman would wear,' from pumps to cravat to topper. The boy's feet are wrapped in rags, his eyes, mouth, and ears are running, and he's lost all his teeth to scurvy. Ned gives him half a crown for his trouble.

The landlord at the Vole's Head is one Nelson Smirke. Smirke is a big man, scabious, with bald patches along either side of his head and a mad electric growth of hair across the crown. The overall effect is vegetal: he looks like nothing so much as a colossal turnip. 'Ah, Smirke!' says Ned over his pigeon pie. 'Draw up a chair, my friend –

I've got a proposition for you.' Smirke sits and folds his massive hands on the table. 'I'll give it to you straight,' says Ned. 'I want to let the Reamer Room for tonight, from eight to maybe three or four in the morning. I'll give you two guineas and no questions asked.'

'Wot's it, a party then?'

'That's right. A party.'

'Yer not plannin' to tear up the cushings and piss in the tea service like ye done last time, is ye?'

'Smirke, Smirke, Smirke,' says Ned, clucking his tongue. 'Have you got no confidence in me? This is a gathering of gentlemen.' The head of a buck hangs on the wall behind him. Coals glow in the grate. Ned lays his fork aside and thrusts a hand into his trousers, plumbing for gold. He takes a deep breath, tears the muslin (and hair) from his abdomen, and digs into the hoard.

'Gennelmen, my arse,' says Smirke. 'I know the sort of turks and derelicts and 'uman garbage wot calls you friend, Ned Rise.'

Two guineas clank down on the table, sweet music. Smirke covers them with a fat fist. Ned looks into the landlord's eyes, then rams down a wheatcake, champing like a refugee. He folds a slice of ham and wads it in on top, then slips a boiled egg up inside his cheek. 'Three,' says Smirke, 'and it's a deal.' Ned chokes briefly, something caught up the windpipe, then spins the third coin across the table. Smirke rises, points a thick finger between the entrepreneur's eyes and snarls: 'There'll be no trouble in my house or be Gad I'll 'ave yer liver out.'

Seven-thirty. Ned stands at the door of the Reamer Room, decked out like a young lord. From a distance, and in the murk of the hallway, he could almost pass for a solid citizen. Up close the illusion fades. First, there is the matter of his face. No matter how you look at it, from whatever angle, in light or shade, extremity or repose, it is at bottom the face of a wiseguy. The face of the young lout who lolls in the class-room with his boots on the desk, sets fire to old ladies, and drinks ink. The face of the teenager who saunters and slouches and terrorizes the fruit-seller, smoking opium, bathing in gin, making a chamberpot of the world. The face of the young panderer arranging something improper, scurrilous even, outside the door of the Reamer Room at the Vole's Head Tavern, the Strand. Then there's the matter of his clothes. The pin-striped trousers and engagé jacket droop like a tailor's nightmare, and the collar, maculated with sherry and gravy until it resembles the hide of some howling jungle beast, has already gone limp as a bath-towel. The gold watch chain? Buffed copper. The bulge in his waistcoat pocket? A stone impersonating a pocket-watch. The stockings are cut from a pair of wool socks and the boutonniere is a scrap of coloured paper. But all this is nothing when compared to the cape, white stars on a cinnamon background which billows round the impresario's shoulders like a gypsy encampment.

Nevertheless, Ned is doing a brisk business. Gentlemen, in pairs, or trios or even individually, make their way down the narrow hallway, press golden guineas and silver sovereigns into his palm, and pass through the doorway of the Reamer Room. Ned deposits these coins in the Bank of the Bulge. And grins the grin of a burglar. Inside, the sounds of revelry: clinking glasses, squealing chairs, yar-hars and yo-hos. Smirke's cue. He appears at the far end of the passageway, a tray of drinks hoisted in one meaty hand, a pair of barmaids sweeping along before him like bubbles riding the crest of a breaker. 'Get yer merrytricious arses in there now and keep the spirits flowin' or be Jozachar they'll tear the fookin' joists down,' he roars. The girls giggle past Ned and into the room to a burst of applause, catcalls and rabid whistling. Smirke pauses at the doorway. 'I'll 'and it to ye, Ned – ye've got yerself an audience of drinkin' gennelmen wot's already been through half a cask of Scots whisky and fifty-three bottles of the grape.'

Ned's grin is sleek and wide. 'Told you so, didn't I Smirke? Leave it to Neddy. You'll be rich.'

A stentorian voice, the voice of a temperamental mountain, calls from within: 'Drink! Goddamn and curse the virgin for a whore, drink!' 'Booza!' shouts another. 'Yaaaaar!' The shouts are like hot wires applied to Smirke's spine. He shudders, stiffens, twitches, his muscles gone clonic, the glasses teetering on the rim of the tray. Then he throws back the door like a soldier and takes the full blast of a sirocco redolent of sweat, sperm, spilled beer and urine. His eyes are like peas. 'Be gad this show better be good Ned Rise or I'll, I'll–'

'Have me liver out?'

'Fricasseed!' he roars, and offers himself up to the din.

Ned slams the door and takes a pull at his flask. It's been a bitch of a day. First there was the business of the carpenters and the stage. Then the advertisements. Shorthanded, he's painted up the sandwich boards himself:

FOR THE BLOOD WHAT'S BOARD WITH PATIENCE
A New Entertainment
The Vole's Head, 8 P.M. Tonight.

TITILLATION.
The V.'s Head. Tonight.

COME TO THE VOYEER'S BALL
The Vole's Head 8 p.m. TONIGHT.

Then he had to pay Billy Boyles and two other reprobates a shilling each to display them outside the gaming houses and gentlemen's shops. They were to answer inquiries sotto voce and fill in the details as delicately as possible. But if he knew Boyles, the flaming ass would be coarse-mouthing it up and down the street till every Charlie and magistrate in town got wind of it. Worries on worries. But that was just the beginning. Throughout the afternoon, in the midst of placating Smirke and hounding the carpenters, he'd had to keep Nan and Sally at a fine pitch of intoxication – soused enough to stay happy and yet not too far gone to perform. And then there was the biggest headache of all: leasing Jutta Jim, the black nigger of the Congo from his master/employer, Lord Twit. Twit wanted three guineas and a firm assurance that his precious manservant would be returned before dawn, 'sweet energies intact'. Shit. The whole thing – the hassles, the tension, the long hours of enforced sobriety – it's nearly crippled him. His head is a suppurating blister and gin is the only tonic.

And so he is standing there in the dim hallway, pulling at the flask, dreaming, caressing the golden bulge at his crotch (thirty-two new guineas so far).... Ned pulls the stone from his pocket and glances at it. The stone is flat, smooth, two inches in diameter. Someone has painted a clockface on its surface. Eight o'clock, it reads. Showtime:

Sally Sebum and Jutta Jim are onstage, performing. Nan Punt, in a broadcloth dressing gown, stands beside Ned, awaiting her cue. 'Uh-uh-uh-uh-uh,' says Sally. 'Uh-aah, Aaah! AAaaahhh!' Jutta Jim backs off from her, bare-assed, buck black naked, his member slick and hard in the light from the oil lamps. Spikes of etiolated bone jut from his nostrils, quills pierce his earlobes, whorled cicatrices vein his torso like a relief map of the moon. The audience is hushed. He turns to them, slow, silent, methodical, and begins to pound at the hogshead of his chest. 'That's my cue,' whispers Nan, slipping out of the gown and tripping daintily onto the stage, drunk as a sow. After parading around and rubbing her bosoms a bit for the audience, she puts Jim's cock in her mouth. The onlookers – they who a moment before had been stomping and whistling and throwing socks, hats, napkins, and silverware – suddenly fall silent. Meanwhile, Sally peels herself from the stage's only prop – a green-velvet confidante – and staggers off into the wings. Ned holds the robe open for her. 'Whew,' she puffs, 'the black cannibal like to've swived me to death.' She's running sweat, her make-up a swamp, the rich black curls plastered to her cheeks and throat. Her breasts are red and white. They strain at the robe like vegetables in a sack. 'And his breath! Like a fookin' chamberpot. He's got a tool on 'em, though – I'll say that for the beast.'

'Glad you enjoyed it, Sal.'

'Enjoyed it?' Indignant, hands on hips. 'You think I enjoys being grunted over and slobbered upon by a stink-mouth nigger bebarian?' But then she winks. 'Easiest four quid I ever made since Lord Dalhousie's milk punch got the better of 'em and 'ee fumbled 'is purse down the front of me sateen dress.'

Ned laughs. 'Just the beginning, Sal. I've got another show lined up here for Thursday and then one for Saturday at the Pig & Pox. And I'll tell you what – if you get back out there and do your histrionical best I'll give you another two crowns on top of it.'

She's about to remark how her mum always wanted her to pursue a career on the stage, but peeps out at the crowd and giggles instead. 'Ned,' she whispers, 'come have a look at this.' Ned looks. The entire audience – Lords and Gartercees, naval officers, shopkeepers, footpads and clerics, even Smirke himself – is caught up in a trance, their mouths hanging open, chins and beards wet with spittle. Jim is stretched out supine now, stage front, Nan riding him like a jockey, leaping the dikes, fences, and water hazards of orgasm, panting and gibbering all the way. There's not a whisper from the patrons, not a cough or snuffle, a golly or gee – they wouldn't have looked up if Halley's Comet had torn the roof off the place. Some are twitching in face and limb, others grip their hats and walking sticks as if they were grasping at twigs on the brink of a precipice. Here and there a handkerchief swabs a brow, restive teeth chew at the back of a chair, feet tap and knees knock. 'Yahoo!' shouts Nan at the peak of a pure gallop, and poor Smirke pitches foward in a typhoon of crunching glass. No one notices.

Sally helps herself to a pull at Ned's flask. Then she laughs. Laughs till she has to put a hand to her ribs.

'What's the joke?' asks Ned.

'Well,' she manages, between bursts of giggles, 'either they've took to wearin' codpieces again or I'll swear somebody's put yeast in all them trowsers out there.'

The Sahel

The Sahel is a strip of semi-arid land girding West Africa like a waist-band, stretching from the Atlantic coast in the west to Lake Chad in the east. It's no picnic, life on the Sahel, let's face it. Talk of scarcity and want, whims of nature: welcome to them. Talk of years when the rains won't come and the sweet bleating herds build monuments of bone to the sun. Or a well that goes salt, sandstorms that shear the whiskers from your cheeks. Then there are the hyenas – making off in the night with kids and goats, disemboweling them and leaving the pissed-on remains for vultures and jackals. And then there's the push south: the farther you go, the greater the risk of a sneak attack by the Foulahs or the Serawoolis. That'd be a fine thing. Your people in chains, cattle butchered, horses raped, kouskous devoured. Of necessity, life is lean. And portable. The entire camp at Benown – all three hunred tents – could be gone in an hour, fata morgana.

Because he lives under the gun, Ali puts his stock in movable wealth, wealth on the hoof – camels, horses, goats, oxen, slaves. If you inventory his material possessions he's practically a beggar. The Emir of Ludamar, ruler of thousands, hegemon of an area the size of Wales, man of the Book and descendant of the Prophet, actually owns fewer things than a Chelsea chambermaid. A goat-hair tent, a change of *jubbah*, a pot, a cookstove, two muskets, a leaky hookah, and a blunt-edged saber that once belonged to Major Houghton – that's about it. Ah, but his horses – moon-white, marbled with muscle, their tails red as an open vein (he dyes them). And his women! If Ali is to be envied, it is for his women. Any one of his four wives could launch a thousand ships – if they knew what ships were.

Chief among them – in influence and beauty both – is Fatima of

Jafnoo, daughter of the shereef of the Al-Mu'ta tribe, Boo Khaloom. Fatima's erotic charms are predicated entirely on a single feature: her bulk. In a bone-thin society, what more appropriate ideal of human perfection? Fatima weighs twenty-seven stone and four pounds. To move from one corner of the tent to another requires the assistance of two slaves. On the sixty-mile trip to Deena, in the north, she once prostrated a pair of camels and a bullock, and finally had to be transported on a litter drawn by six oxen. Ali comes in off the desert, blood and sand in his eyes, and plunges into the moist fecundity of her flesh. She is a spring, a well, an oasis. She is milk overspilling the bowl, a movable feast, green pasture, and a side of beef. She is gold. She is rain.

Fatima was not always a beauty queen. As a girl she was a mere slip of a thing – big-boned and with enormous potential, yes – but nonetheless something of a slim and dark-eyed ugly duckling. Boo Khaloom took her in hand. He stepped into the tent one evening with a rush mat and a pillow. He spread the mat in a corner, set the pillow atop it, and commanded his daughter to sit. He then called for camel's milk and kouskous. Fatima was puzzled: the remains of the evening meal – wooden bowls black with flies, an overturned pitcher – still lay in the corner. All at once she became aware of shadows playing over the walls of the tent, as if a number of people were milling around outside. She asked her father if he was planning to meet with his counsellors. He told her to shut her hole. Suddenly the flap was thrown back and a man entered the tent. It was Mohammed Bello, sixty-three years old, her father's closest friend and advisor. He was naked. Fatima was mortified. She'd never seen a man's legs before, let alone those puckered wattles squirming against the old man's leg like some freak of nature. She thought of the spineless struggling things caught in the muck of a dying water-hole. She was eleven years old. She burst into tears.

Mohammed Bello was not alone. The flap swished and eight other men, naked as babes, stepped silently into the tent. Zib Sahman, her godfather, was among them. And Akbar al-Akbar, the oldest man of the tribe. When they were all assembled, a slave entered with a bowl the size of a bird-bath. The bowl contained camel's milk, a week's supply at least. He was followed by a second slave carrying an even larger bowl filled to the rim with kouskous. The bowls were set before her. Camel's milk is sweet, and rich with nutrients. Kouskous, a sort of porridge made of boiled and pounded wheat, is the staple of the Moors' diet. It is not at all unpalatable, but all things have their limits. 'Eat,' said Boo Khaloom.

At first she didn't understand. Surely all this food must be for her father's guests. Did he expect her to serve them? But then she remembered that they were all naked and she began blubbering anew. Her father was shouting. 'Eat, I said!' he roared. 'Don't you understand Arabic? Have you lost your hearing? Eat!'

She put her lips to the milk and drank between sobs. She took a fistful of kouskous and forced it into her mouth. But she wasn't hungry. She'd just eaten – and eaten more than usual. Her mother had been nagging her about her bones, her coarseness, how no husband would want her, a girl who looked a desert ostrich. And so she had made an effort to eat more. Now she was full: another bite and she'd puke. The porridge caught in her throat.

Boo Khaloom was deranged. He whipped and shouted till his arm throbbed and his throat went raw. 'No more cat's cradle with the other girls, no more lessons, no weaving – nothing. You will sit here, on this pillow, and eat until you come of age. You will eat and you will grow. You will be beautiful. Do you hear? Beautiful!' Mohammed Bello and the others watched. From time to time one of them would nod approvingly. Fatima ate. Wept and ate. 'And when you come of age you will continue to eat – day and night. That is your duty. To your father, and to your husband. He will have a rod!' her father shouted. 'A rod like this one. And he will thrash you as I am thrashing you now and as I will thrash you tomorrow and the next day and the day after that!' Suddenly the venerables were on their feet, as if this were some sort of signal. Fatima looked up, her cheeks swollen with mush, and gasped: a hideous unnatural change had come over them. Where before they'd been flaccid, now they were hard. Wizened old turkey cocks, their members engorged, they closed in on her. 'Thrash you!' her father shrieked and they began pumping at themselves, milking their rods with a whack and thwap, their faces strained and distant, beatific even. Fatima felt as if she were made of wax. Her head was light. She was falling, tumbling down through the eons, chasms in the earth, the abyss. It was then that she felt the first few random drops, like rain.

After that excorating and traumatic night, she ate. She ate

prodigiously, furiously, she couldn't get enough. Sugar dates, mutton, yogurt, slabs of salt, kouskous and dried fish, kouskous and nuts, kouskous and kouskous. There was fruit in the south – tamarind, cassava, watermelon – flat loaves of bread, jars of wild honey, yams, rice, maize, butter and milk, milk, always milk. Goat's milk, cow's milk, camel's milk – she even suckled like an infant at the breast of a nursing slave. She was insatiable. She ate for fear, she ate for vengeance. She ate for beauty.

Tantalus

He is perishing, winding down the long tunnel of waste and death, hurtling toward completion in the dust of generations gone down. He is perishing, quite simply, of thirst. Of hunger too – but the thirst is more immediate. At night, when they remember, the Moors give him a handful of kouskous and half a cup of yellow swill. Tonight they forget. His stomach contracts on air, cells wither and die like jellyfish washed up on the beach. Then the temperature drops and he lies huddled in his jacket, shivering and sweating, the fever an internal weather valve, on and off, sun and sleet. Outside, beyond the circle of tents, jackals shriek and hyenas gather to intimidate the moon. There will be weeping and sorrowing and the gnashing of teeth, he thinks. Then he closes his eyes.

The explorer's dream is immediate and vivid. He is out on the Great Desert in the heat of midday, the sun a torch, his mouth full of sand. There are men behind him, strangers – burned faces, beards, tattered clothes. They trail out over the horizon like ants. In his hand, a forked stick. A man gags and pitches forward. The explorer turns him over and then starts back: the eye sockets are empty, the gums drawn back from the teeth, the skin as crusty as a glazed ham. At that moment a pewter dipper appears overhead, its belly frosted with dew – and then another, and another – a procession of them, dippers full of water, floating overhead like gulls riding an updraft. A feeble huzza goes up from the men. They stretch out their arms and smack their gummy lips – but the dippers hang there, just out of reach. Frantic, they scramble over one another's shoulders, their fingers raking the sky. The dippers are coy, wriggling and sashaying, flirting with the outstretched fingers: but they won't give up a drop. The men despair, dashing their heads against stones and shrubs and rocky crags. 'Do something!' they implore. 'Help us!' Just then the forked stick begins to twitch. Mungo cocks his ear to the wind. He hears something: faint and distant, lilting and lyrical. A wet trickle of sound, like a flute or a harp. Can it be? He is quick, firm, decisive. 'Follow me!' he shouts, and begins jogging toward the swelling sound of it, the roar, the hiss, the sweet syncopation of water rushing over a bed of stones. Dazed, the men stagger to their feet and hobble after him. Across a plain, up a rise and there, there it is! The Niger, clear and cold as an October morning, neat lawns clipped along its banks, punts, coots, and great silent swans coasting over the dimpled surface, salmon leaping, cool ferns and leafy elms fanning the shore. He plunges in, the men whooping at his heels, ecstatic, redeemed, alive. But when he turns round, they've vanished. Waves lap, swans duck their heads: he's alone with his triumph. But no matter, he's having such a time, churning up waves, blowing bubbles and gulping, swallowing, sucking up the smooth, tooth-chilling current till he can drink no more.

He wakes with a stone in his throat. His tongue is dry. His palate is dry. His uvula. What he needs is a drink. Water. Ice. Blood. A cup to tea. Glass of milk. Mug of beer. He tiptoes to the entranceway and peers out. The three guards are asleep, chewing at their beards and snoring like drunken lords. But here's the rub: they're stretched out across the entrance, shoulder to shoulder, the near man flush with the flap of the tent. He'd have to broad-jump the three of them to get clear – and even assuming he could make it, there's still the thump of his descent to contend with. Why they'd be up like starved wolves at even the hint of a sound, cursing and clutching at their daggers. He hesitates.

But then, miracle of miracles, the man in the centre rolls over, exposing a few inches of open ground. It's now or never. The explorer eases out of his boots, takes a deep breath, and steps over the first man. The air is still. Somewhere a bird cries out. But the guard sleeps on, stertorous, lips smacking and lids twitching. Mungo shifts his weight to the front foot and begins to swing the left leg over when suddenly he feels a bit woozy, his mind for some reason flashing on the high-wire artist at Bartholomew Fair. It was years ago. The young explorer stood in the crowd, Kewpie doll under his arm, and watched the man negotiate a wire strung two hundred feet from the ground. The man was in the process of balancing a barge pole in one hand and juggling half a dozen apples in the other, when a pigeon landed at the tip of the pole. The man fell.

Mungo blinks his eyes and finds himself seated on the chest of the first guard. The guard mutters something in Arabic, slow as syrup, and then starts rubbing the explorer's hand against his bristling cheek. The sensation, considering the circumstances, is not at all unpleasant. '*Yum-yum*' groans the guard, as passionately as a lover. '*Hibbah!*' But then he drops the explorer's hand and segues into the stertor of sleep while Mungo steals off into the night.

For more than a month now the explorer has been a captive of the Moors. He is held in solitary confinement. His horse and goods have been appropriated. He has not been charged with any crime. The question of snubbing out his eyes has, praise to Allah, been shelved for the time being. It seems that Fatima, Ali's principal wife, has sent word from Deena that she insists on examing the freak intact – evil eye and all. (In London they flock to see the human caterpillar and the man with three noses: in Ludamar it's albino mutants.) Still, the explorer's life has been anything but idyllic. He's been held against his will, harassed as an infidel, threatened with death and mutilation, starved, bullied, tormented, bored, deprived of conversation, intellectual stimulus, and water. And he hasn't laid eyes on his interpreter for a week. When he last saw him, Johnson was still keeping a tongue – civil or otherwise – in his head. Ali had found that flap of muscle and fatty tissue a *sine qua non* when interrogating the explorer about the arcana of his dress and baggage: the shoes and stockings, the buttons of his coat and trousers, his compass, watch, and razor. 'How does this work? And this?' Ali inquired, directing his questions to Johnson while his sullen dark eyes fixed on the explorer's face. Eventually, he made the explorer step in and out of his clothes thirty-seven times so that successive groups of rubber-neckers could marvel at the ingenuity of it. After the thirty-seventh demonstration, Ali expressed a curiosity as to why Mungo had come to the Sahel in the first place: if he wasn't a trader he must be a spy. 'I'm looking for the River Niger,' Mungo told him. Ali studied his great toe for a moment and then looked up. 'There are no rivers in your country?'

Down a gentle rise from the encampment – no more than three hundred yards – are the wells. Mungo can hear the lowing of the cattle as they crowd round the troughs for their nightly irrigation. When he gets closer he can make out the rounded humps and the wild spiked horns jabbing at the sky like a forest in motion. The cows – more like overweight gazelles than beef on the hoof – stamp and push and bellow for water. He could bellow along with them. He could cry and screech and out-howl all the demons in hell – he's so thirsty. But what's this? Something moving in the stand of acacias up ahead. The explorer sidles up for a closer look.

Six or seven slaves, muffled in their burnooses, are lounging around an open fire, passing a pipe and laughing. Every once in a while one of them dips a bucket in the well and sloshes its contents into a trough, where the cattle snort and shove to get at it. Mungo steps out of the shadows and goes down on his knees to them. 'Water,' he begs. 'Give me water.' And then in English: 'A drop, a taste, a spoonful!'

At first they're startled. But then looking down at the wasted wretch prostrating himself in the cowshit, they begin to laugh. Their eyes are glossy and veined with red. They stagger, whoop, hold their sides, their laughter echoing into the night – 'Yee-ha-ha-ha-haa!' – laughter like the throttling of birds. Then one of them steps foward, pipe in hand. His eyes are tiny, pig's eyes, and his brow swells out over his face like an eroded riverbank. 'Water!' cries Mungo. The man bends, drawing on the pipe, and blows a lungful of smoke in the explorer's face. The odour is strong, aromatic, viscous: are they smoking incense? Mungo coughs. Then the man rocks back on his heels and calls out to his companions: '*Nazarini* wants water?' They laugh. 'Give him water, Sidi!'

Sidi turns back to the explorer and hisses: '*La illah el allah, Mahomet rasowl Allahi.*' Mungo recognizes the phrase: There is only one God, and Mohammed is his prophet. They make him repeat it a hundred times a day. 'Okay,' he says. 'Okay,' and mutters a quick Lord's prayer, begging extenuating circumstances. Sidi kicks him. '*La illah el allah, Mahomet rasowl Allahi,*' says Mungo. 'Water!' shout the others. 'Give the *Nazarini* water, Sidi. Give him holy water!'

The hocks of the cattle rise and fall. Dust settles on the explorer like a parched snow. It is up his nose, down his throat. He can hear them, the stupid beasts, drooling over the troughs in mindless contentment, the precious silken droplets tumbling from their muzzles, catching like jewels at the tips of their whiskers. 'You want water?' Sidi says. Mungo nods. And then suddenly, without warning, the slave throws back his *jubbah* and pisses on him – quick and salt, the hot urine runs down his collar, through his fingers, soaks deep into the fabric of his waistcoat. The explorer leaps up in a frenzy, desperate and homicidal, but Sidi has backed off, laughing, and now the others are bending for stones and bits of wood. Mungo stands there, weak and stinking, as the herdsmen begin to pelt him. 'Drink piss, Christian!' they jeer. He turns heel and jogs off into the night.

It is quiet. The stars fan out across the heavens like spilled milk; mosquitoes whine in the trees. He is turned away from the next three wells in succession, pummelled with fists and sticks. At the last well, an ancient brackish pit set apart from the others, an old slave and his son, a boy of eight or nine, are watering their master's herd by torchlight. Mungo begs them for a drink. The old man eyes him suspiciously for a moment, then lifts a bucket of water from the well. '*Salaam, salaam, salaam,*' says Mungo, reaching out for it, when the boy tugs at his father's sleeve. '*Nazarini,*' says the boy. The old man hesitates, looking first at the bucket, then at the well. He is concerned about contamination, hexes, a well gone dry in the night. 'Please,' the explorer says, 'I beg you.' The old man shuffles to the trough, empties the bucket and points a weathered finger. Mungo doesn't have to be asked twice. He throws himself forward, wedging his head between the big horned skulls of a pair of heifers.

The trough looks like a gutter on a rainy day, the water like sewage, twigs and straw and bits of offal swirling on the surface. The explorer buries his face and drinks, but the competition is fierce, the stream already a puddle, cattle slavering, their great pink tongues like sponges lapping up the last few drops. He turns to the old man. 'More!' he shouts. 'More!' A piebald cow, its eyes big as pocket-watches, bowls him over. And then suddenly a gun-shot barks out, loud as a thunderclap. Then another. The cattle fall back, confused, butting shoulders, snouts and flanks, panicky, running blind. *Ka-bomb, Ka-bomb, Ka-bomb,* they boom off into the night.

When the dust settles, Mungo finds himself looking up at three horsemen. One of them is Dassoud, the hyphenated scar glistening in the torchlight. There is a pistol in his hand. He steadies his mount, levels the pistol at the explorer's head, and pulls the trigger. Nothing happens. Mungo sits there in the dust and cattle droppings, his heart frozen, nerves shot, wondering how on earth to conciliate this madman with the gun. '*La illah el allah, Mahomet rasowl Allahi,*' he says, taking a stab at it. Dassoud is pouring a fresh charge into the priming pan, all the while growling like a dog at an intruder's pantleg. The horses stamp and whinny, the old man and his son cower. Then Dassoud raises the gun a second time, shouts something in Arabic, squeezes the trigger. A flash of light, a sound like hot coals dropped in a tub of water. The pistol has misfired. 'What have I done?' the explorer pleads, edging away. Dassoud curses, flings down the pistol, and calls over his shoulder for another. 'Hua!' shouts the man at his back, tossing him a fresh weapon. Dassoud snatches it out of the air, cocks the hammer, and aims at a constellation of freckles just to the left of the explorer's nose.

'Mr Park!' Johnson, skirts aflap, bursts into the circle of light like a character out of the commedia dell'arte. His chest is heaving and his jowls are streaked with sweat. 'Mr Park, you crazy? Get up on your feet and double-time it back to that tent before they shoot you dead on the spot. You got the whole place in a uproar. They think you tryin' to escape.'

Mungo looks up. Fires blaze on the hillside. Horsemen ride off into the night with torches. There are shouts and curses, random gunshots. Mungo rises. Dassoud lowers the pistol.

Not Twist, Not Copperfield, Not Fagin Himself

Not Twist, not Copperfield, not Fagin himself had a childhood to compare with Ned Rise's. He was unwashed, untutored, unloved, battered, abused, harassed, deprived, starved, mutilated, and orphaned, a victim of poverty, ignorance, ill-luck, class prejudice, malicious fate, and gin. His childhood was so totally depraved even a Zola would shudder to think of it.

He was born out back of a twopenny flophouse in what the wags called 'The Holy Land' – cribs of straw that went for a penny a night. The year was 1771, the month February. His mother didn't have the price of a bed, and so she crept into the outbuilding, the labour pains coming like blows to the groin, a bottle of clear white Knock-Me-

Down clutched in her fist. The straw was dirty. Pigeons dropped excrement from the rafters. It was so cold even the lice were sluggish. She selected a crib in the rear because of its proximity to the horses and what little warmth they generated. Then she settled down with her bottle.

She was a souse, Ned's mother. A sister in the great sorority of the sorrows of gin. At this time in British history, the sorority – and its brother fraternity – were flourishing. When gin was first introduced in England at the close of the seventeenth century (some claim it was brought over from Holland by William III, others say it was distilled from bone and marrow by the Devil himself), it became an overnight sensation. It was cheap as piss, potent as a kick in the head. They went mad for it: after all, why swill beer all night when you can get yourself crazed in half an hour – for a penny? By 1710 the streets were littered with drunks, some stripped naked, others stiff as tombstones. When Sir Joseph Jekyll, Master of the Rolls, introduced legislation to curb the pernicious influence of gin through licensing and taxation, a mob gathered to stone his house and chew the wheels from his carriage. There was no stopping it. As a palliative for hard times, it was sleep and poetry, it was life itself. Aqua vitae. Ned's mother was a second-generation gin-soak. Her father was a tanner. He drank two pints a day and flayed hides. He sold her into service at nine, she was out on the streets at thirteen, a mother at fourteen. She died of cirrhosis, brain fever, consumption, and green sickness before she reached twenty.

There were three other lodgers in the Holy Land that drear winter's night. The first was a tribeless patriarch who coughed like dice in a box and died before first light. The landlord discovered him next morning: clots of blood frozen to his lips, his neck, buried deep in the sere white nest of his beard. Then there was the stone mason – granite monuments and markers – on the tail end of a three-day drunk. He retched in the straw and lay down to sleep in it. Lastly, there was the old woman wrapped in tattered skirts like a dressmaker's dummy, who scraped in after midnight and pitched headlong into the next crib over from the pregnant girl. She lay there, the old woman, her breathing like the friction of rusted gears, listening to the moans of Ned's mother. Moans. They were nothing new. She closed her eyes. But then there was a cry, and then another. The old woman sat up. In the next crib lay a girl of fourteen or fifteen. Her brow was wet. The neck of a bottle peeked out from her jacket. She was in labour.

The harridan crept closer, snatched up the bottle, and held it to her lips.

'Ere,' she keaked. 'Wot's the trouble, little cheese: birfin' a babe, is it?'

The girl looked up, heart in mouth.

'Ee-eeeee!' screeched the old woman, scattering the pigeons in the rafters. 'I've done it meself, done it meself, oh yes. There was a time the babbies dropped from these old loins like pippins from a tree.' Her face was ageless. Who could say how much flesh she'd moulded within her? Or count the years she'd languished in a Turkish seraglio or a Berber hut? Who could guess what twisted paths and dark alleys she'd been down, or what she was thinking when that ring of hammered gold was struck through her lip?

It was a breech birth. First the wrinkled legs and buttocks, then the shoulders and chin, the smooth slick dome of the head. The hour of the wolf came and went, and the old woman yanked Ned from his mother's womb. Her fingers were dry and crabbed. She tied off the cord and slapped him. He wailed. Then she wiped the blood and mucus from his body with the hem of her skirt and tucked him inside her coat. She glanced round, sly and secretive, then made for the door. Baby-snatch!

Ned's mother propped herself on one elbow and felt around her, first for the child and then for the bottle. Both were gone. She focused on the pinched shoulders of the old woman receding into the gloom at the far end of the barn and then she began to scream, scream like sandstorms on the desert, like the death of the universe. The crone hurried for the door, the girl's screams at her back, the horses kicking blindly in their stalls. The bearded patriarch did not wake. But the stone-cutter did. He was in his mid-twenties. He flung slabs of granite about as if they were newsprint, day in and day out. 'Stop 'er!' the girl cried. 'She's got my baby!'

He vaulted the railing and jogged the length of the stable just as the harridan was squeezing through the door. She spun around on him, a rusted scissor in hand. 'Get back!' she hissed. The blow came like a seizure, secretive and brutal. He caught her in the shoulder and she collapsed like a bundle of twigs. Beneath her, there was the sound of shattering glass. And the keen of an infant.

The stone-cutter's name was Edward Pin. They called him Ned for short. He took the girl and her child to his lodgings in Wapping, a fierce hangover raging behind his eyes. She'd washed him in tears and he felt like a hero, no matter how much his head ached. The infant, it seemed, had been gashed across the chest when the bottle broke. Pin lit a few sticks of wood and a handful of coal to take the chill off the room. The girl's hair hung loose as she bent over the baby to dress his wounds. Her name was Sarah Colquhoun. She was drunk. 'I'm going to name 'im Ned,' she slurred. 'After 'is deliverer.' Pin beamed. But then a change came over his face and he took hold of her hair. 'Don't you go callin' 'im Pin, you slut. 'Ee's none of mine.'

'Rise I'm callin' 'im!' she shouted back. 'Ned Rise, you son of a bitch.' It was the metaphoric expression of a hope. 'You know why?... Cause he's going to rise above all this shit 'is mother has had to eat since I could barely say my own name.'

'Ha!' he sneered. 'Baptized in blood. And gin. And with a ginswill of a whorin' mother. I bleedin' doubt it.'

Ned's memories of his mother are sketchy. A drawn face, all cheekbone and brow, the skin stretched tight as leather on a last. A persistent hacking in the night. Phthisical pallor. Too much green round the gills. She was dead before he was six. Pin, needless to say, was a violent drunkard with the temperament of a cat set afire. When he worked, he came home white with stone dust, his eyes bleeding alcohol. Then he would settle down to torture the boy for the sheer joy of it, like a ten-year-old with a frog or rat. He tied Ned's feet together and hung him out the third-storey window like a pair of wet pants. He clamped the chamber-pot over Ned's ears, stropped a razor on his back, submerged his head in a tub of water for sixty seconds at a time. 'Drown you like a rat, I will!' he growled.

When the boy was seven the stone-cutter decided it was time he earned his keep. He appeared in the doorway one night with a fistful of baling twine, caught the boy round the neck, pinned him down, and trussed up his leg at the knee. Then he cut Ned's trousers high up the shin, fashioned a crutch from a broomstick, and set him out on the street to beg. It was cold in the wind, and the bindings chewed at the boy's flesh. No matter. Seven years old, shrink-bellied and filth-faced, he teetered like a drunken stork and pleaded for pennies in Russell Square, Drury Lane, Covent Garden. But mendicity was popular and the competition was fierce. An army of amputees, lepers, pin-heads, paralytics, gibberers, slaverers, and whiners lined the streets shoulder to shoulder. There was the legless man planted in the chamber-pot who hopped around on his knuckles like an ape; the limbless woman who polished boots with her tongue; the man-dog with a withered tail and spiked yellow teeth hanging over his lip. Ned didn't have a chance.

When Ned came home with two farthings the first day, Pin thrashed him. The following day, after sixteen hours of entreating, imploring, and beseeching, Ned had nothing to show but a bit of string, three chestnuts, and a brass button. Pin drubbed him again, this time giving special consideration to the nose, mouth, and cheekbones. As a result, Ned's face took on the colour and consistency of a fermenting plum. This development improved the take somewhat, but then there was always the necessity of raising fresh welts each day. After a month of it, Pin pulled something in his thrashing arm. There's got to be a better way, he thought. Then he hit on it. 'Ned,' he called. 'Come over 'ere.'

Pin was sitting at the table with a tumbler of gin. The floor was ankle-deep in rags and papers, the bones of chops and chickens, scraps of wood, fragments of glass, smashed earthenware, feathers. Ned was in the corner, feigning invisibility. The stone mason jerked his head round. 'Come over 'ere, I said.' Ned came. A meat cleaver lay on the table, cold and tarnished. When Ned saw it he began to blubber. 'Shet yer 'ole!' roared Pin, forcing the boy's right hand down on the table. His own grimy fist smothered it like a hood. Trembling, vulnerable, the boy's fingers lay there on the block, pale as sacrificial lambs. There were black semicircles under the nails. The cleaver fell.

With his arm in a sling to display the mutilated hand to advantage (Pin had excised the first joint of each finger, thumb included), Ned's take began to improve. In a month or two he was pulling in seven or eight shillings a day: a small fortune. Pin gave up the lapidary profession to sit through the long afternoons in taverns and coffee houses, bolting duck with orange sauce, swilling wine and laying his broad calloused palms across the bosoms and backsides of women of pleasure. Ned froze his ass off on the street, choked on crusts, and cabbage soup, the loss of his fingertips an ongoing horror to him, a waking nightmare. He wanted to run off. He wanted to die. But Pin kept him tractable with blows to the back of the head and threats of further mutilation. 'Like to lose the rest of them nubbins? Or the 'and maybe? Or 'ow bout the 'ole arm?' Then he would laugh.

One grim afternoon, as the ex-stone-cutter was reeling across the street from the Magpie and Stump to inspect his ward's pockets, a landau drawn by four handsome bays dashed him to the pavement. He became involved in the rear spring mechanism and was dragged about a hundred yards up the street. A woman screamed. He was dead.

For the next several years Ned lived on the streets: begging, filching, eating garbage, occasionally finding shelter with a loon or pederast or axe murderer. It was a tough life. No hand to comfort, no voice to praise. He grew up like an aborigine.

Then, when he was twelve, his luck turned. He was at Vauxhall Gardens one morning, picking pockets and stripping bark from the trees, when he was arrested by a sound trembling on the warm still air, an unearthly fluting like something out of a dream. It seemed to be coming from beyond the fountain, near the flowerbeds. When he got there he found a scattering of park-goers – rakes and gallants, ladies and tarts, nurses with infants, fops, cutpurses, itinerant hawkers – all gathered around a man blowing into a wooden instrument. The man was bald, his face and crown red as a ham, his cheeks puffed. Jollops of flesh hung over his collar and quivered in sympathetic response to the keening vibrato of the instrument. He was dressed like a gentleman.

Ned watched the clean athletic fingers lick up and down the keys, lighting here, pausing there, lifting, darting and pouncing like young animals at play. The pansies and jonquils were in bloom. Forget-me-nots and peonies. He sat in the grass and listened, the music reedy and sweet, like birds gargling with honey. The man's foot tapped as he played. Some of the listeners began to tap along with him, the buckled pumps and slippers and wooden clogs rising and falling in unison, as if manipulated by a string. One woman swayed her head in a soft glowing arc, almost imperceptible, the sun firing an aureole of curls round her face. Ned's foot began to tap. He couldn't remember a happier moment.

When the musician took a break, the crowd dispersed. Ned lingered to watch him. The man twisted the mouthpiece from his instrument, unfastened the reed and balanced it like a wafer on the tip of his tongue. From a leather-bound case he produced a brush, with which he swabbed the hollowed body of the instrument. The keys glistened in the sun. 'You find all this stimulating, do you?' the man said. He was addressing Ned.

Ned sat there, chewing at a blade of grass, ragged as a field gone to seed. He'd lived his life in the muck of the street, pissed in the Thames, scavenged his clothes from dust-bins, comatose drunks, the stiffened corpses stacked like firewood beneath the bridges. He could't have been wilder and filthier had he been raised by wolves. 'What of it?' he spat.

The man drew the reed from his mouth, examined it, then slipped it back between his lips. There were ten thousand shit-faced orphans like this one out on the streets. They were at his elbows everywhere he went, insinuating themselves, offering their mouths and bodies, whining for coppers, bread and beer. But something in this one appealed to him: what it was he couldn't say. He made an effort. 'I don't know – it just seemed as if you appreciated my little performance... the tunes, I mean.'

Ned softened. 'I did,' he admitted.

The man held up the instrument. 'You know what this is?'

'A fife?'

'Clarinet,' said the man.

Ned wanted to know how the sound was made. The man showed him. Could he learn to play? Ned asked. The man stared down at Ned's hand, then asked him if he was hungry.

Prentiss Barrenboyne owned a block of houses in Mayfair. He was in his mid-fifties. He'd never been married. His mother, a fierce and acerbic empiricist with whom he'd lived all his life, had died a month earlier. He brought the boy home that night and let him sleep in the coal cellar. In the morning he instructed his housekeeper to wash and feed him. It was a foot in the door. By the end of the week Ned Rise had become a habit. Officially he was established in the house as a servant, but Barrenboyne, won over by the lad's ingenuous and consuming enthusiasm for the clarinet, came to treat him more like a member of the family. He bought him clothes, gave him milk and chops and drippings, taught him to read and how to balance a teacup on his knee. There were trips to the concert hall, the theatre, the shipyard, and the zoo. A tutor was engaged. Ned acquired the rudiments of orthography, geometry, piscatology, a phrase or two of French, and a profound loathing for the Classics. He was no Eliza Doolittle. His progress – if the bimonthly absorption of a date or sum merits the appellation – was as leisurely as the drift of continents. The tutor was beside himself. He looked at Ned's face and saw the face of a wiseacre. He accused him of drinking ink and flogged his backside as he flogged his memory. Ned bore it with patience and humility. There were no tantrums, no fits, no funks. He did what was expected of him, sang hosannas to his redeemer, and polished his prospects. He knew a good thing when he saw one.

Seven years passed. In France they were sending out invitations to a beheading, across the Atlantic they were knocking down forests and bludgeoning Indians, in the East End they nabbed the misogynist known as 'The Monster' who for two years had been goring women's backsides in the street, and in Mayfair Ned Rise was eating three meals a day, sleeping in a bed, bathing at least once a fortnight, and stepping into clean underwear each and every morning. Seven years. The memory of the streets had begun to fade. He'd never eaten offal, witnessed perversion, theft, arson and worse, never huddled over ash pits with ice crusting his lashes and a cold fist clenching at his lungs – not Ned Rise, pride of the Barrenboynes.

Over the years Ned and his guardian had grown as close as palate and reed, wedded by their love of music. A week after the old man took him in the music lessons began. His face and crown suffused with blood, the hoary mutton chops bristling, Barrenboyne grinned his way into the room one night, a wooden case in hand. Inside was an ancient C clarinet, the one he himself had played as a boy. He handed it to Ned. Within the year Ned was playing passably in spite of his handicap, capable of sight-reading practically anything by the following summer, and in five years' time proficient enough to accompany his mentor to the park for his public debut. They sat there on the very bench on which Ned had first seen the old man, he with his C clarinet, Barrenboyne with his B-flat, and played airs from Estienne Rogers' tunebook. People gathered round, tapped their feet, swayed their bodies, while Mozart, dying in Vienna, composed his great Requiem Mass. Ned rose to the occasion.

One morning, just before dawn, Barrenboyne stepped into Ned's room and shook him by the shoulder. 'Get up, Ned,' he whispered. 'I need you.' His voice trembled. His face and jowls were redder than Ned had ever seen them, red as tomatoes, flags, the jackets of the King's Hussars. Ned was nineteen. 'What's the matter?' he asked. No answer. Birds began to whistle from beyond the windows. The old man was breathing like a locomotive. 'Get dressed and meet me out front,' he said.

Barrenboyne was waiting at the gate. He was dressed in the suit he'd bought for his mother's funeral, beaver top hat, silk surtout. Under his arm, a leather case, the rippled skin of some exotic reptile. A new clarinet? thought Ned. He'd never seen it before. They walked at a brisk pace: through Grosvenor Square, down Brook Street, across Park Lane and then into the soft green demesne of the park itself. The place was deserted. Fot, like milk in an atomizer, hung low over the wet grass. A crow jeered from a tree branch. 'You know what a second is?' Barrenboyne said.

It was a slap in the face. 'A second? You're not–?'

The old man took hold of his sleeve. 'Just take it is easy now,' he said. 'You're a grown man, Ned Rise. Prove it.'

Two men – figures out of the gloom – were waiting for them by the edge of the Serpentine. One of them was a blackamoor, short, fat as a sow. He wore a feather in his hat, doeskin breeches, lisle hose and an iridescent waistcoat. A real buck. Barrenboyne strode up to them, bowed, and presented the leather case. It was seventy degrees at least, but the negro was shivering. His second, who kept inhaling snuff from an enamel box and sneezing into his handkerchief, took the leather case and opened it, between sneezes, for the negro. The negro selected a pistol. There was liquor on his breath. Then the sneezer offered the case to Barrenboyne. The old man lifted the weapon from its case as gently as if he were unpacking his clarinet for a breezy concert on the green. It began to drizzle.

The sneezer was snuffing snuff in a paroxysm of nervous energy, snapping open the box, pinching a nostril, gasping and slobbering into his handkerchief, all the while jerking his limbs and shuddering like an epileptic. The negro dropped his gun. The drizzle turned to rain. Barrenboyne's wattles began to vibrate as if he were exploring the upper register of the clarinet, and Ned found himself trembling in sympathetic response. Finally the sneezer managed to walk off twenty paces and set the principals on their marks. 'Ready!' he bawled. Two harsh metallic clicks echoed over the field, one in imitation of the other. 'Take aim!' Barrenboyne and the negro slowly raised their arms, as if saluting one another or taking part in the opening movement of a revolutionary new dance routine. Ned could picture them, jetéing over the greensward to leap through one another's arms. 'Ffff–' came the aborted command, tailed by a septum-wrenching sneeze. There was a flash and a snap. Birds cried out at the far end of the field. The negro's pistol was smoking and his eyes were still buried in the crook of his elbow. Barrenboyne lay on the ground. Dead as a pharaoh.

Laying It on the Line

Dawn. The sun breaks over the Sahel like a cracked egg and takes up where it left off the day before – scalding, incinerating, searing the life from everything within its compass. Carrion sniffers and night-roving reptiles creep back to their dens, and the big battered Nubian vultures sail out over the plain to check out the leavings. Rocks begin to expand, stunted shrubs dig deeper into the earth, mimosas fold up their leaves like parasols. By eight in the morning the horizon is shirred.

Mungo Park lies motionless on his back, watching a millipede trace a series of blind circles across the roof of his tent. Since the night of his 'attempted escape' things have gone hard on him. Six men now doze outside his tent each night, and his food and water ration has been cut by half. It begins to occur to him that he may not make it after all, that he might just lie here and waste away, dauntless discoverer of the interior walls of a Moorish tent. His bones will dry and crack and fall to dust under the alien sun and the wheeling strange colossi of misplaced constellations. He begins to feel daunted.

Suddenly the flaps part and Johnson ducks into the tent. In his hand a goatskin water-bag, known as a *guerba* in these parts. The explorer lies there, racked with fever, riddled with worms, his stomach shrunken, sphincter open wide, barely able to raise his eyes. He is weak and stinking, tabescent, at the far edge of hope. Johnson kneels beside him and feeds the leather nipple into his mouth. His lips grope, pulse quickens. It is water, cold and clear, water dipped from the shifting porous depths of the earth. It stirs the roots of his hair, firms his toenails, sings to his brittle bones. 'I'm saved!' he gasps, and then vomits.

'It's all right, Mr Park. Take it easy: you got the whole thing to yourself.'

'Wha?' The explorer's eyes are crusted and yellow, cheeks drawn, his beard a playground for ticks, fleas, lice and maggots.

'You heard me right. Chief Jackal, he tells me to come in here and give you the water-bag and then a pan of milk and kouskous.'

'Milk? Kouskous?' Johnson might just as well have announced haggis, finnan haddie, and sheep's-head soup. Mungo goes into peristaltic shock, then jerks himself up, clutching at the *guerba* and ransacking the tent with his eyes. 'Where?' he pants, struggling to his feet. 'Where? Tell me for God's sake!'

At that moment a boy enters with a wooden bowl. Milk and kouskous. The boy makes as if to lay it at the explorer's feet, but Mungo snatches it from him and buries his face in the thick ropy paste with all the desperation of a man stranded on the desert for forty days and forty nights. Which is precisely what he is.

Afterward, he pats his abdomen. 'Johnson,' he says. 'Oh-ho Johnson, Johnson, Johnson, how I needed that . . .'. But what has he done? The bowl's been scraped clean and here's his faithful guide and interpreter languishing before his eyes! 'Johnson,' he stammers, staring down at the ground, '. . . can you ever, can you ever forgive me? I'm afraid I went into a bit of a frenzy there . . ., I–I forgot all about you.'

Johnson holds up his palm. 'Oh they been feedin' me right along, don't you worry about that. Got to. Else how am I goin' to bust my ass for them? Mend this, mend that. Scrub this pot, milk them goats, oil up Akbar's sandals, and skim some cream for the horses. Shit. It's like bein' back on that plantation again. Sometimes I wish they'd just let me lie here and languish along with you.'

Mungo strokes the soggy grain from his beard and systematically licks the kernels from his fingers, then takes a long pull at the water-bag. Colour trickles back into his cheeks. 'So what's up?' he says. 'What's made the bloody camel drivers so charitable all of a sudden?'

'Fatima.'

Fatima. The syllables flow like wind on water. First she'd saved his eyes, and now the rest of him. Hope glimmers. 'She wants to see me?'

Johnson nods. 'Ali says you got to be fed, washed up, and made presentable. He won't have his wife examinin' a unwashed Christian. And he gave me this too,' handing the explorer a pale folded garment.

'What is it?'

'*Jubbah.* Ali says you got to cover up your legs – he finds your trousers objectionable, high-quality nankeen or no.' Johnson laughs. 'You ever get back to London you can sweep all the beaux and noodles under the table, start a craze: skirts for gentlemen.'

Mungo laughs along with him, drunk on food and water. The two chuckle and wheeze, wiping tears from their eyes. Then Johnson looks up, suddenly serious. 'She'll be here tomorrow night,' he says. 'Don't blow it.'

Plantation Song

On this sub-Saharan evening awash with pale light and tapering shadow, Mungo Park, for the first time in nearly three months, finds himself out of the tent and back in the saddle again. His horse has been restored to him (cachectic as ever, looking like one of the gutted nags the Druids used to impale for decoration), his beard, locks and loins cleansed and anointed, his rags exchanged for a spanking white *jubbah.* On his head, a battered top hat; around his shoulders, the blue velvet jacket he wore while addressing the African Association at St Alban's Tavern, Pall Mall. Ali and Dassoud flank him on their chargers. Ali's mount is white, Dassoud's so absolutely black it cuts a hole in the horizon (an illusion he enhances by blackening the animal's hoofs and anus, and staining its teeth). Johnson brings up the rear on an Abyssian ass.

They are bound for Fatima's tent at the far edge of the encampment, a distance of perhaps six or seven hundred yards. Ali and Dassoud are silent, while Mungo, sotto voce, rehearses phrases from his Arabic grammar: 'I am honoured to bask in your presence.' 'Allow me to make obeisance to the undersides of your feet.' 'Hot, isn't it?' As they pass through the heart of the camp, dogs dart out to yap at the Christian's stirrups, children gather to bombard him with nuggets of camel dung, adults step from their tents to squint up at him and denigrate his race, creed, and colour. 'I piss in your mother's hole!' a man yells. But then Ali holds up his hand and the voices fall silent, the children run to their mothers, the dogs vanish. 'Thanks,' says Mungo. Ali's face is impassive. His gesture has had nothing whatever to do with compassion or fellow feeling – he just doesn't want his wife inspecting a washed Christian in a shit-stained *jubbah*, that's all.

Fatima's tent is two or three times the size of any of the others in camp, and distinguished by broad bands of colour: grey, beige, indigo. Mungo recognizes the huge Nubian out front. The Nubian stands there, on guard, flexing the black bulges between his elbow and shoulder. Off to the right a woman squats in the dust, busily milking four or five she-goats. The explorer observes the pale soles of her feet, the yellow torpedoes of the goats' teats. A fly lands on the explorer's nose. The sun touches the horizon.

'Dismount!' shouts Ali, as he and Dassoud spring from their steeds like a pair of Russian tumblers. Johnson, ambling up on his ass, relays the command to his employer, while the Nubian steps forward to take charge of the animals.

It should be said that the explorer's mind is labouring under a Sisyphean strain at this juncture: he is keyed up, jittery, acquiver with apprehension and doubt. The success of his mission – yea, his life itself – may depend on the impression he makes in his forthcoming interview with the Queen. His stomach sinks with the same nauseated, socked-in-the-kidney feeling that used to assail him at school before end-of-term exams. Butterflies, they used to call it. Stage fright. Heebie-jeebies. The Choke.

And so, sweating like a marathon runner, he steps down out of the saddle, catches his left foot in the stirrup, and slaps to the ground in a storm of dust and goat hair. He lies there a moment, thinking Christ in Heaven what have I done now, while Dassoud and Ali exchange glances and Johnson rushes to his aid. After steadying the horse, loosening the stirrup and finally thinking to remove the explorer's boot, Johnson succeeds in extricating him. But this is just the beginning. The ground here, it seems, is a mecca for the costive denizens of the Sahel, an unspoiled latrine for mother nature and all her feathered, furred and squamate creation. Goat herds here, cheek by jowl with hyena ordure; grainy bars of camel dung, dogshit, cowshit and sheepshit coil around the withered ropy leavings of adders and skinks; there's even a stray ibex turd or two. Mungo rises from this morass, brushing at his *jubbah* and dusting his hat. 'Sorry about that,' he says. Ali shrugs. Then gestures for him to follow, and disappears through the soft contiguous flaps of Fatima's tent and into the mystery beyond. Mungo, reeking like a zoo, his back an abstract collage of mauves, siennas, and dun yellows, the representative of King George III and all of England, follows the Emir of Ludamar into the sanctum of the Queen.

It is dark inside, a pair of oil lamps burning fitfully. There are tapestries, mats, urns, a perch on which two birds of prey – saker falcons – are calmly disemboweling a jerboa. The explorer glances up just as one of them finds a long strand of intestine and begins to tug at it, like a robin with a worm. '*Salaam aleichem*,' says Ali, and there she is, seated on a pillow the size of a double bed. The explorer is stunned. He'd expected a big woman – but this . . . this is impossible! She is gargantuan, elephantine, her great bundled turban and glowing *jubbah* like a pair of circus tents, her shadow leaping and swelling in the uncertain light until it engulfs the room. Her attendants – two girls in billowy pantaloons and a hoary old woman – sit at her feet like olives flanking a cantaloupe in a surreal still life.

Mungo cannot make out her face, which is concealed behind a *yashmak* –the double horse-hair veil worn by Muslim women in public – but he is immediately struck by her feet and hands. Petite and delicate, they float at the tips of her bloated extremities like ducks on a pond. He is fascinated. Each of her digits is ornamented with a ring, and for some reason – perhaps to draw attention to their charms her hands and feet have been stained saffron. The effect is dazzling. When finally she turns her head toward him she gasps, and gives out a faint squeal. Ali rushes to her, jabbering in Arabic. When she answers him, her voice is soft and sensual as a sunshower.

Mungo nudges his interpreter.

'She says she's afraid,' Johnson whispers.

'Afraid? I'm the one whose giblets are on the line here.'

'You're a Christian. To her that's like bein' a cannibal or a werewolf or somethin.'

'What about you?'

'Don't look at me, brother – I'm a Animist. Shhh . . . now she's bitchin' about the smell . . . "Do they all smell like that?"'

Suddenly Ali barks out a command. 'He wants us on our knees,' says Johnson, easing himself down.

The explorer follows suit. They pose like this for a long while ('I'm beginning to feel like a ostrich,' Johnson quips), until a high nasal voice begins yodeling out the evening prayers. It is the *muezzin*, stationed somewhere outside the tent. Ali and Dassoud likewise prostrate themselves, and Fatima comes down off her throne like a thunder-cloud rolling down the side of a mountain. As she tilts her forehead to the earth, the explorer can feel her rich black eyes on him.

When the prayers are finally finished, Fatima lumbers back to her pillow, settles herself primly, and softly dismisses Dassoud and her husband. She then turns to Mungo and his interpreter, and asks them to be seated. Behind them, the Nubian edges into the tent, scimitar in hand. For a long while the room is silent, Fatima and her attendants ocularly feasting on this blond apparition in the blue velvet jacket. Finally the Queen addresses him, a single sentence, her voice rising as if on the crest of a question.

Mungo looks at Johnson.

'She wants you to stand up and take your jacket off.'

Mungo complies, and one of the girls slips up to take the garment from him and deliver it to the Queen. Fatima regards the jacket silently, running her hand over the material against the nap, taking one of the brass buttons between her teeth. The explorer stands there in his *jubbah* like a child in a nightgown. 'Give it to her,' Johnson whispers.

The explorer clears his throat, and in his best Arabic offers her the jacket. She looks up at him and politely declines, but does appropriate two of the brass buttons. 'For earrings,' she explains, holding them up to the corners of her *yashmak*. From the shadows one of the falcons begins to crow: ca-ha! ca-ha! Fatima wets her lips. 'Does he want any pork?' she asks.

'Tell her no,' says Johnson.

At that moment One-Eye appears with a bushpig on a leash. The bushpig has an elongated snout randomly disfigured with lumps and ridges, several yellowed tusks, and a nasty look in its eye. With a leer, One-Eye offers Mungo the pig. 'Snark-snark,' says the pig.

'Look disgusted,' Johnson coaches.

The explorer does his best to express horror and loathing, knowing full well how deeply the Moors abhor pork. He backs away, fingers atremble, slapping his forehead, and tugging at his lip while the bushpig, squealing like an accordion, stamps and stutters and jerks at its leash. The performance seems to be reassuring Fatima, and so the explorer gyrates even more wildly – really hamming it up – until he accidentally stumbles into the falcons' perch. This, he immediately realizes, is a mistake. At the touch of his elbow the birds rear up and shriek in his face, their beaks and talons like scissors, wings beating round his ears. Then the larger of the two springs onto his shoulder. He is terrified. In his anxiety to brush it away he ducks directly into the path of the bushpig, who has been waiting for just such a chance. In a flash the pig lurches forward and savagely bites the explorer six or seven times in rapid succession. During the panic that ensues, the explorer somehow manages to collapse half the tent and wind up spread-eagled across the Queen's voluminous lap. The Nubian eunuch intercedes to behead the pig with one swipe of his scimitar, while One-Eye and the pantaloon girls try to dislodge the shit-caked and bleeding explorer from the Queen's person. Through it all, Mungo can hear the strains of Johnson's voice raised in song – it seems almost as if he's singing a dirge, downhearted and mournful, one of the old plantation songs Johnson likes to call 'the blues'.

'You done blowed it now,' he's singing. 'Blowed it now. Lord God Almighty, you done blowed it now.'

New Continents, Ancient Rivers

But he hadn't blown it. Not by a long shot. In fact, as things turned out, the Queen didn't seem at all indisposed by the presence of a porcipophagic albino infidel in her lap – perhaps, in a strange way, she even welcomed it. The explorer's first intimation of this came almost immediately. As he lay there, stunned and bleeding, cradled in the trembling aqueous flux of her lap like a ship come to harbour, he felt he detected a movement deep within her. A ripple, a swell. An undulation as soft and inevitable as the rings which fan out over the waters of a pond after a stone has broken its surface. Was she laughing? Tittering deep in the omphalos of that magnificent flesh-factory? Was he a hit, after all? Unfortunately he had no chance to find out, for Dassoud, murder in his eye, was already hacking at the deflated wall of the tent. Mungo sprang from the Queen's nave and planted his brown in the earth, following Johnson's example. '*La illah el allah,*' he chanted by way of amends, '*Mahomet rasowl allahi.*'

There was the shriek of rending goat hair – *zit! zat! zoot!* – and Dassoud leaped into the tent, inflamed with the notion that the Queen was in danger, thirsting to exact a hasty and savage retribution. 'Aaarrrr!' he growled, whirling his terrible swift sword – but then he stopped in his tracks. What was going on here? The hand-maidens were in hysterics, tent poles shattered, blood spewed, and feathers strewn from one end of the place to the other... and yet there sat Fatima, just as he'd left her, while the *Nazarini* and his slave lay quailing on the ground, One-Eye and the Nubian standing over them like executioners. 'What in the name of Allah is going on here?' he demanded.

The Nubian, who had never spoken a word in his life, said nothing.

The pig sprawled in the corner, still quivering, gouts of blood issuing from its severed throat. It's head lay at the Nubian's feet.

'Lord have mercy!' whimpered Johnson, addressing the sand.

Finally the hand-maidens' lamentations wound down to an easy gagging mewl, and One-Eye launched a rapid-fire narration of what had transpired, playing down his own involvement as best he could and emphasizing the reckless and irresponsible behaviour of the *Nazarini* and his slave. Dassoud listened impatiently, rocking on his feet, twisting the saber in his hand, until finally he cut the story short and insisted that the transgressors be led out into the dunes and disemboweled. At this point Fatima cleared her throat. Dassoud fell silent. Her tone was firm, her diction spare. The sense of it blew right by the explorer, but the upshot of the whole thing was that he and Johnson were led back to his tent, where a seventh comatose guard was summoned to complement the six men tried and true who were already dozing before the entrance-way.

An hour later an unwonted aroma charged the air. It was lingering and piquant, redolent of hearths and basting and relishes. It was the smell of meat. The explorer swallowed twice. 'Johnson – do you smell what I smell?'

'Prime rib. I'd know it anywhere.'

Just then the flaps parted and the savoury rich aura filled the tent. It was one of the pantaloon girls. In her hand, the haunch of an addax, still hissing from the spit. She gave it to the explorer. 'For you,' she said. 'From Fatima.' Then she winked and disappeared into the night.

Mungo tore a mouthful from the bone, then passed the joint to his interpreter. He was laughing. 'We're home free now, old fellow – guess I must have done something right after all.'

'Maybe she's big on slapstick,' Johnson suggested.

'Who knows? But one thing's for sure: she's an angel. First the *guerba*, then the milk and kouskous – and now this!'

'Yeah,' said Johnson, chewing. 'It was big of her.'

The next morning she sent him a dish of yogurt and bittersweet hoona berries; in the evening it was scrambled brains and rice. He was astonished. After two months of water and mush, here was something he could sink his teeth into. And this was only the beginning. In the ensuing days Fatima's girls brought him sheep's liver, camel's hump (braised), a stew of chickpeas and sweetbreads, buttermilk pudding, three dozen bustard giblets, and a whole roast kid. 'Soul food,' Johnson called it. 'It's your inner-man that's got her worked up – never mind your disreputable and shit-caked outer-man.' Inner-man, outer-man – what difference did it make? Red meat fed them both. Why, he must have dropped a good four stone since he left Portsmouth. He glanced down at his yellowed toes and drawn ankles, the sticks of his forearms: couldn't weigh much more than ten right now. But then he grinned, and muttered a little prayer. If this kept up he'd put it back on in no time. And then – who knows? – maybe he'd be strong enough to make a run for it.

There were other changes too. He was allowed to wander round the camp at will (shadowed by his seven keepers, of course), spend as much time as he liked with Johnson, and even have a first-hand look at some of the Moors' customs and ceremonies. This last, above all else, lifted his spirits. After all, he *was* an explorer – and here he was, exploring. He witnessed two circumcisions, a funeral, the death of a dog that had lifted the leg against Ali's tent. He watched the slaves pounding millet, tanning hides, churning butter in a *guerba* suspended between two sticks; he watched them reciting prayers, defecating, throwing pots, chewing roots, tattooing infants and dogs. It was all very illuminating. But ephemeral. He couldn't keep track of things from one day to the next.

Then one morning, as he sat watching a slave tie up the nipples of a camel to keep its calf from suckling in the heat of day, an idea hit him like a blow to the back of the head: he'd write a book! He'd write a book and be famous like Marco Polo or Gulliver or Richard Jobson. Why not? Here he was, seeing and smelling and tasting things no white man had ever dreamed of – it would be criminal to miss his chance to document it. He marched back to the tent, tore the leaves from his pocket Bible, and began writing, filling sheet after sheet with his impressions of the climate, the flora, the geological formations, the habits and physiognomies of the Blackamoors, Mandingoes, Serawoolis, and Foulahs. He described Ali's beard, Dassoud's scowl, the heat of midday, the solitude of the baobab. Talked of Fatima's graciousness, the tang of the hoona berry, woodsmoke on the night air. He filled thirty sheets that first day, and secreted them in the crown of his hat.

One evening he witnessed a wedding. It was strikingly similar to the funeral he'd attended: keening hags, howling dogs, a solemn procession. The bride was a walking shroud, veiled from head to foot, even her eyes invisible. He wondered how she was able to see where she was going. The keening women followed her, their stride measured by the beat of a *tabala.* The groom wore slippers with upturned toes. He was accompanied by a retinue of Mussulmen in embroidered burnooses and a cordon of slaves leading goats and bullocks, and carrying a tent. At an appointed spot the tent was struck, the goats and bullocks slaughtered, a fire ignited in a depression in the earth. There was a feast. Beef and mutton, songbirds, roasted larvae and other delicacies. There was dancing, songs were sung and tales told. And then there was the pièce de résistance: a whole baked camel.

BAKED CAMEL (STUFFED)

Serves 400

500 dates
200 plover eggs
20 two-pound carp
4 bustards, cleaned and plucked
2 sheep
1 large camel
seasonings

Dig trench. Reduce inferno to hot coals, three feet in

depth. Separately hard-cook eggs. Scale carp and stuff with shelled eggs and dates. Season bustards and stuff with stuffed carp. Stuff stuffed bustards into sheep and stuffed sheep into camel. Singe camel. Then wrap in leaves of doum palm and bury in pit. Bake two days. Serve with rice.

A regular feature of this expansive period were the explorer's daily meetings with the Queen. Each afternoon – immediately following the *dhuhur* or midday prayers – he was summoned to Fatima's tent for a question-and-answer period. She questioned, he answered. Insatiable, she never tired of quizzing him. She was an anthropologist, sociologist, a comparative anatomist. She wanted to dissect and absorb his habits, thoughts and beliefs; she wanted to taste his food, wear his clothes, sit at his box in the theatre. England, Europe, the vast and uncertain oceans – she wanted them built of words, words supple and evocative, words that would calcify in her imagination. She wanted visions. She wanted the memories behind his eyes. She wanted to digest him. Why had he come to Ludamar? How did his father manage the herds without him? Why did he wear so asinine (*jalab*) a covering on his head? Did all Christians have cat's eyes? What was the sea like? Had he ever been crucified? The explorer, grinning like a monkey and trying his clumsy best to radiate wit and charm, answered her questions as fully and patiently as he was able.

One afternoon she asked if the *Nazarini* practised circumcision. 'Certainly,' Mungo replied. She wanted to see for herself. The explorer looked at Johnson. 'What do I do now?' he whispered.

'Tell her you'll be more than happy to demonstrate – but it'll have to be in private. Then toss your eyebrows a couple of times.'

Mungo told her. He tossed his eyebrows. For a moment the tent was as silent as the dark side of the moon. The Queen's black eyes burned over the fringe of her *yashmak*. Then she slapped her thigh and tittered.

That night the explorer ate leg of lamb.

On this particular morning, three and a half weeks since his first meeting with Fatima, the explorer is sitting in the shade of an acacia, writing. *The Moorish women,* he writes, *wear their hair in nine plaits, which they divide as follows: two on either side of the face, six thinner braids over the crown, and one stout coil at the base of the neck. The hair is washed and oiled once a month, dressed and replaited weekly. For sanitary reasons, and because it tends to bleach the hair somewhat, the women prefer a rinse of camel's urine, which is collected for this purpose. (One can always see a slave or two, cup in hand, pursuing a micturating camel about the camp.) The urine is a powerful astringent, and serves to destroy vermin and other parasites. Indeed, I have had the opportunity to assess its efficacy personally, as my pubes, axillae, side-whiskers and locks were infested with lice and desert mites. I found it refreshing, if somewhat mephitic....*

There is a bloom on the explorer's cheek. A clarity in his eye. Worms, grippe, scabies, the fever, and racheting cough – they're things of the past. Nasty memories. He's a meat-eater now, a man of broth and blood, as befits a Scotsman, and gaining strength day by day. The heat enervates him, of course, and he still suffers attacks of confusion – but all in all the change in diet and the fresh air have gone a long way toward resurrecting him. And the peace and quiet have had something to do with it too. Just a month ago it would have been impossible for him to sit here: the very sight of him drove the average Mussulman into a frenzy. Within seconds he would have been beleaguered by a stinking, spittle-spewing mob of Moslem zealots. Now it's different. They know he's under Fatima's protection, and aside from isolated incidents (some unseen adversary walloped him in the side of the head with a pig's pizzle not more than twenty minutes ago), he is left to himself.

The Moorish men, on the other hand, never bathe. They do, however, have a biannual ceremony know as asíla má, *during which they bury themselves in hot sand for some forty-five minutes to an hour just prior to sunset. They are then disinterred, rubbed down with the sweat of an estruating mare, and thrashed with the under-branches of the* seríf *bush. I am told that the operation is congenial to long life and sexual vigour.*

As the explorer looks up to wet his quill, he is startled to discover that he is not alone. Standing there before him, her chocolate eyes following the dip and rush of the pen, is the plumper of the pantaloon girls. 'What is it?' he says.

'Fatima says you must come to her.'

Come to her? At ten A.M.? What could she possibly want with him

at this hour? 'All right,' he says, getting to his feet. 'I'll fetch Johnson.'
'No,' says the girl. 'Fatima says he will not be needed.'
The explorer shrugs. 'Lead the way,' he says.

As he pushes through the flaps and into the tent he is instantly engulfed in darkness. Blue spheres pulsate before his eyes, yellow cartwheels drift off into space. He can see nothing. There are the familiar odours of frankincense and camel urine, and from the corner, the rasp of the saker falcons chewing at their wings. But why hasn't she lighted a lamp? And where's that damned girl gone off to? Ah well. No matter. May as well ride with the current. '*Salaam aleichem*,' he says, addressing the shadows.

'*Aleichem as salaam*,' comes the reply, soft as the beat of a moth's wing.

He jumps. She's sitting right beside him – he could have stumbled over her.... Christ, it's dark. Can't very well move for fear of upsetting something. 'Braaaaak!' says one of the falcons. Maybe he should ask her to light a taper – but then how in the name of God do you say 'taper'? He settled for '*Kaif halkum?*' – how are you?

'*Bishára*,' she answers, which he takes to mean she has no complaints.

Silence.

He shuffles his feet, picks his ear and jerks at his knuckles, wondering if he should risk taking a seat. It's an awkward moment. After ten or twenty seconds of ear picking, he makes a stab at conversation, hoping to express how pleasant it is to see her again – though he can barely make her out. Unfortunately, what he actually says is: 'My sight is rabid pleasure.'

Fatima titters.

Encouraged, he goes on, addressing the shadowy bulk before him. Battling case endings, syntax, verb tenses, and spotty vocabulary, the explorer waxes eloquent as Antony, Demosthenes, and the Speaker of the House all rolled into one, telling her how much he's appreciated the attention she's given him, not to mention the jellied calves' feet and purèed mung beans. At that moment, however, the elderly attendant enters with a taper and the explorer discovers that he's been addressing a hand loom. The Queen is actually seated on the far side of the tent, rising up out of her enormous pillow like an Alp rising from the foothills. The explorer is bewildered. 'Come over here,' she says.

At the sound of Fatima's voice the old woman starts, then hurries about her business. She fixes the candle in the upturned palm of an ivory figurine, gathers her skirts and sweeps past the explorer with a lickerish grin. Mungo starts forward, but then hesitates. Something is wrong here – but what? Suddenly it hits him: Fatima's head is bare, the thick braids fanning out over her shoulders like the runners of a plant. He's never glimpsed so much as a single hair before – unless you count her eyebrows. 'Come here,' she repeats.

The explorer steps up to her and bows, trying to think of something witty to say. She pats the pillow. 'Up here,' she motions. Mungo shrugs. Then scales the pillow and sinks into its vastness. The old woman is nowhere to be seen. Nor is there any trace of the pantaloon girls. It occurs to him that he has never before been alone with the Queen. But now the pillow has begun to quake, flowing along its length like a wind-driven sea. He looks up. The Queen is pulling the *jubbah* up over her head, grunting daintily as she labours with the flashing fields of cloth. Beneath the *jubbah*: naked flesh. The explorer begins to get the idea.

'Help me,' she moans, the gown smothering her head and upper torso. Mungo leans forward and seizes the nape of the stupendous garment, thinking of sheets and flags and circus tents. He tugs, she grunts. Her arms ripple beneath the cloth like animals in a sack, she gasps, and then suddenly her breasts jog free, shuddering mightily with the concussion, colossal orbs, heavenly bodies. They come to rest over the multiple folds of her abdomen like the twin moons of Mars. The explorer is suddenly stung with hurry and necessity. He jerks at the recalcitrant cloth with all the meat-eating fervour he can rouse, panting and moaning, until all at once the *jubbah* gives as if it were made of paper. He falls back, and there she is – the Queen – naked and ineluctable as the great wide fathomless sea. '*Yudhkul*,' she whispers. '*Yudhkul alaiha*.'

He flings the boots, paws at the buttons, jerks at his *jubbah*. Moist and mountainous, she waits for him, eyes aglow, veil lowered, her flesh smoldering like Vesuvius. He wheezes with haste and anticipation. It's a minor attack of fever: no mere mortal could approach this magnificence. He scrambles atop her, feeling for toeholds – so much terrain to explore – mountains, valleys and rifts, new continents, ancient rivers.

O That Sinking Feeling

February, 1796. Wordsworth has been in and out of France and Annette Vallon, Bonapart has put the screws to Babeuf and is vigorously pounding at Joséphine's gate, Goethe is living in sin with Christiane Vulpius, and Burns is dying. In Edinburgh Walter Scott fights a losing battle for the hand of Wiliamina Belches, while in Manchester a snot-nosed De Quincey wanders the streets and wonders what a whore is. In Moscow it's snowing. In Paris they're plugging holes with *assignats* for lack of anything better to do with them. And in Soho, at the Vole's Head Tavern, they're sucking and fucking. Onstage.

Ned couldn't be more pleased. Jutta Jim's been going strong for better than an hour now (if you discount the two brief intermissions during which he chanted tribal lays and quaffed a pint of chicken's blood to keep his spirits up). Nan and Sally have enlarged their roles admirably, and the audience has been too preoccupied to wreak mayhem or piss on the carpet. What's more, Ned's throat, limbs, liver, and lights haven't been threatened in over an hour (Smirke's been running around with a hard-on all night, peddling drinks like an oasis owner in Araby, and Mendoza hasn't said boo since Jim strutted out onstage), and his gross take has far exceeded his rosiest estimate (nearly thirty-six pounds against an outlay of twenty-three and two, which includes a new suit of clothes, tips, and refreshment for himself and his cast).

So why all this anxiety? He's been through a flask and a half of gin already, smoked three pipes, and paced the room twenty-two times, and he's still jittery as a case of rat-bite fever. He can't understand it. He's even starting to develop an itch in the missing joint of his pinky. Of course, deep down, he already knows the answer – things are going too well. And that means he'd better dodge, duck, and flinch, because when things start going too well that's when the Powers That Be swoop down on you like a dozen hurricanes and leave you buried under half a ton of flotsam and jetsam.

It reminds him of the time at Bartholomew Fair when he and Billy Boyles just couldn't lose at the gaming tables, had themselves a couple of tarts for nothing, then fell into the way of a champion fighting cock worth fifty quid easy. And then, as they were skulking off the fairgrounds with their booty, there it was – Zeppo the Eleusinian's star-spangled cape – just hanging out to dry like a gift from the gods. On the way back Boyles led him down a lampless lane, and sure enough, a pair of dacoits pounced on them. 'Stand and deliver!' a voice growled, and Ned found that the barrel of a pistol had been inserted in his ear. 'Oy'll jest disburden yer of yer loose coin,' the voice rasped, 'while me accomplice 'ere bleeds yer pal.'

The accomplice was a dwarf, no more than three feet high, with a mass of carrot flaming hair round his cheeks and crown like a brush fire. Ned handed over his purse and watched as the dwarf limped from the shadows, ordered Boyles to sit in the road, and began probing his rags with the point of a dagger. ''Ere!' the dwarf exclaimed. 'Wot's this then?' It was the fighting cock, nestled in Boyles' breast, its legs and beak bound with strips of blue ribbon. The dwarf plucked the bird from its cachette, throttled it with a twist of his knotty hands, and held it up for the gunman to admire. 'A bit of somefin for the pot, then, 'ey Will?'

'Good show, Ginger,' growled the gunman. 'Now strip the beggar raw and see if 'ee's got any coin of the realm about 'im.' Down with the trousers, up with the shirt: Billy Boyles was naked as a jay inside of ten seconds. 'Now you, pretty boy,' the gunman said.

Ned appealed to the gunman's compassion and sense of fair play. 'But I already gave you my purse,' he snivelled, '– 'have a heart, will you?'

'Ha!' the gunman laughed. 'Think I doesn't know river sand when I feels it? Wot yer take me for, a dyspertic baboon or somefin? Off with yer drawers, sucker!'

The game was up. Ned dropped his trousers and there it was glowing in the moonlight like a luminescent diaper – the strip of muslin stuffed with the day's winnings. The dwarf tore it from his abdomen and coins rained to the ground. 'Hoo-hoo!' he sand. 'We've 'it the buggerin' jackpot this time, 'asn't we, Will?'

Just as the dwarf was scooping up the last of the coins, a coach-and-four tumbled around the corner and the muggers vanished. Boyles crouched against the wall *in puris naturalibus* while Ned wrapped the magician's cape around his bare legs and flagged down the coach.

'Ho!' bellowed the driver. The coach came to a stop with a rattle and screech. 'We've been robbed!' Ned shouted. The door shot back. Inside was Sir Euston Filigree, magistrate and gamecock fancier. Beside him sat an officer of the law with a cocked pistol. 'What a coincidence,' said Sir Euston. 'I've been robbed too.'

'Get in,' said the officer.

'Three months at hard labour,' said the judge.

It never fails. Whenever things start to look up, whenever fantasy begins to jell into possibility, the Hand of Fate intercedes to slap you back to your senses. Frightening. Enough to make you paranoid. Ned takes another pull at the bung and glances around him like a lamb at a convocation of wolves. Up onstage Jim, Sally, and Nan are approaching the climactic finale – an impossible, multi-limbed, sinew-straining, *tour de force* feat of sexual acrobatics – heads, tongues, and hips undulating in a quickening tempo, *allegro di molto*, the audience spilling from chairs, upsetting tables, panting like a dog-show in mid-July. The moment suspends here, ticking along at the edge of release, sublimely attuned to the functions of the body and the sway of the planet – when suddenly the door flies back and the voice of authority booms through the chamber: 'CEASE AND DESIST IN THE NAME OF GOD ALMIGHTY AND ALL YE HOLD DECENT!'

The gilded youth is the first to react. 'Holy shit! It's the constabulary!'

'It's a raid!' someone shouts, and the room erupts in confusion. Regimental commanders trip over their swords, baronets, and shopkeepers collide, clergymen hit the floor, while rogues, rakes, noodles, beaux, bucks, and bloods make for the rear exit, Ned Rise leading them by a length. Up onstage Jim vacates Sally and Sally strips herself from Nan who in turn releases Jim and reaches for her gin and water. 'SEIZE THE PROPRIETOR!' bellows an officer, and Ned, already at the door, looks back to see poor Smirke in the grip of two burly Charlies. "Ee's the one!' roars Smirke, pointing a thick finger at the entrepreneur as he squeezes through the door. 'The clown in the cape!'

'AFTER HIM LADS!' booms the co-ordinating officer.

Ned is in the alley already, off like a fox at the first woof of the hounds, passing bucks and bloods as if they were standing still, the gin coming up in him, feet flying, the cape beating round his shoulders like the wings of the Furies. Unable to flee in their high-heeled pumps, the bucks and bloods fall easy prey to the pursuing officers – the dread Bow Street Runners – and shout curses at Ned's retreating back. 'You slimy weevil, Rise – you'll pay for this!'

'Gallowsbait!'

'Clystermonger!'

Ned pays them no mind. He is caught up in the pure frenzied ecstasy of flight, in the astonishing coordination of heart, lungs, joints and feet, in this fearsome momentum fueled by alcohol and driven by panic. Down the street to his left, over the cobbles – just a blur – and into the dark close on the far side. The shouts and curses receding now, almost safe. But what's this? Footsteps at his back, regular as a drumbeat. He turns to look over his shoulder and an icy dagger punches at his ribs: two grim and athletic Runners pad along the alley, barely winded, confidently working into the easy loping stride of marathon men. Good God, he doesn't stand a chance. These Bow Street Runners are relentless, tireless. Word has it they've even run down men on horseback.

He gives it all he's got, heading for the river. His chest is heaving, there's a fire in his lungs, the coins dig at his crotch. 'STOP IN THE NAME OF THE LAW!' Never. The law's a joke and only losers get nabbed. His feet slap on the pavement. Now he's rounding the corner into Villiers – and there's the river! If he can just make the cover of the docks or jump one of the boats... but they're gaining on him, the bleeding jocks, and *chink-chink*, there go the first two coins. He grits his teeth. Churns harder. And then suddenly the boards of Charing Cross Pier resound under his feet, nowhere to go, the jocks thumping at his heels – a hand on his collar – and then he's free, plummeting through the dank night air. There's a crust of ice, the coins like a ship's anchor, the water an icy cudgel. SLOOSH! And he's gone.

The Runners stand at the edge of the pier, plumbing the shadows. The ice is the colour of slate, the water black. Nothing moves. 'Well Nick, I guess that's that,' says the grimmer of the two.

'Right you are, Dick,' comes the reply. 'Case closed.'

Lisa St Aubin de Terán

Keepers of the House

Lydia Sinclair was just seventeen when she arrived on her husband's estate in the Andes. Her first day went by in a haze of mosquito bites and heat and a swarm of new faces. The farm workers and visitors saw her swathed in a long dress and with a wide-brimmed hat, and were struck by her likeness to the tall women who had lived in the valley before her time. The children laughed a little at her strangeness and her height, but the older ones recognized in her a vision of the past.

The whole estate was badly neglected when she arrived, but, after the first few months, when her husband, Diego, took an interest in the running of the hacienda again, she soon learned how to put things in order. The rings and pouches under Diego's eyes had grown and stayed, and his natural tendency to sleep at every opportunity was exaggerated by a new malfunction of his kidneys, which Benito dosed with a potion that he brewed himself from the savage ñongue plant. She soon learned how to put things in order. Perched on her horse, or striding in high boots through the grass, Lydia reviewed the fields like an officer his troops. Her aide-de-camp was a large scraggy-necked turkey-vulture who followed her everywhere in blind adoration. He was called Napoleon, on account of his military pose. The bird had been a present from an eccentric friend of her husband's who had given him to her in an unseemly hessian sack, saying,

'Take him, Doña, he'll soon settle down with you.'

She had opened the sack and the bird had flapped out and hidden in the undergrowth behind the house. When she had stooped to pick him up, his curved black beak had twisted in a death clasp around her wrist.

'Hold him tight, Doña,' the man had cried, 'he doesn't want to wound you.'

She had laboured with the pain, while the blood drained from her hand. The Napoleon had let go, and neither of them had known who held whom.

The vulture had arrived on her second day; on her third day, an old man called Natividad had hobbled up to her to tell her that his only daughter had left him for a man with a donkey, and that he would live on his own now. Lydia had been at a loss for words, so she had nodded and watched him go wheezing back to his empty hut. There seemed to be no escape from the sound of his wheezing, which the wind carried down the hill to drift up around her house.

She took her bearings and adjusted herself to the Momboy valley with the same ease with which she had adjusted herself to her hammock. It was particularly easy for her to think, stretched out flat between the two pillars that supported her. She liked to feel herself enclosed by greatness, rocking between extremes. It was the extremes that first attracted her to her husband, Don Diego Beltrán. She had been fascinated by his debauched good looks and his pride. They had met in London, when she was sixteen and he was thirty-five. He had found her there, and followed her, and by his constant presence she had come to love him. He had been like a great rare fish washed ashore, whose lungs had been unable to adapt to the twentieth century. It was the first time that he had ever left the Andes, and had he not been exiled for political offences, he would never have left them at all. But he had landed in London, and fallen in love with Lydia as a school-girl in love with the past, and after two years of honeymoon in Italy he had taken her back to what he always referred to as his 'little place in the Andes'. To Diego it may have seemed like a little place, coming as he did from a family who had once owned every mountain range from Trujillo to Mérida and the icy páramo to Pamplona and across the plains of the Orinoco to Barinas and Niquitao. But to his wife, Lydia, the 'little place' was a vast estate, such as she had never seen before, where the sugar-cane stretched for as far as she could see along the valley, and grove after grove of avocados clung to the terraced slopes of the surrounding hills.

Diego and Lydia had what was really more of an understanding than a marriage. Even when Lydia's Spanish had become second nature to her, they spoke very little, because Diego was an unusually silent man. It was only when he talked about the hacienda, or about the past, that he shone as a conversationalist. And he was only angry with the time being–with its bought power and its petrol dollar and its war on the environment. So the estate became the missing link in their silent marriage, and 'the family' assumed the life that Diego lacked. He was more like his ancestors than any other member of the family, and despite his present apathy had done more to change its future. However, all his plans had aborted one after the other, like a machine-gun-fire of miscarriages.

Diego divided his time between sleeping and reading, and he would spend every day either in his rooms or locked in the upstairs library, where the shelves of tattered leather volumes were always thick with the crumbled remains of bookworms and cockroaches and paper-dust. Sometimes he would visit what was left of his family, in ritualized rounds in the neighbouring town, some fifteen miles away. And Lydia would be left on her own. For company, there were Benito Mendoza, who was eighty-nine and had worked for the family since he was a boy; the beagle hounds that she had brought over with her on the ship from England; and four girls to help in the house.

Benito looked and moved like a man of fifty, and was always in excellent health. La comadre Matilde said that he was preserved in alcohol. Whatever the reason, he was always steeped in liquor. He drank more in a week than most people did in a month. It was almost as though he kept his stock of life in the assorted bottles of fermented cane-juice that he kept around him. He had a kind of superstitious fear of running out at any time, so he hid some of the bottles, small flat quarter-litres, all over the outhouses and gardens. Wherever Lydia chanced to look she would see one, in the fork of a tree, in the hen house, under a bush, by the side of a drain, all with one last drink in them. Benito's great age, and the security that this army of concealed bottles brought him, gave him an air of serenity.

He would sit on the stone edge of the veranda, or on the long carved bench that had once been in the cathedral at Trujillo but was now in the main corridor of the house. His skin was tawny yellow and his eyes were brown and bleared with drink. He looked very straight ahead, and he teetered rather than walked; and yet, other than an aura of liquor that he carried about with him like eau-de-Cologne, there was no other sign of his alcoholism. His mind and voice were as clear as the pool of water that he had shown her filtering through a wood on top of the hill, filling a basin made by the roots of a huge bucare tree. The new Doña was kind to him, and Don Diego seemed pleased to see him talking to her, night after night. He himself rarely spoke, and Lydia was locked in his silence. She had time for Benito, who was alone with his memories. They were the only secrets and surprises he could offer her.

One night, when Diego had gone early to bed and the house was even stiller than usual, he confided to her: 'You are special, Doña, and different, and very like the people that I shall tell you about. You'll survive when I and all in the valley, and the valley itself, are dead and it's through you that we won't be forgotten.

'Do you know, Doña, I have given my whole life to the service of the Beltrán family; and even though they are declining now, I'm proud of it, and of them. The mountains have always upheld the old traditions: and the Beltrán family are like a fortress within the mountains: they are the last survivors. When they fall, I myself and all of us will fall as well. They are the weather-vane of our own failure. I am their oldest retainer and I've outlived most of them and I know more about this valley and its people than anybody else. Someday the Beltráns may be remembered as tyrants or fools, but who will see their splendour and their suffering?'

Benito wedged himself into the corner of his seat, intent on squeezing out his words.

'Who will see how willingly we've all turned on the wheel of their favour, or how we all strove to stay in the wake of their movement? We used to cling inert to the petrified violence of the hills. And then we were all swayed by their energy, and their action. The Beltráns, when they came, rode rough-shod through the valley, as though with a chariot of fire, like meteors. They didn't ride just any horses, they rode the wild horses that roamed the hills, and they never quite broke them. On clear nights I can see them bucking and rearing in the distance. They have all gone now though. Only the nags are left.'

Time passed, and Diego planned new ways to irrigate his fields, but the dry banks failed him. He showed Lydia how to renew the crops, but a strange fungus burned them. Lydia planted the garden, and her own dogs dug it up. She fed the stray cats, but the stray dogs killed them. She bound the cracks in her home, and the machete wounds in the cane fields. She learned to lower fevers, and to raise hopes, and she learned to decipher movement in the stillness of the people. She and Diego saw the power wagon, known as 'La Povva', trundle across the bridge on its last trip. Laden with damaged sugar-cane, and held together entirely by chains and scrap metal and ropes, La Povva lurched past them to the mill with men and boys hanging from its sides like flags. Diego had retired to his rooms for four days after that, grieving for the sugar-cane.

Two years had passed and the Povva had always been there,

swaying to and fro, strange in its camouflage paint, an ex-army lorry waging war on the crumbling roads. Now there was no more cane, no more working mill or wheel, just disused monuments, and La Povva rusting in a field. Natividad, too, was dead now.

For the Christmas of 1955, Don Diego called his sixty-five workers to him, and, dividing the arable lands of his estate into equal lots, he gave one lot of land to the care of each man there, together with a share of his mules and seeds. He had kept a similar lot for himself, and one for Lydia, and he kept most of the unterraced hill-slopes. But there was a new tyranny rising in the valley – the drought.

With the change of crop and the changing climate, the structure of Lydia's life changed too; even her hammock worked itself loose and began to sink to the ground. She stroked Napoleon, and watched the moon's phases and the vultures rise. Napoleon hardly ever flew: he strutted and hurried in his strange-necked way. He seemed to have no desire to leave her. Even though they sometimes fought, he would remain. In these middle years, in the face of her own marriage's failure, Lydia fought and challenged everything that threatened to erode the valley's strength. In 1956 she acquired a special status and was grafted on to its blood: after three years of infertility she was with child. Even Diego, who practically never spoke now, not to her or to anyone, rallied at the prospect of a child. Their unborn heir sank slowly towards her pelvis and waited, and she herself waited for a pattern to come back to her life.

Meanwhile, she challenged and defended until her teeth ached from the effort. First she summoned her housekeeper:

'Comadre Matilde, why do the corn and beans taste of stale dust?'

La comadre turned her slow, bovine face to the corridor and said, 'Doña, there are weevils in the bales and jars. A scum of brittle bodies floats on the soak-water of every pan of beans. It is a sign.'

And she crossed herself.

'Just as the maggots in the cheese are a sign.'

Here she put down the lump of dough that she had been kneading and crossed herself again. Collecting up the huge mass of raw bread she stepped into the corridor, and, opening her eyes wide to give weight to her words, Lydia asked, rhetorically, 'And what about the milk souring no sooner than it leaves the cow?'

Almost reluctantly, Matilda set aside her dough, studded with grey shell-like corpses, and turned to face Lydia, who had followed her. Then, in a voice of constant apology she said, 'Doña, long before Don Diego was born, when Benito was a young man, and I was a child, the sky turned the colour of blood and fell to the ground. There was a thundering like the river crashing down the valley in flood. Before the end of the day, the cloud rose in a continuous sheet. It just rose and left with an even louder whirring. Afterwards, the light returned, but all the land was bare. They had ripped away every tree and stalk and leaf, leaving the valley like a desert fringed with bedraggled banana palms. That was the year of the locust, Doña.'

Lydia was shocked. She had heard of the plague of locusts before, many times, but she was always surprised by the devastation they had caused. She urged her old housekeeper on. 'What did you do, Comadre? What did you eat?'

'We collected up great mounds of dead locusts, Doña, creatures so strange that they could not be God's creatures. They were evil and we scraped them together and burnt them. Then, for nearly a year, we just ate bananas: fibre, juice and skin. Death never took such a good harvest, not even in the years of the black vomit.

'Every time a scrap of food is wasted, I remember. Every time the young ones say things are bad, then I remember how bad they can get. And every time I peel and cook the green bananas for your table, I think: the locusts are coming, slowly now. This time they are eating out the land and the trees. This time we can't see them.'

'But this is different, Comadre.'

'Yes,' said the old woman, turning painfully towards the kitchen once more. 'This time it is different. Now the fires are burning before the plague. The forest fires are taking everything. These are the years of ashes!'

That night the child was crowned, and Lydia prepared the carved oak cradle that had been in the family for years; the local midwife was called, but she found the delivery difficult. She told Don Diego that the umbilical cord had wound itself five times around the baby's foot, and while he was being disentangled he breathed in the amniotic fluid. 'What does that mean?' Diego had asked her dully. 'It means it's bad, Señor.' The boy was born and was called Alejandro Beltrán Sinclair. His face had a strange, wax-like beauty, and he seemed restless and cried all through his first night. La comadre Matilde began to spread the news that the new heir had water in his lungs.

Doña Lydia was exhausted and tearful; she felt the child's death in her veins and she could not bear it. The women from the estate hung around her house, and from her room she could just hear them chattering, and she guessed by the tone of their voices what they were saying. From the kitchen she heard la comadre crooning to herself:

'Sleep, my little lord, sleep while you are able.
This long night and the moonlight are yours,
But not the morning.
In this land of cradle-cap,
Yours is the fairest cradle.'

La comadre was always making up songs.

Doña Lydia shut herself in her rooms with the child. Her husband wandered in and out, not quite sure what to do; he paced around for half an hour at a time and then left. By her bed, Lydia piled up soiled plates and clothes, and new ones took their place. For days and days she just watched and held her baby, listening to his breathing for the least sign of improvement. The christening came and went. The child was hurried into the church at Mendoza, the first Beltrán to be christened without a cardinal or even a bishop there. But Lydia was too tired to know or notice.

Napoleon tapped on the mud-mortar of the wall of her room. He wanted her back. His tapping was growing frantic. Each day of the baby's life was a triumph for Lydia, and a source of fury for the outraged vulture.

One day, she dozed in her rocking chair and awoke to see Napoleon's head sticking through the wall. He had opened a hole in the brickwork and his turkey neck was poking through. His skin hung down the wall like an elderly scrotum, and the glint in his eye was evil. He glared at the baby with jealous savagery. Lydia looked up at his grotesque neck framed in plaster, and she knew that he would have to go.

That day, the baby's breath came more sharply. His face tightened and seemed to stick in a gasp of pain and then the breath was released in a wheeze of relief. The pattern accelerated until the whole room shook with the tremor of his lungs. She held him up to the sun as though it might be able to ease his pain, but it only showed up even more the paleness of his skin that was turning steadily bluer as his breath failed him. Racked by spasms, the child lost consciousness every time he managed to exhale. His pulse stopped, and his mother breathed for him, kneading his heart and giving him breath. He relaxed a little, and she kept on helping him, and then he stiffened, and still she cradled him. Nobody dared to take his rigid body from her arms. They were locked together and she sang to him in a strange language that no one could understand.

When they finally took the child from her, he would not fit in his little white coffin, but she would not let them break his bones to straighten them, and another, wider, box had to be made. She had reached the beginning of the end.

Diego Beltrán had always wanted but never had any children; the baby's death left him winded as from a fist in the groin. He drank a lot, and when he was alone he wept, and all the while he worried about his wife, who would let no one near her. Lydia had locked herself upstairs in the library. Her eyes stung and the room swayed, but she could not cry. Exhaustion had dulled her brain. She felt a thud on the edge of her consciousness: Diego was knocking at the door of the next room.

'Lydia, let me in'.

Through a missing knot in the woodwork he could just see her, staring out towards the river and the mill. The night would hold her in its chill cramp, and by day she would be much too hot, but she didn't move.

Her friend the doctor came, and spoke to her through the door, and he begged her to weep. Benito hovered outside her rooms, a fixture among the changing visitors. He tugged at the rim of his hat, and he, too, wanted her to weep. The whole valley besought her to weep as they had done – the river could not hold their tears. Their acceptance of death was not callousness: they were like serfs on its lands.

On the third day, Diego broke open the door. She turned her face away but he knelt beside her, reasoning quietly with her:

'We pay tithes,' he said, 'but we are never free. Death is a part-time lodger in all of us. We all differ, but we do have a common denominator: there is no guarantee of survival. Life is more than living here, it is constant war. We cannot win, but if we stick together we can, at least, keep fighting. To avoid disputes as to whom to support and defend, we are moved by what is family. Our loyalties are firstly to our family, and then to our dead.'

He pointed to the women waiting outside the house:

'Every single one of those women has lost a son, if not several.'

Lydia looked up, and towards them, and then slowly away.

'If you think that they cry too readily for our son, whom they never knew, it is because they are crying for their own dead as well as for yours and for you. For most of us there is no horizon further away than the crest of the hill, and we have no refuge other than in each other. We cling together like threads in a cloth, and death is our undoing. We are threadbare, Lydia, and you are one of us. In spurning our help you spurn our grief as well. We try to live a little more, a little better, and in that extra bit are the lives of our dead. It is too hard for them to die and let nothing remain in their stead, so we carry them with us, as added strength. We do this despite the strain, but so many have died that there is always a certain sadness inside us. Whenever someone else dies – and there is always someone – then we come together and share our grief. It is the one time when we allow ourselves to weaken. What hope is there for us all if we cannot see the shadow of our sorrow in the eyes of friends?'

Diego stroked her hair and his voice became more insistent:

'Don't harden towards us, Lydia – life is hard enough already.' He stood up and walked towards the door. When he turned, he found that she was crying to herself. He sat with her for a while, holding her in a relieved silence, while she felt the chill leave her bones, and a warm patch like a hot poultice spread over her chest.

After this, when she looked back, Lydia came to feel that there had been a clear succession of catastrophes, accumulating their debris in great dunes that changed the pattern of her life. It was in her sixth year on the estate that the sheep's disease brought a change. They stared as though with stale eyes. They moved stiffly and with difficulty, their joints seeming to crunch. It was hard for her to believe that they were really ill. They lowered their heads and trembled, huddling together in the ruins of Natividad's, the dead goatherd's, hut, and then they began to wheeze. It was this ordered convulsion that distressed her most. It seemed that death itself wheezed through many lungs in a sick cloud of heavy breath from which there was no escape. Ever since her first night on the estate, silence had incorporated the cicadas and wheezing. It was the only rhythm left in the hills. She tried, to the last one, to save her straggling flock, but she knew from her manuals they had anthrax: she could hear the oedema in their tissues, like ground glass under their skin.

They burned their carcasses, and the half-charred remains brought down the vultures. There was such a glut that they picked and chose and a mass of rotting offal was left. The fires on the ground were matched by fires in the scrubland on the hill. It was as though the peasants were hurrying towards their end by burning the last few stalks and leaves. Benito told her that it was an old custom of the Timotoquican Indians to burn down the hills as a sacrifice to the sky in times of drought. It was meant to make it rain; in fact, it sealed the drought. Many people died, and many left. Lydia and Diego, Benito and Matilde huddled together. Benito made coffee, and told them about the past. Whenever Don Diego came down, Benito told him anecdotes about his father. They all believed that it would rain, with time, and they were all waiting.

Years passed and only their crippled cousin Cristóbal came by, hobbling on his one remaining leg. It was a lonely way to live. Lydia remembered how she had once hidden in the reeds of a little ditch that ran by a ridge of trees, avoiding some particularly irritating visitor. Benito told her that that was exactly where Cristóbal used to hide when he wanted to be alone. She was pleased by the coincidence – it seemed to draw them closer.

Diego then saw his people leave, and what was left of his will-power drained away with them. He had a bed made up for him in the library – the same room where his baby son had died years before – and he took to it and turned to the wall. He slept that way for the best part of a year. He would prop himself up to eat and to reach out for his chamber pot. Otherwise, he slept.

La comadre Matilde left one day and the last they saw of her was her limping shapeless back struggling down the road in a dust cloud. Her cousin and the children had disappeared long before. Benito gathered up stores from abandoned homes and carried them back by the sackful. His booty included a vast supply of moonshine liquor which he surreptitiously drank, and the two of them sat alone, immune to the sickness, staring out at the hills, and watching for the passage of Cristóbal; and waiting for rain.

Most of the days were then spent sitting on the edge of the chimney's plinth in the disused mill or upstairs with Diego, in his shuttered room, or sorting papers from one room to the next. Diego had become like a sepia print of his ancestors. His silence was like a main joist and his eyes were sad like Napoleon's and, like his, they followed her around. Lydia was shifting the dust and the moths from the study when she heard him bellow, 'Lydia!' and she turned and went to him. She saw that he looked like her father had done the moment before he died, and she knew at once that Diego, too, had had a stroke. She held him as he arched and then went limp, and she knew that the paralysis would stay with him until the day he died. She held his inert hand and, cradling his head, she wept for him and his stillness. Looking out over hectares of dried weeds she remembered sadly that something always happened on the third stroke of a time signal. She knew that for her, on the third stroke, it would be time to go.

The next few days found her sitting by the mound, cleaning out the rust and the sand from the engine of the last jeep on the estate. She knew that there was petrol in a deposit in the sugar-mill. Time was running out again, and she had to hurry to leave.

On the morning of the 3rd September, 1962, Lydia awoke feeling more tired and cramped than ever before. It was dawn and she lay back, enjoying the short respite from the sun: the early morning was the only time when the high altitude of the surrounding hills could defy the climate. The sun was slowly climbing over the mountains, and soon the still, airless heat of the day would take over, flaying the fissured skin of the valley once more. She eased herself down from the high, mahogany bed inlaid with satin-wood and, dressing quietly, she left her husband, Diego, sleeping in his massive immobility. She paused in the doorway for a while to watch his inert body in its seventh month of paralysis, and its second year in bed. His hair and beard had grown long and grey, making him look more than ever like his distant cousin, Cristóbal, who still limped by their house every day.

From the wide balcony that adjoined their suite of rooms, she could see the thick dead leaves of the malaguetta tree, whose aromatic leaves sweetened the air, and the brittle remains of tangled jasmine; and to the far side of the house, at the foot of the nearest hill, there was a single row of palm trees each older and taller than the next, and each with a cluster of withered fruits high in its crown.

Downstairs in the kitchen she made some coffee and then leant on the balustrade overlooking the road, and watched for Cristóbal to come limping into view. Her coffee was thick and muddy, and, like everything else in the house, it tasted of weevils. Yet, that day, it tasted especially good to her, in the knowledge that it would be the last cup of coffee that she would drink there: it was her last day on the hacienda. After three days and nights of work, she had finally managed to assemble and equip one complete jeep from the fleet of broken cars in the stables. As she stood there, looking down the valley, her bones ached at the thought of not seeing Cristóbal once more before she left.

It was eight o'clock before she saw the familiar vultures heralding his approach. Then he followed, close behind, leaning on his staff. As he neared the archway where Lydia stood, she tried to imprint on her mind every rag and detail of him for future reference. She memorized his dishevelled mane of grizzled hair, and the ragged stump of his mutilated leg. When she left later on that day, taking her paralysed husband with her, Cristóbal would be the last Beltrán left in the valley and (possibly) the last man. But he had been there for so long that he almost was the valley. Benito had said that he remembered him as old when he himself was still a boy. He had patrolled the banks of the River Momboy for over a hundred years. He moved like a pendulum in an endless coming and going, and he became so regular a feature that he seemed like the land itself. Even death had not overtaken him as it did other men: his age was not a mortal age. He would never die in any way that involved the usual phase from death to decomposition. He would just become part of the valley itself, and together they would drift into sand. The steady advance of the drought was clogging his veins. His mass of beard and hair was as scorched and brittle as the last charred weeds, and his once ruddy complexion was burnt to dry flakes that fell in his wake.

Lydia watched him coming towards her that morning, like a slow ghost. His clothes seemed more torn than ever, and the string that held up his trousers was trailing behind him. Benito had told her the story of this giant scarecrow and his lameness many times, and yet its strangeness never ceased to surprise her. Cristóbal was the third son of Ernesto, who had been both Minister of Finance in Caracas and a famous judge in Trujillo. When Cristóbal was six, his mother died while giving birth to a baby brother who also died, and his father retired with his grief to the capital, neglecting his three remaining sons in favour of his former career.

The two elder boys ruled the household and the family's estates with fanatical authority. Their premature burdens had made them unusally self-conscious, and they would tolerate no flexibility in their reign of terror. They sensed that some of their former power was slipping from their grasp; the River Momboy seemed to be washing away the customs and beliefs of their workers, and they saw it as their duty to set a solid example. However, Cristóbal could not be brought to understand this. The welts of their whip made no impression on his mind, and the more they punished him, the more his physical condition deteriorated, and the less he repented.

After their father's death, Cristóbal's refusal to conform seemed to insult them personally. Perhaps what most angered them was the knowledge that this brother possessed energy such as they could never even hope to feel – the boy had the unchannelled strength of a pacing tiger. They believed that if only he could be made to conform, he would not only cease to embarrass them, but also attain great heights. Yet he was stubborn and wayward, and he strayed from home. He was otherwise sweet-natured and amenable in all things save in his insistence on his freedom to wander the hills. Cristóbal claimed that he could not breathe unless he roamed so, and he complained of fever in his body when he stayed still. There was a wave of restlessness that welled up inside him like physical pain that roaming alone could ease. So he never stayed long at home, and could not sit still; he frequently missed his mealtimes, and constantly ran away from his tutor. Cristóbal ignored his punished and battered flesh, and he ignored his brother's wrath, and every morning he would set out for yet another day of rambling on the hills.

Cristóbal grew somehow, despite his solitude; and, in lieu of any family love, after his mother's death, he turned to the hills. For at the age of six, he, who had been his mother's pet, became a scapegoat for everybody's grief. Instead of soothing his own sense of lack, his brothers somehow blamed him, the youngest, for the loss of their mother: they had been very close to her too and now all that was left them was this whining child. His cousins came, from the Hacienda La Bebella, and offered to take him and bring him up with their own young sons. But Cristóbal's father would have none of it – he must stay with his brothers, who would be an example to him. Thus he was left to mourn alone and only the hills were there to cradle him and fill his sense of loss. He grew up there, on the highlands, on the borders of the cold pármo; and from the outcrops of rock that he climbed, he could survey the whole valley stretching out below; and it was then that he swore his allegiance to the hills that had become his only solace.

His brothers tried everything to keep him at home.They kept him for months on cornbread soaked in milk, allowing him no meat or beans or coffee. They confiscated his books, and forbade him to visit his cousins; they set him extra tasks and lessons, and they beat him until their own arms ached. His face often bore the shadow of rainbows rippling on his cheeks when he blinked, and blues and greens and yellows shifted under his skin and over the bumps and contusions that their many blows produced – and still he would pay them no heed. They locked him in his room, but he escaped through his barred window, leaving a wreckage of splintered wood behind. They locked him naked in his room – yet still he escaped, and found clothes. They locked him in a windowless room, with no clothes and no light, and he nearly died there, plagued by insects and his festering sores. Then the servants told the villagers, and the villagers complained.

'Beat the boy, cleanly, but don't torment him.'

And it was in the light of this interference that his brothers' anger turned cruel. They would force him to conform. Even the vultures in the sky seemed to say, '¿Qué dirán? ¿Qué dirán?' and Cristóbal's two brothers knew well what their neighbours were saying; they would be holding them to ridicule; they would be whispering behind their backs that they could not control this wayward child. But they, too, would see. They would all see what real authority could be. It was his feet that offended them – so they would punish his feet.

They burned the sole of his right foot with a white-hot cattle iron. At fifteen, Cristóbal had the strength of a wrestler, and it took some time for him to slump into a pale sweat of pain, so the iron was driven in, further, perhaps, than had been intended. His foot was branded deep into the flesh, scorching a piece of bone as the whole room filled with the smoke.

Cristóbal lay salved and bandaged in his bed for five long days until a restlessness drove him back to the hills. It was they alone that could cool his blood and ease what seemed like ice grating over his wound. Every cell in his body was singed; it was as though the back of his head had opened up, revealing the inside of his skull; and his brain was sucking and swallowing directly from his surroundings. The whole world was crawling into his head – settling in this or that lobe, fitting into the fissures and lumps. Cristóbal stood in his massive beauty on the hilltops; and the frangipani trees, the bucare, and black cedars seemed to sit under his crown, and they sheltered him during the hardest moments of his unhealed wound and his strange self-trepanation. The thin scabs on his foot tore open, and the flesh became swollen beyond all recognition. The edges gapes and oozed, and he was pursued by the clinging smell of infected burns that filled the air, following him like a river of sewage wherever he went. Undaunted, he stripped a thick staff, and took to the mountains like a wounded bear.

It was old Benito's father, Lysandro, who had healed his foot, long before Benito himself was born; he had bathed it with a solution of wild rosemary and salt that stung on the cuts, He bandaged Cristóbal with cool fibrous palm leaves, and lowered his fever as he lay on a woven mat on the floor of his smoke-grimed hut. Each day, Cristóbal lay on his own, waiting for the man to return from his work, laden with odds and ends that he had picked up on the way, such as vultures' eggs for supper, or a pocketful of tiny rose-scented plums that grew wild in the surrounding woods. Sometimes he would bring back a chip of porcelain or a rattling clay doll made and buried by the Indians centuries before. The fields were full of relics, and this man had his own special way of explaining their presence, more enthralling by far than that of Cristóbal's former tutor.

Only one theme had ever interested Cristóbal in the long imprisonment of his lessons. He had had no time for theology or mathematics or Latin grammar: he was interested only in history. He had sat for hours listening to his boring tutor come alive as he told the story of his namesake, Cristóbal Colón, and his discovery of America. His own ancestors had come, on the third of these voyages, stopping first at the island of Santa Dominica, and then sailing on to the mainland. They had come with the vision of the great future of El Dorado, and a desire to be present during its rise to glory – they themselves would guide its course whilst thriving on it riches. And they had stayed, the de Labastidas and the Briceños, the Aragons and the Gabaldons and the de Melos. But Cristóbal felt a strange mixture of these ancestral feelings: he foresaw a continued rise in the fortunes of the valley, but he also saw the ravages of its decline. The land would slowly turn to dust, and Cristóbal determined to be present when the drought that his thoughts prophesied took a strangle-hold on the hills and plains, and throttled every last drop of life from his homeland.

No one else had any idea of what was to come: they did not know that their ordered society would crumble like a pack of cards. The black vomit, the Massacre, the famine and the drought would all come by surprise; no one would believe in them until their force had undermined the land. Everything was to change: only Cristóbal would be there – as the one constant amidst the upheavals and the decay. Cristóbal would be the valley what the hills had been to him.

It was not long before his brothers found him, and when they did, they had lost every christian feeling in them, and all their natural pity had drained with their loss of pride. They spoke with their jaws set in a rigid grimace. Old Benito's father was turned out of his hut and off their estates. He loaded his mule with his belongings, and journeyed away from the uplands and the páramo where he had been born, and travelled down to the neighbouring lands and hills. The two brothers kept back ropes and an axe from their departing worker, and when he was gone, they bound Cristóbal to a long wooden bench. They had brought their cattle branding iron with them, and they put it in the fire on the deserted hearth. Cristóbal said nothing – too shocked by the sudden departure of his new-found friend. From the moment that Benito's father set off down the track with his overloaded mule, and his heavy sackful of stones and trinkets, Cristóbal felt a final severing of his family tie. What was to follow was merely the confirmation of what he felt: they were all strangers. And then and there, Cristóbal renounced the lands that were his inheritance, forfeiting his wealth, denying kinship to the many different branches of his family, shunning all human company, speaking to no one, no matter whom, choosing rather to patrol the banks of the Momboy, watching and waiting.

When the iron was hot, and the two brothers impatient, one of them took the axe and the other the brand. The rough blade, ground on a weathered whetstone, swung down and shattered the boy's flesh and bone, while the other brother rammed the red-hot iron on the spurting pulp and cauterized the wound. Cristóbal had seen the hatred in his brothers' eyes, and he had seen the scraped blade catch the light as it fell, then he too had fallen after the first flicker of pain. When he came to, strapped down by leather thongs on his own bed in his brothers' house, he was still falling, and only the edges of his bed were there – the rest had slipped away. He was aware of a gnawing pain in his right foot – the old burn in his sole was nagging him. It was only after the delirium faded that he realized that he had no foot to ache, and that the whole of his right leg had gone amputated to the upper thigh.

The household was hushed, and servants rustled in and out of his room with pails and swabs, and he guessed the censor of his mutilation in their red eyes and sullen faces. In their world, there was no place for the maimed, and death was preferable to disablement. Such things, they knew, could not happen further down the valley: it was only here, on the uplands, that the cold wind had warped their brains. One by one the peasants left, heading for La Bebella, and the lowlands. Meanwhile, Cristóbal healed and hardened his ungainly stump, and choosing a strong staff as tall as a vaulting pole, he swung himself away from his brothers' house, determined never to return. The rest of his life was entirely dedicated to patrolling the crumpled foothills for a distance of some twenty miles, from the market town of La Caldera to the small mountain village of Timotes and back again. His itinerary was as regular as a railway train, and his staff and one foot furrowed the track of the Camino Real.

Lydia felt so reluctant to leave the hacienda that her every movement had become slow and ineffectual. Each trip to the jeep and back was taking an unusually long time. Her feet dragged as she walked, willing her to stay; there even seemed to be a shimmer of life on the parched slopes, and she could have sworn that there were birds other than birds of prey in the fields around her. But it was merely the sun catching on skulls and stones or dry gourds, hanging from the telegraph wires or knotted around dead trees. The only live beings left were herself and Diego, and their dog, and Cristóbal, and the turkey vultures frantic for a corpse. She knew that they would try to get her husband, Diego, when she brought him down, because he seemed too lifeless, and they would sense the death in him. She found an old tarpaulin in which to wrap him, like a winding sheet, as a shield against their horny beaks.

Cristóbal was sitting outside her house, on the road, leaning against a rough milestone. Over his shoulder she could still decipher the familiar number chipped out of the white rock: four hundred – it was four hundred miles to the capital, four hundred miles to the sea, and more than four hundred years since the first of the family came searching for gold. Now only Cristóbal remained, who had limited the roundness of his world and its discovery to the pacing of the whittled slopes and their disastrous erosion. And it struck her that his appearance was as strange to herself and her peers as that of Cortéz and his men had been to the astonished Aztecs on their arrival in Mexico.

At times Cristóbal shifted his gaze from the stone balustrade where Lydia had been leaning, turning his eyes alternately to the once seething town of La Caldera, and, in the other direction, to the chill uplands where he had been born. Lydia climbed the uneven staircase to her library, where legions of cockroaches had feasted, reducing it all to shreds and dust, and she watched Cristóbal's every movement through the dull cedar doors that led out on to one of the many balconies.

The house was built along three sides of a square; Diego lay as though in state at one end, and she stood at the other, looking out at Cristóbal and the caked remains of the River Momboy, and, beyond them, the disused factory and mill. One side of the house lay open, and the high whitewashed corridors all led directly on to what used to be a formal rose-garden enclosed by high gates and a wall. But now the gates hung awkwardly on their hinges, and the gaps that they made in the courtyard wall were like unhealed wounds through which the displaced sand and decay swept in and stayed.

The burnt orange tiles of the uneven roof flared like bonfires in the sky. Lydia looked down the long quadrangle of flames, and the tightness in her brain shrank from the roof's furnace. She had still to fetch one of the tiles from the old floor of gold and pack it safely in the jeep, and she had still somehow to carry Diego down the main stairs. The library, which was really two large rooms, had been her tower, her solace now for ten long years. The cracks in the walls were full of her whisperings, and the hollow beams and bats' nests under the boards knew how much she missed all that was lost and gone. The whole room seemed to weep and sigh in echo to her sorrow.

And yet, she thought, would ten years seem a long time to Cristóbal? She decided that it would, but she did not know how long. She didn't know that under his immutable mask every day was one of torment. Nor did she realize quite how much he suffered from his ill-severed limb, nor how the valley's death was his own slow dying. With all the diligence of a natural farmer, he had roamed landless through the valley, observing every blade and detail of the hills and fields that he knew so well. Even when the crops had grown easily, he had foreseen the time when the hills would become barren and deserted, and deserts would shape themselves where there had been woods. And he himself would finally wither and dry so much that not even the vultures would stay for him, and he would fade into the mist of dry ashes, and be covered over by sand.

When the locusts came, he alone had known that the famine would pass. Afterwards, he had pitied La comadre Matilde with her premonitions of destruction. She had urged every family she could reach to fear the land, little knowing that the land itself would also be destroyed. He had watched the frail hut of Matilde's blind aunt over the years. A young girl used to tend to the old woman's needs; and he remembered her in the rain. He could remember vividly what the valley used to be like when it rained – it seemed to wash off caked mud and release new possibilities of movement. When it rained, the whole world relaxed.

With the first warm drops a bout of almost clockwork bustle would break through their routines. In every hut and household, preparations were made for the forthcoming downpour. There was a rush for pails and pans to catch the drops, shutters were drawn, and the bunches of beans, hung over poles to dry, were covered. Mounds of coffee were hauled into outhouses, and the multi-coloured flags of drying clothes were jumbled together and stuffed into hammocks. Then everyone would sit back, and an undertow of well-being needled its way through their veins. The rain came in a distemper of relief, and not all those who heralded the first showers were there to wave out the last. There were always some of the very old and young who succumbed to the colds and fevers of the rains, and those who died of the many forms of dysentery that the wet weather brought in its tow. In the days when it rained regularly, and each year was divided into two seasons, the dry and the wet, the month of May was the wettest. And there was even a name for the illness that came at that time – it was called the mayera – and it appeared in the records as the cause of death of many children.

La comadre Matilde's aunt grew older, and the cataracts over her blind eyes grew bluer, and yet she did not die. Cristóbal remembered how he had walked by one afternoon and seen her slumped against the limed wall of her cluttered veranda. She had been hauled out there by the girl who nursed her, and her cloths and petticoats were draped around her to dry. As signs of a storm gathered overhead, her nurse had run home to help seal up her own hut, and the old woman had lain huddled and silent under her canopy of damp laundry. Her legs had grown as pale and bony as an old woman's legs can grow under the waxen knots of arthritis. She had been taken out with the washing and everyone had forgotten to take her in. Her knees and wrists were too weak to help her crawl more than a few feet, and she could not find her own door. She called to the girl, who was far away and out of earshot; and she called to Matilde, who was nowhere near; but all that came by way of reply was the rumbling of the storm, and rain so hard that it scarcely let her breathe. When she opened her mouth to cry out, the fat drops of water threatened to drown her like a duck. She had watched ducks drown, many times, in their own element. They lifted their necks as though to give thanks for the rain, and, opening their throats in adoration, the rainwater choked them. So the old woman ceased to call, muttering instead at her niece's neglect. In the long hours of her drenching, she cursed Matilde – who would have lain down her life for her – and she cursed her indifference – even though she cared for no one but this one blind aunt.

Matilde never knew how harshly her absence had been taken that day. Nor did she know that her aunt became a child again as she lay beaten by hour upon hour of heavy rain. Only Cristóbal saw her skinny bones and skull plastered to the floor at the mercy of the tempest and her truant nurse. He foresaw that the girl would come and haul her in again, and he foresaw that much later the old woman would die despite Matilde's broths and pains; and he knew that her body would be a mere heap of deranged swellings, and that Matilde would be lost without her.

The sun was moving steadily across the charred slopes, and Lydia needed no dial to see that she would have to hurry. Even if the roads were still in fair condition, it would take her from twelve to twenty hours to reach the sea. The back of the jeep was stacked with cans of petrol, water and gourds. The battered canvas roof was stretched and tied in position, and her old Winchester rifle lay across the front seat, together with a small Colt revolver, and a sawed-off double-barrelled shot-gun. The glove compartment was well-stocked with cartridges, and she had packed matches and string, food and knives, and such spare parts as she deemed necessary. All she needed now was to fetch Diego.

She felt that the vultures were watching her too closely, so she dropped her bundle of canvas and picked up the rifle, and pressing the butt hard against her shoulder, she took her aim and shot down one of the birds, and the others all flapped after it, squabbling in a frenzy of torn feathers. Now Lydia knew that she would have the time it took them to pick clean its bones to carry her husband downstairs. All that was left were the stairs. Lydia had been avoiding them all morning. They implied too definite a finality. They had assumed massive proportions in her mind, and become almost too high to climb. When she first arrived in the house, she had been unusually impressed by their size and splendour, and their mottled green marble was engraved in her head. Even the stairs held many memories, and the slight dips in the dreads were worn by her own and others' feet through centuries of routine.

But Diego was neither to walk nor fall down these stairs as so many others had done before him. He would descend quite differently: he would be hauled down by Lydia. His body was too heavy for her even to attempt to carry, so she wrapped him in the old tarpaulin and dragged him down. She held his shoulders and let his legs trail and bump on the treads. There was no banister, and it was all that Lydia could do to keep from falling. She winced as Diego's body hit the steps, and she could almost feel him bruising.

The house was like the bubble of an hour-glass. Sand drifted in from the hacienda to the halls in a steady trickle until the fields seemed empty, and house seemed full. Lydia heaped Diego's body into the back of the jeep as best she could, finding that one half of him invariably slipped down once she had got the other half in. But after some tugging and pulling, she succeeded in wedging him between the seats. Cristóbal was still down on the road to the side of the house, and therefore could not see her. Megan, her last beagle hound, hurried her thin ribs across the hall, and scrambled into the back seat, twisting and turned around Diego's face, until she had found a comfortable space for herself. Megan was Lydia's one compatriot in that strange and newly barren land: she had sailed with her from England ten years before, crated in a sheep pen on the upper deck of the *Montserrat*, the Spanish ship that had rocked them across the Atlantic.

Once they were all in, Lydia started the engine. She had started it several times the day before, but even so she held her breath, in case it would not go. Then, with only one last look back, she drove down the bumpy, almost impassable track to the road. The jeep lurched, and her two passengers were thrown from side to side against the fastened cans of petrol. Halfway down, the wheels stuck in a drift of sand, and she had to work with her hands and a shovel to clear the way. The drive from the house to the road was just under a mile long, and lined with dead avocado trees. When she finally reached the road, Cristóbal had already risen, and was walking away uphill. She could see only the back of his head with its massive mane of hair and his staff which gave him an almost supernatural height. Ahead of him flew a straggling band of vultures which turned to follow her as she drove away. They seemed to know that Cristóbal would not die, but slowly desiccate, and the drought in their gullets bade them turn tail and follow Lydia and the Beltráns.

Lydia drove on to the town of La Caldera, stopping only once to shoot down one of the troop of vultures to decoy its brothers from Diego and herself. She passed the Plaza Bolívar, and the other square with its statue of General Mario and its derelict mansions; and she passed street after deserted street of rubble and clay. Even the cathedral had broken doors and windows, and what looked like a sand dune in its open aisle. The covered market-place flapped shreds of coloured canvas and the looted stalls were overturned. There were pieces of bone and skull in the most unexpected places, and many of the doors on many of the houses were barricaded and marked with a black cross as though for plague. The whole place was desolate. Lydia left the town behind her, and the cemetery that hemmed its outskirts, overflowing in endless skimped additions. Then the road took her downhill, past a disused barracks, to a wide bridge across the dry bed of the River Momboy, and she climbed once more with the road, to the hill that lay outside the town of La Caldera. It was a suddenly high place in the slow descent to the sea, and because there had once been a prison there, it was known by the name of Calvary. Lydia shot down one more vulture, buying her own time with its death; and, keeping her engine running, she stepped down for a moment to take one last look at the valley she was about to leave.

As she faced the highlands, she saw Cristóbal standing on a distant outcrop like a statue of rock; and the sun seemed to shine directly upon him so that his shock of wild hair became a blaze of gold, and around his head there was a strange halo.

Despite the distance, Lydia could see him very clearly, more clearly, in fact than ever before, and it seemed to her suddenly that the halo was composed entirely of splintered bones. He turned and walked away, taking with him his strange head-dress of a lifetime's hunger; for the bones were the discarded bones of the salt-fish they had all eaten in the times of plenty; and they were the bones that yellowed nails had dug for, when the drought began, to boil again; and they were the bones that old men had sucked and dribbled as they chewed their cud of thistles. They were all of their bones, and they were splinters of china, and hidden wish-bones too, and Cristóbal had been storing them in his trepanned head for a long time. And now there was no one left to see, he had shaken them loose, and Lydia's last vision of the valley was of this one mutilated man whose strength of mind and body dominated the land as surely as his forefathers had done before him. He was a part of the hills themselves: the hot sands would bury him, and only then would he lay down his staff and end his marathon.

GRANTA

JOHN L'HEUREUX

THE ANATOMY OF DESIRE

Because Hanley's skin had been stripped off by the enemy, he could find no one who was willing to be with him for long. The nurses were obligated, of course, to see him now and then, and sometimes the doctor, but certainly not the other patients and certainly not his wife and children. He was raw, he was meat, and he would never be any better. He had a great and natural desire, therefore, to be possessed by someone.

He would walk around on his skinned feet, leaving bloody footprints up and down the corridors, looking for someone to love him.

'You're not supposed to be out here,' the nurse said. And she added, somehow making it sound kind, 'You untidy the floor, Hanley.'

'I want to be loved by someone,' he said, 'I'm human too. I'm like you.'

But he knew he was not like her. Everybody called her the saint.

'Why couldn't it be you?' he said.

She was swabbing his legs with blood retardant, a new discovery that kept Hanley going. It was one of those miracle medications that just grew out of the war.

'I wasn't chosen,' she said. 'I have my skin.'

'No,' he said. 'I mean why couldn't it be you who will love me, possess me? I have desires too,' he said.

She considered this as she swabbed his shins and the soles of his feet.

'I have no desires,' she said. 'Or only one. It's the same thing.'

He looked at her loving face. It was not a pretty face, but it was saintly.

'Then you will?' he said.

'If I come to know sometime that I must,' she said.

The enemy had not chosen Hanley. They had just lucked upon him sleeping in his trench. They were a raid party of four, terrified and obedient, and they had been told to bring back an enemy to serve as an example of what is done to infiltrators.

They dragged Hanley back across the line and ran him, with his hands tied behind his back, the two kilometers to the general's tent.

The general dismissed the guards because he was very taken with Hanley. He untied the cords that bound his wrists and let his arms hang free. Then slowly, ritually, he tipped Hanley's face toward the light and examined it carefully. He kissed him on the brow and on the cheek and finally on the mouth. He gazed deep and long into Hanley's eyes until he saw his own reflection there looking back. He traced the lines of Hanley's eyebrows, gently, with the tip of his index finger. 'Such a beautiful face,' he said in his own language. He pressed his palms lightly against Hanley's forehead, against his cheekbones, his jaw. With his little finger he memorized the shape of Hanley's lips, the laugh lines at his eyes, the chin. The general did Hanley's face very thoroughly. Afterward he did some things down below, and so just before sunrise when the time came to lead Hanley out to the stripping post, he told the soldiers with the knives: 'This young man could be my own son; so spare him here and here.'

The stripping post stood dead centre in the line of barbed wire only a few meters beyond the range of gun-fire. A loudspeaker was set up and began to blare the day's message. 'This is what happens to infiltrators. No infiltrators will be spared.' And then as troops from both sides watched through binoculars, the enemy cut the skin from Hanley's body, sparing – as the general had insisted – his face and his genitals. They were skilled men and the skin was stripped off expeditiously and they hung it, headless, on the barbed wire as an example. They lay Hanley himself on the ground where he could die.

He was rescued a little after noon where the enemy, for no good reason, went into sudden retreat.

Hanley was given emergency treatment at the field unit, and when they had done what they could for him, they sent him on to the vets' hospital. At least there, they told each other, he will be attended by the saint.

It was quite some time before the saint said yes, she would love him.

'Not just love me. Possess me.'

'There are natural reluctancies,' she said. 'There are personal peculiarities,' she said. 'You will have to have patience with me.'

'You're supposed to be a saint,' he said.

So she lay down with him in his bloody bed and he found great satisfaction in holding this small woman in his arms. He kissed her and caressed her and felt young and whole again. He did not miss his wife and children. He did not miss his skin.

The saint did everything she must. She told him how handsome he was and what pleasure he gave her. She touched him in the way he liked best. She said he was her whole life, her fate. And at night when he woke her to staunch the blood, she whispered how she needed him, how she could not live without him.

This went on for some time.

The war was over and the occupying forces had made the general mayor of the capital city. He was about to run for senator and wanted his past to be beyond the reproach of any investigative committee. He wrote Hanley a letter which he sent through the International Red Cross.

'You could have been my own son,' he said. 'What we do in war is what we have to do. We do not choose cruelty or violence. I did only what was my duty.'

'I am in love and I am loved,' Hanley said. 'Why isn't this enough?'

The saint was swabbing his chest and belly with blood retardant. 'Nothing is ever enough,' she said.

'I love, but I am not possessed by love,' he said. 'I want to be surrounded by you. I want to be enclosed. I want to be enveloped. I don't have the words for it. But do you understand?'

'You want to be possessed,' she said.

'I want to be inside you.'

And so they made love, but afterward he said, 'That is not enough. That is only a metaphor for what I want.'

The general was elected senator and was made a trustee of three nuclear-arms conglomerates. But he was not well. And he was not sleeping well.

He wrote to Hanley, 'I wake in the night and see your face before mine. I feel your forehead pressing against my palms. I taste your breath. I did only what I had to do. You could have been my son.'

'I know what I want,' Hanley said.

'If I can do it, I will,' the saint said.

'I want your skin.'

And so she lay down on the long white table, shuddering, while Hanley made his first incision. He cut along the shoulders and then down the arms and back up, then down the sides and the legs to the feet. It took him longer than he had expected. The saint shivered at the cold touch of the knife and she sobbed once at the sight of the blood, but by the time Hanley lifted the shroud of skin from her crimson body, she was resigned, satisfied even.

Hanley had spared her face and her genitals.

He spread the skin out to dry and, while he waited, he swabbed her raw body carefully with blood retardant. He whispered little words of love and thanks and desire to her. A smile played about her lips but she said nothing.

It would be a week before he could put on her skin.

The general wrote to Hanley one last letter. 'I can endure no more. I am possessed by you.'

Hanley put on the skin of the saint. His genitals fitted nicely through the gap he had left and the skin at his neck matched hers exactly. He walked the corridors and for once left no bloody tracks behind. He stood before mirrors and admired himself. He touched his breasts and his belly and his thighs and there was no blood on his hands.

'Thank you,' he said to her. 'It is my heart's desire fulfilled. I am inside you. I am possessed by you.'

And then, in the night, he kissed her on the brow and on the cheek and finally on the mouth. He gazed deep and long into her eyes. He traced the lines of her eyebrows gently, with the tip of his index finger. 'Such a beautiful face,' he said. He pressed his palms lightly against her forehead, her cheekbones, her jaw. With his little finger he memorized the shape of her lips.

And then it was that Hanley, loved, desperate to possess and be possessed, staring deep into the green and loving eyes of the saint, saw that there can be no possessions, there is only desire. He plucked at the empty skin and wept.

GRANTA

TED MOONEY

THE SALT WIFE

Martha worked in a radio-biology lab in Manhattan, and when Larry, her husband of seven years, left her at last for the cause of art, she decided to accept the long-standing invitation from a lab in Los Angeles to visit their operation and talk about her work. She left her Alsatian with someone she knew from her women's group, packed her suit-case first with clothes she imagined to be appropriate to L.A. and then with those she imagined to be wildly inappropriate, and after picking up a small lead-lined attaché case of radio-active samples from the lab, she boarded an enormous jet that transported her without the least sensation of motion to Los Angeles.

Katherine, whom she had not seen since college, met her at the airport in a white GTO convertible. They had some trouble recognizing each other at first because in the ten years since their last meeting, Martha had come to pay less attention to her looks and Katherine more, but it was really only an instant of uncertainty, and Katherine had told her to watch for the car. 'I'll be wearing a white convertible in my button-hole' was actually what she'd said.

They embraced when they met, and Katherine, who was now an actress, cried, proving once again to Martha that you become what you imitate, since Katherine had never before been histrionic in any way. Still, Martha was touched. Then they drove. While they drove they talked, and while they talked they smoked. When they got off the freeway, Katherine took advantage of a traffic-light to open her door and empty the car's ashtray onto the street. Martha, looking out her window, saw that the man in the MG next to them was emptying his ashtray too. He smiled at her and waved.

'This is a funny town,' she said to Katherine.

Martha found Katherine's apartment in Hollywood funny too. First of all, there was nearly as much space for the GTO in the parking lot downstairs as there was for Katherine upstairs. Then there was Katherine's aesthetic sense, which, in some appalling tic, had caused her to decorate all the walls, chairs, sofa, and smaller accessories in a pale-green calico fabric dotted with tiny white and yellow flowers that looked like protozoa. Even the picture frames were covered in it. And that was the third thing: all the pictures in the apartment were colour photographs of Katherine: nude Katherine in the bathroom, frocked Katherine over the sofa, night-gowned Katherine in the foyer.

'A drink?'

Martha looked at her watch, decided to leave it at New York time for now. 'Yes,' she answered.

They drank Campari and soda at a marble-topped table by the window. Katherine, who had never met Larry, wished to know if it bothered Martha to talk about him. It did not. Martha related several entertaining stories about the man who, it had to be admitted, was still legally her husband. There was the time he had run out of canvas and had therefore painted their bathtub, throwing his dealer into ecstasies and their apartment into chaos for the two weekends it was the annex to his show. There was the year they had lived in New Orleans. There was the year she had had to eat yellow pills in order to stand the constant presence of his friends. There was the time, the year after that, when they were arrested for a veiled yet public indecency in Lincoln Center Plaza, were fined, and fell thereafter deliriously in love for another eight months. And so on.

Martha, as she spoke, grew fascinated by the sight of palm trees on the street below and had to keep reminding herself to look at Katherine. Katherine, for her part, kept looking at the lead-lined attaché case in the far corner of her living room.

'What about your work?' she asked when Martha ran out of entertaining stories about Larry.

'What about it? It's very important to me.'

'Doesn't it scare you? All that radio-activity stuff?'

'Yes,' Martha answered after a moment. 'It does.'

Then they had another drink, after which Martha yawned, set her watch back three hours, and retired for a nap upon Katherine's lace-covered, doll-infested bed.

That evening, they went to a small dinner party at the house of Katherine's lover. The occasion being celebrated was the recent casting of Katherine as the ambassador's mistress in a high-budget movie about some terrorists who hold the Super Bowl hostage. Since this was to be an 'action' movie, the ambassador was not a very important figure, and his mistress less so, but it was the first real role Katherine had had.

'I'm twenty-nine,' she said as they drove to the party. 'In another year I'll be too old ever to be called "starlet".'

'And you know,' said Martha, summoning up one of their routines from college, 'how very much we all want to be called "starlet".'

At Gregory's party, there were eight adults and a child of five who, when Katherine and Martha walked in, was insisting loudly that Elton John had a special cape that bestowed upon him the power of flight. This idea was being entertained with mild enthusiasm by the adults.

Martha thought she was beginning to get a sense of L.A. To test herself, she made five calculated guesses about the things around her, then checked herself against Katherine. She guessed (1) that the house, which was divided vaguely into screened-off 'areas' rather than rooms, had been designed by Gregory (it had); (2) that the sugar bowl on the table contained not sugar but cocaine (correct); (3) that the child was Gregory's by his first marriage (incorrect; his second); (4) that the man in the denim jump-suit was an est instructor (wrong; he sailed); and (5) that Elton John did indeed own such a cape (answer not known). Martha agreed to have a drink.

Soon enough she was peering over the tilted gin horizon of her third and noticing that the man in the leather shirt was, just as she'd thought, too hot, sweating in fact. Everyone was talking about why there are more good restaurants in New York than in L.A.

'What are you thinking?' asked Gregory, who was sitting next to her. She turned her head to face him. Gregory was a record producer.

'Very little,' she answered. 'As little as possible in fact. I think I'm getting the hang of it.'

'Jet lag,' he sympathized.

'I don't think so.'

Then, during the uncomfortable pause that she had so expertly induced, she remembered what it was she had wanted to ask him.

'What,' she inquired, 'is the purpose of that?' She pointed to the far corner of the living area where a stack of seven colour televisions, each tuned to a different channel, conveyed police cars, newscasters, Handi-Wrap, and what appeared to be a Zulu village. There was no sound.

'Oh, those,' said Gregory, who clearly considered this the correct question. 'Well, think of it this way: if this room were full of ghosts, you'd want to know about it, right? Well, I don't know anything about ghosts, but this room *is* full of very high-frequency versions of Walter Cronkite, Telly Savalas, and previously owned Cadillacs: TV waves, you dig? Invisible without a tube. And I, for one, am just paranoid enough to want to know what's in the room with me.'

Martha nodded. She understood. She swallowed the last of her drink and let the ice rest a moment against her upper lip as she looked at Gregory.

Dinner, in deference to the complicated vegetarian diet that Katherine followed, was eggplant dish *imam bayildi*, which loosely translated from the Turkish means 'so good the Pope fainted'. It was not good. Martha had wanted to sit next to Gregory in honour of his having said the first intelligent thing she had heard in L.A., but at the last moment she was stuck between the five-year-old and a very blond flight instructress named Laura.

'How old are you?' Martha asked the five-year-old, who was wearing an Alice Cooper T-shirt.

'Seven,' he answered.

Martha poured herself wine. Ever since she had decided not to risk having children, other people's children distressed her. She felt she ought to apologize for having contracepted their playmates and future spouses.

'I'm twenty-eight,' she volunteered, knowing perfectly well how stupid that must sound to a crypto-five-year-old like this one, but believing firmly that guilt's obligations must be discharged. In her hand, the wine glass again advised her of its emptiness.

Which is how it went and went until, by the time they all returned to the living area for coffee or, one assumed, cocaine, Martha was a deal drunker than she'd been in months.

She cornered Gregory by the sliding plate-glass panels that led to the sun deck and back property. He was flicking switches as previously hidden spotlights were picking palm trees out of the darkness. Martha remembered something she had seen on TV about night combat in Vietnam.

'Get those snipers,' she said.

'What?' said Gregory.

'Joke,' she said, and smiled encouragingly. He smiled back. Then Katherine arrived with coffee for the three of them.

Martha had forgotten that Katherine always did that, always arrived engagingly in the nick of time. Not that Martha herself could remember just then what she had intended to grill Gregory about. 'We were talking about sniping,' she said, half to Katherine, half to herself.

Sometimes, when Martha got very drunk, she talked about radio-activity. She did this because she had discovered that radio-activity was for most people a topic of conversation only slightly less compelling than sex. She did it only when drunk because this extreme interest frightened her.

It took Martha a moment to realize there was a record playing, quite loudly in fact – something light and electric that sounded like the Eagles but was not. She looked at Katherine, and decided the whole thing might be more gracefully endured with a few snorts of coke. She fetched the sugar bowl from the table, over the objections of Leather Shirt and Laura.

'Gregory likes his work,' Martha observed to Katherine as she raised the tiny silver spoon to her nostril. Gregory had closed his eyes and was making professional sounds at the music.

'Yes, he does,' she answered, and accepted the sugar bowl gratefully. 'He likes it very much.'

'What about you?' asked Gregory with his eyes shut. Then he opened them and stared with a blue intensity that surprised Martha. 'How do you dig relating to all those invisible busted-up quanta zipping around?'

'Well,' she said, savouring the descending numbness in her throat, 'if this room were full of ghosts, you'd want to know about it, right?'

Katherine drove Martha home by way of the Strip, that boulevard named after sunsets made famous and beautiful by smog. As they passed Schwab's drugstore, a song came on the radio, something light and electric that sounded like the Eagles but was not, and Katherine said she knew what Martha was thinking but you had to live somewhere. Then Katherine ran out of cigarettes and Martha gave her one of hers.

'Don't be silly, Kathy,' she said. 'We understand each other.' Katherine looked stoned and grateful. Out of the corner of her eye, Martha watched the car's antenna tearing radio waves from the air. There was a crowd outside the Whisky as they passed, and Katherine wanted to know who was playing.

In the parking lot of her building, however, in the orange light of the sodium lamp, Katherine cried. Katherine wished to have babies but could not do so without compromising her career as an over-aged starlet. So: no babies. Soon it would be too late and risky. Martha hugged her. While they were holding each other, a man in a red Gran Torino pulled up and asked them if they wanted to go to a party. Katherine gave him the finger, and he rolled slowly away.

Upstairs, Katherine showed Martha where the pale-green towels were, meanwhile washing her own face to rid it of tearstains. They agreed to meet for dinner the next evening, after Martha's laboratory lecture; then Katherine gave her the apartment key, kissed her good-bye, and returned in her white GTO to Gregory.

Martha swept the dolls off Katherine's bed with her arm and turned down the lace coverlet. She was hungry, but the refrigerator, when she opened it, had nothing in it but a half-bottle of seltzer, so she tracked down the Campari and mixed herself a nightcap. She drank half the drink then took off her clothes, got in bed, and turned out the light. When her eyes adjusted to the dark, she got up again, turned on the television at the other end of the room – picture but not sound – and returned stumblingly to bed. Gregory Peck was leading his company up Pork Chop Hill. She slept.

In her dream, she was strolling across an arched wooden bridge that spanned an estuary. It was night, and in the moon-light the sea was visible beyond. Half-way across the bridge, she heard a great splashing, and she leaned over the railing to see what was causing it. In the water, which seemed to be lit from below like a swimming pool, thousands of gold and silver fish had risen to the surface and were leaping into the air and over each other in small arcs. It came to Martha that they were speaking to her and that she understood what they were saying. In the distance, by the shore, she saw her mother squatting over the water to speak to an enormous, coral-coloured fish.

Martha awoke in the dark with a mouthful of lace coverlet half swallowed. Panicked and confused, she pulled it free, sat up, and was copiously sick over the side of the bed. The digital clock flickered, then rearranged itself to say 2:16. Gregory Peck had been replaced by Alan Ladd on horse-back.

Several dizzy seconds passed before the rest of the world sifted back into place and Martha was able to turn on the light and stand up. Then she fetched pail and mop from the broom closet and, as quickly as the constricted capillaries of her brain allowed, cleaned up the vomit.

Back in bed, she was reaching for the light switch once more when the lead-lined attaché case caught her eye, reminding her in its ruthless way that she had forgotten to refrigerate the sodium 22 and iodine 131 solutions. Her plan had been to take them out to the lab at UCLA that day, but Los Angeles had intervened.

Wearily, she swung out of bed again to rummage around in her suitcase for the new pair of protective gloves she had brought. There were skirts and shirts and pants and dresses – more clothes, it seemed to her, than anyone could possibly wear – but she could not find the gloves. She sat back on her haunches and hugged her naked knees. As sometimes happened when she was drunk or high, she felt that extraordinarily difficult things were being required of her. Alan Ladd, on the other hand, was clearly feeling very at home on the range as he galloped after an escaping bad guy. She closed her eyes, and for a moment she thought she was going to cry.

Then she shivered – a single, small convulsive shake from head to foot – rose, and walked over to the attaché case. Squatting in front of it, she dialled the combination, sprang the ancillary locks, and carefully drew it open. She removed the two vials, put them down, closed the case, picked them up again, and took them over to the refrigerator. She concentrated her attention on the vials as she tried, with the crook of her arm, to unlatch the refrigerator door, and she kept noticing over and over again how naked her hands looked without the gloves. Then she succeeded with the latch, and the door swung open on the empty, white interior. Martha carefully slipped the vials onto the top shelf, directly under the plastic freezer compartment. She stared in at them, verifying once more with her eye that the refrigerator was otherwise empty. If this refrigerator were a body, she found herself thinking, those vials would be its heart. Still staring, she touched one exploratory hand to her breasts, whose nipples had gone taut in the chill air. Then she shut the door, washed her hands, and stumbled back to bed and sleep.

In the morning, in the shower, while trying to decide whether or not to use Katherine's Golden Placenta Hair Conditioner, Martha swore to herself that under no circumstances would she be so careless again. This was the second time she had handled hot solutions without protection, and neither time had it been necessary. She thought with disgust and sadness of her chromosomes, those spindly centres of her history and future, and imagined them shattered by invisible enemies whose names were beta and gamma. Then she squeezed an ounce of hair conditioner into her palm and studied it. She read the label on the bottle, hoping it would say where the golden placentas came from, but it didn't. Cows, she thought, and began working it into her hair.

At the rental agency on Franklin Avenue, Martha asked first for a Pinto but then changed her mind and requested a Cordoba. She took Sunset Boulevard west, scientifically straightening the order of her thoughts and glancing from time to time at the lead-lined attaché case, which sat on the seat beside her like a hitch-hiker. This morning she had of course had no trouble finding the protective gloves in her suitcase. Consequently, her hands continued to look disturbingly naked to her as she held the wheel, but she was happy to be driving and began to occupy herself with a skilful series of lane changes. Short stretches of the highway had recently been resurfaced, and Martha found peculiar comfort in the periodic jolts. She sought them out. When she turned on the radio, Linda Ronstadt was comparing her heart to a wheel.

Martha arrived at UCLA twenty minutes before she was due but spent all the extra time wandering from building to building and from floor to floor, trying to follow the directions Dr Epstein had sent her. When at last she did locate him, she was fifteen minutes late. He did not seem to mind.

'I'll tell you straight out,' he confided as they walked upstairs to the lab. 'Dr Kellerman and I hope to have a position to offer you before you leave L.A.'

Martha made sounds of pleased non-commitment. She had not expected anything so definite, and the business of having to acquire her own Cordoba and sun-tan seemed at the moment unwarrantedly difficult.

'I'm flattered,' she added, in order to dispose of the subject temporarily. They exchanged smiles, and as Dr Epstein raised a hand to adjust his glasses, Martha saw he wore a gold-plated ID bracelet around his wrist.

In the laboratory, an exceptionally well-equipped complex of six well-ventilated rooms, Martha was introduced to Dr Kellerman and the twelve assistants, technicians, and students who had gathered to hear her lecture-demonstration.

'We've all been eagerly following your work with oestrogen in *The Journal of Radiobiology*,' said Dr Kellerman, beaming. 'Very exciting.'

'Thank you,' said Martha.

She put on the lab coat, gloves, dosimeter, and shoe covers offered her, then, picking up the lead-lined case, followed her hosts and audience into the adjacent hot lab. There, lined up in their metabolism cages, were the six Patagonian cavies she had requested: healthy female rodents the size of rabbits. She unlocked the attaché case, listening absently to the high keening of the cavies, then drew it respectfully open. The top to the vial of iodine 131 had been jarred slightly askew; she promised herself to avoid hitting the highway bumps with such gusto on the way back.

'Shall we begin?' she began.

And, diving gracefully into the lengthy lake of technical speech and process, Martha talked and talked. By way of illustration, she injected the cavies, which had come for that very purpose all the way from the plains of Argentina, with a variety of steroids and radio-active tags. She collected samples of their blood and held the wand of a Geiger counter to the glass tubes where fright had caused them to deposit their golden urine. She spoke so intelligently and concretely of what was coming next in the world that at the end of the three-hour lecture-demonstration, her audience surprised her suddenly with its solemn applause. Pleased and slightly amused, Martha thanked them, locked up the lead-lined attaché case once again, and retired with them to the low-level lab next door. There, gossiping professionally with Kellerman and Epstein, she awaited her turn for the decontamination shower.

When it came and she found herself alone in those precautionary waters, scrubbing her body for the second time that day, she thought, as always, of her husband. The decontamination ritual had never ceased to depress her profoundly, with all that it implied about the nature of her work, and she had long ago developed a reflex to counter that depression: she thought about making love to Larry. It amused her and hurt her that the reflex remained, even now, when Larry did not. Drawing the wash-cloth across her breasts, she noticed that her nipples were erect, and the image of herself naked and stoned in front of Katherine's refrigerator came rushing back. In that image, it seemed to her that the top to the iodine 131 vial was askew. She turned up the hot water and quickly washed again.

When she was dried and dressed, Martha knocked on the door to signal she was done, then left by the other door, following the arrows to the monitoring room. She sat on a stool in that windowless cubicle, switched on one of the three Geiger counters, and held the mica-window tube to her left palm. A slow static blossomed. That's me, she thought; my atoms. The thought spread out in her mind like a spilled liquid, and she had just decided to scrub down Katherine's refrigerator that evening as an extra precaution when she noticed that a man was standing in the doorway, watching her and listening.

'Not good,' he said, and walked in.

Martha looked at his neat, blond goatee. She remembered he had asked the right questions during her lecture. 'Not all that bad, though,' she answered, handing him the counter tube. 'Much better than I'd thought.'

The man switched off the Geiger counter without using it. To do this, he had to reach over Martha.

'In this business,' he said, 'as in many, it's possible to know too much.'

Martha studied the man's face, liking it, liking what it said. She shrugged. 'When you're hot, you're hot,' she said. 'And when you're not, you're lucky.'

Martha, in her rented Cordoba, followed the man to a restaurant he had suggested. He had said his name was Victor. As she drove, Martha groped in her bag for her sunglasses, and in so doing missed the turnoff Victor had just that moment taken. She took the next left and ended up in the Aqua-King Swimming Pool Company's parking lot, adjacent to the restaurant's lot but separated from it by fifteen yards of Astroturf and a sparse line of eucalyptus trees. Thinking there might be a passage in back, Martha began following the divider strip around, but when she saw Victor roll down the window of his Camaro and beckon her, she drove carefully up over the Astroturf and joined him. The smog had lifted and it was getting hot and it appeared they were going to lunch in something called the Mai Tai Lounge.

'Rather a peculiar place,' said Martha when they were safely ensconced beneath plastic palm fronds, pink and yellow spotlights, and a ceiling hung from wall to wall with artificial oranges.

'It's a peculiar town,' said Victor. 'I bet you've noticed that.'

'It has crossed my mind once or twice,' replied Martha, lighting a cigarette.

'But after a while,' he continued, 'you get used to it. And after another while, you get to like it. The next thing you know, you don't take your sun-glasses off even to go to bed.'

Martha smiled. 'Is that how you are?'

His hands mimicked prayer, and his pale eyes met hers.

'The day,' he answered, 'shall surely come.'

Martha ordered one of the house rum drinks, which proved to be disappointingly anaemic, then switched on the second round to bourbon, which Victor had been drinking from the start. Victor had been born in Tyler, Texas, and had an accent that surfaced with the liquor. He ordered the Mahi Mahi, she the Tropical Delite.

They talked for some time about Epstein and Kellerman, with whom Victor had worked for three years; then they began to tell stories from their respective pasts. Martha liked very much the stories about his father.

They had one more drink; then Martha, in her car followed Victor, in his, to Sunset Boulevard and the Carolina Pines Motel, where, beneath a paint-by-number harlequin, they made prolonged and oddly peaceful love. Though Martha knew her diaphragm was in her purse, she did not use it, in part because she suspected it was no longer the right size. She started to think about this, the size question, but at that moment Victor gave her a monitory squeeze, and, anticipating him, she began to come.

Afterward, they peered through the window's louvered plastic blinds at a middle-aged man drinking gin and tonic alone by the pool. Despite the heat, he was wearing a full-length tweed top-coat over his bathing suit like a bath-robe. As they watched, he began lobbing the ice cubes from his drink one by one into the pool, where an inflatable plastic dolphin floated on its side.

'What's he doing?' whispered Martha.

Victor kissed her behind the ear. 'Freezing to death,' he said. Then Martha lay back down and slept.

When she woke, Victor was dressing.

'Time to go?' she asked.

'Have to,' he answered, sitting down on the side of the bed to put on his shoes. He buckled them in silence, then looked at her. 'You staying?'

'For a bit. Kiss me.'

He did, and when the kiss grew lengthy, it was she who broke it.

'So Victor,' she said then, running a hand through her hair. 'Should I take the job those two lizards are going to offer me on Thursday?'

He mimed deep thought. 'Yes,' he said after a moment. 'I think you should.'

'But will I?'

'No,' he said. 'Of course not.'

Martha liked his smile very much, and thinking about it after he left, she fell asleep again.

It was dark when the telephone rang, and as she groped to answer it, she knocked the bedside lamp over. The manager wished to know if she was going to stay the night, since it was nearly eight. She was not. She hung up, then groggily felt her way to the bathroom and switched on the light. It was a blue-white fluorescent, very bright, and it buzzed. Martha was half-dressed when she remembered the dinner date she had made with Katherine and Gregory. She returned to the bedside and called, twice dialling the wrong number before Katherine answered.

'Hi, Kathy, it's me.'

'Well. Madame Curie. You just caught us. How'd it go?'

'They're going to offer me a job.' Martha stooped to turn on the lamp she'd knocked over, but the bulb was broken.

'Marvellous!' said Katherine. 'Are you going to take it?'

'I don't know.'

There was a pause.

'Sounds as if you're considering it though,' said Katherine.

'I don't know. I guess it depends on whether I get used to wearing my sun-glasses to bed.'

'What?'

'Nothing. Listen, I just called to tell you not to wait dinner. I got held up.'

'Oh, don't worry; Gregory and I have already eaten, I'm

embarrassed to say.'

'Don't be silly; I should be embarrassed for not showing up.'

'No, I mean I'm embarrassed because of *what* we ate. We got stoned at my place, and of course there was nothing to eat but these two disgusting TV dinners that I've had sitting in my freezer since I turned vegetarian, which is what? two years?'

Martha had the uncomfortable feeling then that something was passing her by, that something had been decided without her knowing it.

'What?' she said vaguely. 'What are you saying?'

'TV dinners,' said Katherine. 'Gregory insisted.'

'Oh,' whispered Martha. And then she understood that she'd actually been hoping something *would* pass her by, but now it hadn't, and that something was the word 'freezer'.

'Oh my God,' it appeared she was saying. She said it again. She was afraid she was not going to be able to stop saying it.

'What's the matter?' asked Katherine. 'I mean, it's not *that* disgusting.'

Martha closed her eyes for a moment, and in the dark swimming of her head she thought she saw fish. Then she opened them again.

'No, no. Everything's okay. Listen, I've got to go. I'll talk to you later.' And she hung up.

Martha took stock of things. She was sitting on the carpet next to the bed, and one of her hands was bleeding, and the reason it was bleeding was that it had been in a pile of broken light bulb glass. And the lights were not on, and the television was not on.

She stood up, walked over to the television, and turned it on. Walter Cronkite looked at her.. She remembered that one time Walter Cronkite had cried on television because someone had been assassinated – a President, she thought. It was hard to tell what Walter Cronkite was thinking about now. Martha finished dressing and left without turning off the television.

She drove so carefully that the cars behind her honked until she understood what was the matter. She kept the radio on but tuned it to a frequency where there were no stations. From time to time she looked at the lead-lined attaché case on the seat next to her, and as the rhythms of the driving began to take hold, she began to reason.

The vials had been a few inches away from the freezer for about eight hours. The freezer compartment had been plastic, not metal, and had been open at the back. If the vial of iodine 131 had in fact been less than perfectly sealed, it would certainly, in its gaseous state, have contaminated any organic substance in the refrigerator. Ingestion of radio-active material was the most damaging kind of exposure because it was ongoing. It was extremely unlikely that Katherine or Gregory would display any symptoms for ten or fifteen years.

After circling once through the parking lot of Katherine's building to see what was parked there, Martha let herself into the apartment, slipped the night latch to, behind her, put on the protective gloves, and, using a plastic bag in place of a bucket, scrubbed the refrigerator's pristine white interior clean. The soapy water she flushed down the toilet; the bag, gloves, and sponge she put in the lead-lined case. On her way out, she hesitated over the telephone pad until she remembered the pen didn't work. Anyway, her luggage was still there.

On Sunset, though, without actually having decided anything, Martha got directions to the airport. For some reason, all three of the attendants had red bandannas tied around their throats. She was going to ask them why until she remembered what Victor had said about knowing too much; maybe it was some bizarre California death cult.

She turned in the Cordoba at the airport, and when the Avis girl took her Master Charge card, Martha had a sudden horror of signing her name. She longed for the touch of legal tender. 'Let me pay you in cash,' she said, rummaging in her purse for her wallet. But when she found it, she realized she was short, and she ended by signing the charge form after all.

In the terminal, she bought her ticket, then killed the hour until her flight drinking Bloody Marys and feeding quarters to an electronic Ping-Pong game. It was her right hand against her left hand, and her right invariably won. She thought again about calling Katherine, but there was nothing in her luggage she needed right away.

The jet was not full, but she sat next to a seventy-six-year-old Chicano who was flying east to see his son, a school-teacher in Massachusetts. The man had never flown before and tried not to show his fright, but during the turbulence over the Rockies, Martha awoke to find his gnarled hand desperately clutching hers. He did not look at her. They held hands the rest of the way to New York.

Getting into the cab at Kennedy, she gave the driver her address, then fell asleep. When she woke up, they were in Manhattan, driving to the rhythms of Tito Puente on the cabby's cassette recorder. It was morning rush-hour. She imagined her apartment as she had left it three days previously, then knocked on the partition and gave the driver Larry's studio address instead.

The Greenwich Street entrance was locked, so Martha walked around the corner to the back door on Laight and up the four flights of broad wood stairs. She had years ago given up on the elevator, which was prone to stopping between floors. The building itself was at least eighty years old.

The door to the studio was ajar, and the light was on. Martha had not seen Larry for three weeks.

'Hello?' she said, coming in.

He was standing with his back to her, working on a huge canvas that ran the length of the loft and filled the air with the smell of acrylic. He looked briefly, curiously, over his shoulder at Martha, then went on painting.

'Hi, Martha.'

'I didn't call,' she said.

'I know,' he answered, thinking she meant him. He changed brushes and dipped the new one in a can beside his feet. It came out blue, the blue of a Gauloise package. 'But you're here anyway, and I've had a dream about you.'

'Tell me,' she sighed, leaning her back against the wall, then sliding down until she was sitting on the floor. She had left the attaché case at the door.

Larry started filling in an area of the canvas with the brush.

'In this dream,' he began, 'you and I are driving up the West Side Highway. We start from all the way downtown, and I'm at the wheel. The highway is in even worse shape than it was when they closed it – full of holes, and in some places whole sections have collapsed – and we're the only car. You're giving me directions, helping me avoid the dangerous parts. Then, just past the George Washington Bridge, as we get onto the Saw Mill, something zooms out of the sky over New Jersey and splashes into the Hudson. I barely catch it out of the corner of my eye, but I get very excited, asking if you saw it too. You get kind of shifty and evasive. Then I see that you knew it was going to happen.

You turn your head away from me and say: "It's spacemen, but we don't need to worry until they announce themselves over the radio."'

Larry paused, then traded the brush for a ruler and began using it to push the blue paint across the canvas.

Martha put a hand over her eyes.

'Then, next thing I know, we're in Vermont at your parents' summer place. Somehow I understand that they're living in caves under the house and that they're also, at the same time, dead. We're in your room, in bed. You tell me that you've changed your mind now and really do want to have children. I draw back the sheet, and you're enormously pregnant. "Get me a glass of water," you say, and I go down to the kitchen to get it. On the way back upstairs I hear you laughing, and by the time I get up into the hall, you're in hysterics. I come in. You're in labour, and, while I watch, you give birth to passenger pigeons, dodoes, reindeer, pumas, bison, grizzly bears, bald eagles, wild horses, blue whales, condors, orang-outangs. The room is full of animals – their smells, their noises, their movements – and more keep filing out from between your legs. Whooping cranes, alligators, tortoises. It doesn't stop.'

There was a long silence, then Larry said, 'That's the end.'

Martha uncovered her eyes. He had stopped painting, had let his arm drop while he inspected the results, and for a moment Martha privately watched the blue acrylic paint fall from the ruler in slingy furls to the old wooden floor. Then, he turned around to face her, and in the atoms of what has passed between them in this populated world, that look remains fixed forever.

GRANTA

Jorge Ibarguengoitia

The Dead Girls

The Casino del Danzón

For years the Baladro sisters had the idea of opening a third place of business. They were aware that since both their houses, the one on Molino Street and The *México Lindo*, were located within zones of tolerance – that is, red-light districts – a certain type of apprehensive customer was inhibited from visiting for fear of being recognized in such a neighbourhood in the early hours. Serafina Baladro, the younger sister, felt that for this reason Concepción was the perfect town: it was well situated, being twenty kilometers from Pedrones and twenty-three from San Pedro de las Corrientes, and so small and so seldom frequented that its existence was practically a secret from the world.

Hardly a week after Serafina saw Concepción for the first time, Captain Bedoya, her lover at the time, brought news that he had found a lot that was made to order for putting up a building for the business. Twenty-two meters frontage by eighty-eight meters deep. It was owned by two elderly ladies who had to raise the money to put their brother into an institution for the insane run by the Sisters of the Divine Word in Pedrones. The asking price was 33,000 pesos.

Before making a decision, the Baladros consulted a lawyer, *Licenciado* Canales – who held an important post in the state government – regarding possible problems that might arise in obtaining a licence to operate a new business. He assured them that there would be none. This was at the time Governor Cabañas had just taken office, long before anyone could have dreamed he might crack down on prostitution.

Serafina and Arcángela Baladro decided to buy. They put up the money in equal parts and the property appears in the deed in both their names. It should be noted that Captain Bedoya received a commission from the sellers for discovering a customer willing to pay their stiff price, and he collected another commission from the buyers for finding such a reasonable property; he was given 500 pesos of the fee paid to the notary and kept the 1,500 pesos for himself that the sisters gave him to distribute among important persons of the township.

This was accomplished by the middle of February and on the 28th, the Baladros commissioned an architect to draw up plans for 'a whorehouse the like of which had never been seen in these parts.'

The House before the House in Concepción: A History

Señora Eulalia Baladro de Pinto states:

The newspapers wrote that my sisters inherited the business from my father, that my father was notorious in Guatáparo for his dissolute life, and that he was shot by the *federales*. Lies! My father was a respectable shop-keeper who never set foot in a house of ill repute and who did not live in Guatáparo but in San Mateo el Grande, where we were born and where he is still remembered with respect and admiration. He never had trouble with anybody, least of all the *federales*. He died of natural causes in the year 1947 in San Mateo, having confessed and received Communion and, fortunately, without ever knowing that my sisters were involved in a kind of life that would have disappointed him.

My sister Arcángela became the proprietress of a house of vice by accident. She was a money-lender. One of her borrowers defaulted on his loan and she had to take over some of his properties, including a small bar in Pedrones on Gómez Farías Street. She tried various managers for months but each was so dishonest that she had no choice but to run the place herself. She made such a success of it that in a couple of years she was able to open the house on Molino Street in Pedrones. In a short time, it too was famous.

Years after, thanks to a politician friend of hers, she got a license to operate a business in San Pedro de las Corrientes. She came to see me at that time and said, 'I am moving to San Pedro. Would you be interested in taking charge of a little business for me that I have on Molino Street?'

I was married to Teófilo and had all I needed but I was curious to know what sort of business it was. That was the first I knew of what my sister did. I could hardly believe my ears.

'Better dead,' I told her, 'than running one of those places.'

Arcángela took offence and we were not on good terms for years. When I turned her down she made the offer to my sister Serafina. Whatever her faults, Arcángela was always in favour of keeping business in the family. Serafina accepted because she was young and inexperienced, had just been disappointed in love, and was working in a textile factory as a spinner. She took over the house in Molino Street and Arcángela went to live in San Pedro de las Corrientes where she opened the *México Lindo* which was to become the most popular cabaret in the city.

For years it seemed like God was with them. While my husband and I lost everything three times through honest work, my sisters were getting rich off immorality.

Arcángela Baladro states:

The prostitution business is simple. To succeed you must only keep strict discipline.

The girls come down from the rooms at eight o'clock in the evening and file by so that I can make sure they are clean, neatly dressed, and have combed their hair. The man behind the bar sets the cash register on zeros. The juke-box is plugged in and the metal curtain raised. The customers then start arriving. Some, already familiar with the place, go directly to the girls they know, while others feel strange or shy and prefer to have a drink or two until they make up their minds. When I notice that after some time they are still at the bar, I send a girl over to attend to them. Most men will follow the first one who invites them to a table. In my houses it is forbidden for the girls to drink at the bar.

Sometimes, a customer will prefer to wait for a particular girl who is busy working upstairs. Provided he pays for what he drinks he is welcome to stand at the bar as long as he pleases. Sometimes, a group of men will sit at a table without feminine company, which is all right, too. They can do anything they like, as long as they pay. There is one thing I will not permit, however – which is usually done by students – and that is to pick a girl, dance piece after piece with her, and then leave without spending a peso. To prevent this, the juke-box is rigged so that there is an intermission between numbers for a rest and a drink. Everybody has to go back to the tables when a number is over. After each round, the waiter hands the customer a bill and gives the girl a token. The customer is required to pay his bill before leaving, in a nice way, and in cash.

All drinks served in my houses are legitimate. In twenty years nobody has ever been able to say he was not served exactly what he ordered. Even the girls are served what they ask for. If somebody wants rum, a bottle of rum is uncorked, and what goes into the glass is what was originally inside that bottle.

The cabaret has two doors, one to the street and one to the house.

Whoever has paid can leave by the street door. When a customer with a girl feels like spending some time alone with her, he asks to be taken to her room. She will say yes because it is forbidden to say no. The customer pays his bill and the two of them leave the cabaret through the door to the house. This door opens into a hall. Here, at the foot of the stairs, is the room-attendant's table. She tells the customer the price: not all the girls cost the same. The customer pays the attendant and she in turn gives the girl a token and the man a towel. The customer and the girl go upstairs to her room where they may stay for as long as he has paid for. When they are through, they must come down together. This is important, so that the room attendant can be sure that the customer has not mistreated the girl. The customer may, if he wishes, return to the cabaret or he can leave the house by the street door. The girl returns to the cabaret and continues working. A good worker earns three, four, and up to ten tokens a night.

Testimony of the employee Herminia X:

I was born in the village of Encarnación, State of Mezcala. We were very poor. I was the third of eight children. I had a job as a nursemaid when I was fourteen. I earned twenty-four pesos a month.

A woman by the name of Soledad came to my house one afternoon and spoke to my mother. She said she could get me a job as a servant in Pedrones where I would get food, a room, and two hundred pesos a month. My mother wanted me to go that night. There were two other girls in the bus who were also to work as servants. When we got to Pedrones, we slept in Señora Soledad's house. I knew as soon as I went into that house that this family was not like other families because there were women standing around in the hall in their slips. Señora Serafina accepted me but not the other two girls who left with Señora Soledad and I never saw them again. Señora Serafina took me upstairs to a room and said, 'This will be your room. You can keep your things here and have nothing to worry about.'

As soon as she said this she went off and left me in the room by myself. I sat there for a long time and didn't dare to go out. In the afternoon, Señora Serafina opened the door. I was frightened because there was a man with a mustache with her.

'This Señor is a very good friend of the house.' Señora Serafina said. 'His name is Don Nazario. He wants to see if you've been broken in yet.'

(A detailed description follows of her first experience which is harrowing. She says that she suffered terribly in the beginning but that she became used to it and even got to enjoy the life. She says she earned many red and blue tokens and owned as many as fourteen dresses at one time. She complains that no matter how much she made it was never enough to pay off what Serafina deducted for room, board, the clothes she bought, and the two hundred pesos Serafina was sending to her mother each month – the declarant and her mother were never in touch by mail because the former did not know how to write or the latter how to read. She also complains that the two hundred pesos never reached her mother. She found this out eight years later when she met her by chance in a market. She says that she never wanted to see her family for fear that they would be ashamed of her because of what she had become.)

Testimony of Juana Cornejo, known as The Skeleton:

I met the Señoras Baladro by accident. I lived on a farm and needed money because my little girl was ill. I went to Pedrones to look for work and walked from house to house knocking on the doors until I came to the one where Señora Arcángela opened. She said to me, 'Sure, there is work in this house but not for a servant. If you are willing to be a whore I have a job for you.'

The new house in Concepción was named The *Casino del Danzón* and it was opened by the Baladros on the night of September 15, 1961, the anniversary of Mexico's independence. Among those attending the celebration were: *Licenciado* Canales, the private secretary of the Governor of the State of Plan de Abajo; *Licenciado* Sanabria, the private secretary of the Governor of the State of Mezcala; Congressman Medrano; one railway union leader and two peasant leaders; the manager of the San Pedro de las Corrientes branch of the Mezcala Bank; a number of businessmen; and the proprietor of a stable of over a hundred cattle. Two of the three invited mayors arrived at two in the morning, immediately after officiating the Independence Day ceremony in their respective townships. The Baladros had reached the pinnacle of their social career, of which they were unaware because they assumed other heights remained for them to scale.

At midnight – the fiesta started somewhat late – the doors of the balcony opened and Arcángela stepped out, a bell in her hand, together with *Licenciado* Canales, who carried his country's flag. Arcángela rang the bell to attract the attention of those below and everybody applauded. When there was silence, *Licenciado* Canales waved the flag and pronounced the following version of the traditional Cry of Independence: *Viva* Mexico! *Viva* national independence! *Viva* the heroes who won us our liberty! *Viva* the Baladro sisters! *Viva* the *Casino del Danzón*!

Licenciado Canales's words were received with shouts of approval.

(This was the first incident. Congressman Medrano and one of the peasant leaders were of the opinion that *vivas* jointly for the national heroes and the Baladro sisters constituted a blasphemous juxtaposition and brought word of the incident to the ears of Governor Cabañas who at once dismissed *Licenciado* Canales from his post and broke off their friendship, thereby removing the only influence the Baladros had at the State House of Plan de Abajo.)

At the opening, the Baladros, wearing evening gowns for the first time in their lives – Serafina describes her dress as iridescent – received their guests in the dining room, and waited until everyone had arrived before moving into the cabaret. The decorations made an impressive and unforgettable impact. When the exclamations had died down, the girls entered, elegantly dressed and coiffured. Serafina then announced that everything was on the house for the evening, a statement occasioning some confusion: the guests assumed that 'everything' included the girls, whereas the girls assumed that as nobody was paying they were under no obligation to work.

After the 'Cry of Independence', witnesses say, Arcángela led the guests to the Baghdad Salon where the 'show', in which three women participated, was presented for the first time. Several of the spectators grew over-excited and would have joined the spectacle had Arcángela not stopped them. When everybody had returned to the cabaret, the dancing began, and the second incident occurred.

What happened was this: *Licenciado* Sanabria, who had never been suspected of equivocal tendencies, was suddenly overcome by a murky passion and felt impelled to dance with Ladder, the taxi driver, who had just come to deliver a message. The two men danced a *danzón* entitled 'Nerëidas' from start to finish in front of a horrified assemblage – nobody else daring to dance. At the end, Ladder thanked his partner and left. *Licenciado* Sanabria then tried to dance with various other gentlemen who declined his invitation. He realized, finally, that he had cut a sorry figure and held a grudge ever after against all who had witnessed his disgrace and against the Baladros in particular for having been instrumental in his succumbing to temptation. This ill-will is to play an important part in the story, as will be seen later.

The major snag, however, was the following:

Something got into Governor Cabañas. Something caused him to do what no one had ever dreamed of trying in the one hundred and forty years of independent government: the banning of prostitution.

The various reasons offered to account for this mystery are like branches originating in a single root: Cabañas was the most stubbornly ambitious governor in the history of the state of Plan de Ayala. His provincial predecessors were all played out by the time they took office. Governor Cabañas, on the other hand, came to the governorship fresh and determined to attain new heights in his career. The fact that he was the very first native son of Plan de Abajo to govern the country in some one hundred and twenty years served only to kindle the idea that he was presidential timber.

He reorganized the state government along the lines of a small-scale republic – for instance, the Tax Office was renamed the Ministry of the Treasury or the Board of Improvements became the Ministry of Public Works. He was out to show that, as a brilliantly capable leader of a mini-nation, he would likewise be a brilliantly capable leader of the larger one, if only the powers-that-be would give him the chance.

Besides changing the names of departments, Cabañas embarked on a number of monumental and expensive public works – a state office building, a highway, a tunnel – which produced an enormous deficit. As a consequence, Cabañas had to increase taxes. To placate the disgruntled – who said that the government was a pigsty undeserving of what it currently received and who complained about everything, from the diameter of the sewer pipes to the inadequate water supply to the plague of vice to which the authorities continually shut their eyes –

he remedied the grievance that cost the least: he decreed that all houses of prostitution throughout the State be closed down.

The Plan de Abajo Moralization Act – banning prostitution, pandering, and even the delivery of soft drinks to a brothel – was presented to the State Congress under the sponsorship of Governor Cabañas, debated for half an hour, and passed unanimously to applause on March 2, 1962.

The Moralization Act was enforced with a stringency unprecedented in the history of the State. By the end of the winter, not a single brothel would remain in operation.

That night, in the dining room, Serafina discussed with Captain Bedoya what they should do in order to vacate the three houses they ran. Arcángela, apparently, took no part in this conversation.

Captain Bedoya asserts that, as all the houses belonging to the sisters were now closed, he advised Serafina to dismiss the employees and devote herself to some other activity.

He says that Serafina refused to take his advice for two reasons. First, because a judge was now involved and he would unquestionably compel her to give each dismissed girl separation pay. Secondly, *Licenciado* Rendón was going to take legal steps to revoke the closure order since he considered it unjustified and certainly not final, and had promised her that in two months' time or three, at the most, she and her sister would be reopening.

After dismissing the idea of getting rid of the girls, Serafina and the Captain discussed what to do with them until they were back in operation. They considered various possibilities: putting up the twenty-six women at a hotel, which was rejected because of the expense; distributing them among various whorehouses of the region, which Serafina vetoed because of the risk that the hospitable procurers might refuse to return them later on. The solution finally adopted was illegal but very simple: to move out and then quietly move back in. They decided to bring the girls from all their houses to the *Casino del Danzón*, which had fifteen rooms and all the conveniences, and where they could spend two or three months without anybody being the wiser. The seals would not have to be broken because they could enter the building by crossing over from the roof of the house next door which belonged to Señora Agustina Benavides, a kind-hearted lady who would be incapable of refusing the Baladros a favour.

In a short time Señora Serafina Baladro and her neighbour Señora Agustina Benavides had made an oral agreement in which the latter would permit Eustiquio Natera (known as Ticho) to break through the wall between the vestibule of her house and the dining room of the Baladro house so as to permit persons in number 85 Independencia Street to have access to number 83 without having to jump across the roofs. In consideration for this favour, Señora Baladro agreed to pay Señora Benavides the sum of two hundred pesos on the first day of each month.

Another agreement was also made on that date in which Señora Benavides would permit the said Eustiquio Natera to connect a wire to her electrical service in order to pass current to the house next door. Twenty pesos.

Both agreements were kept by the two parties for the thirteen months that elapsed between the time they were entered into and the day Captain Teódulo Cueto found the bodies buried in the yard.

My name is Radomiro Reyna Razo. I am a native of Concepción. I am the person who sold *Los Pirules* farm to the Baladro sisters but I would like to point out that when I signed the deed I had no idea who they were or what line of business they were in and I certainly never imagined what they were going to do on the property I sold them.

What happened was this. I had to pay back a loan and did not have the money, so I decided to sell off part of my properties. I made this intention known to a number of people and one day, Captain Bedoya, whom I knew by sight, came over to me in the bar of the Gómez Hotel and said to me, 'How much commission will you pay if I get you a buyer for that land you are interested in selling?'

I made him an offer, he accepted, and two days later the Señoras Baladro arrived at my house in a taxi.

Nobody would ever have taken them for procuresses. On the contrary, they looked so respectable that I invited them into my lounge and introduced them to my wife. They were dressed in black. The older one, who had the greater authority, wore a shawl, as if she were going to spend the rest of the afternoon in church. She kept an eye on her sister as if she were a maiden. When the younger one crossed her leg, the older one said, 'Serafina, cover yourself.' And the other one tugged on her skirt until she got it down over her knee.

They made such a good impression on my wife that she served them vermouth and biscuits which they accepted. They drank in a very refined way and did not get drunk or use foul language. Then, I offered to drive them out to the property and my wife came along. Who would have believed we were riding, my wife and I, in the same car with two procuresses?

The day we signed the deed, they arrived at the notary's office carrying a brown paper bag with grease stains on it out of which they took fifty thousand pesos in five-hundred bills. Captain Bedoya was present but he made a sign to me not to pay him his commission in front of the Señoras. We went outside on some pretext and I gave him the money.

After the signing, when they and the Captain had left, the notary, who knew them, told me what kind of women I had been dealing with. But, it was too late, the papers were already signed, I had the money in my hand, and I really needed it.

Eulalia Baladro de Pinto (the third Baladro sister) states: Teófilo, my husband, had just lost everything we had in the world for the third time. When my sisters' letter arrived, the *Licenciados* were confiscating the front room furniture. The letter said:

> Dear Eulalia,
> Since the business that has been giving us our livelihood for so many years is getting more and more troublesome all the time to operate, we have decided to go in for farming. We would like your husband Teófilo, who knows so much about farms, to manage ours for us, etc....

The letter was written by Arcángela but signed by both her and Serafina. Teófilo and I saw a ray of hope in this and the next day we packed our things and went to Concepción.

When we saw the farm for the first time, it was the beginning of the rainy season and the corn was sprouting – Eulalia Baladro de Pinto says – but the place seemed very desolate to me. (She describes the farm-house, the ruined barn, the shed falling to pieces, and the depression that gripped her when, as she looked around, she realized there was not another inhabited house as far as the eye could see.)

Teófilo drew up a plan – Eulalia explains – of what had to be done on the farm to make it productive and estimated what it would cost. The plan sounded good to my sisters but they considered the price very high. They gave my husband less than half the money he needed, and in dribs and drabs. He was able to fix up the house with that amount but could not connect the water or electricity. He managed to repair the barn but there was no money to buy cows and he could plant only corn but not alfalfa. And, in place of essentials, they gave us something we did not need.

One morning, my sisters arrived at the farm with a long package wrapped in newspapers. Arcángela put it on the kitchen table and told Teófilo to open it. It was a rifle.

'I brought it for you,' she said to Teófilo, 'to use on anybody who tries to steal our cows.'

There weren't any cows ever, then or later.

On July 14, the Baladro sisters made a picnic on *Los Pirules* farm. They invited a priest to bless the land just purchased and to baptize it with its new name – formerly, it was called *El Pitayo.* The list of guests who attended the picnic suggests the change in the Baladro fortunes. Instead of local congressmen, mayors, labour leaders, and bank managers, those present were Captain Bedoya, a subaltern of his named Brave Nicolás, Ladder (the taxi-driver), Ticho (formerly the bouncer), and Teófilo Pinto. Fifteen girls were also there. While they were waiting for the priest to arrive, the men and women formed teams and got up a soccer game with a ball Ladder had in the trunk of his car.

After the priest left – to officiate at a christening – the guests opened bottles and toasted the occasion. The food was late – red *mole* prepared by The Skeleton, the rice by Eulalia – Ladder played the guitar and the girls sang. It did not rain.

Three days later. Blanca died.

The Story of Blanca
(Blanca X: b. Ticomán, 1936 - d. Concepción, 1963)

The sand in Ticomán is white and soft, and your feet sink into it as you walk. The beach is spacious. A stony creek flows by it into the sea. As far back as memory goes, the locals have dug wells in the creek bed during the dry season. The Ticomán people are inlanders and ignore the sea. The men work the corn-patches on the slopes of the hill; the women feed the pigs in the corrals. Nobody knows how to swim; nobody ventures into the sea; nobody expects anything from it. The sea's only use is in its driftwood. The Ticomán people wait for it to be swept down the creek during the rainy season and for the waves to cast it up later on the beach.

Two white cliffs can be seen in the distance along this neglected sea and, beyond that, ships continually pass without ever stopping.

The families are large. When the men get drunk they talk about going elsewhere to work. When the boys grow up, they leave. Most of the females remain, but not all.

One can imagine Blanca as a little girl doing what the other children of her age did in Ticomán, walking along the beach with a dog, gathering driftwood, drawing water from the well – until an old woman with a shawl took to sitting in a rush-bottom chair by the sea. She saw the child pass carrying an armful of driftwood.

The story now moves from the beach to the annual fair in Ocampo. Many devout people come to this fair to keep their vows to the Virgin of Ocampo: some carry heavy beams on their backs from the hermitage – where the spring of miraculous water is; others walk barefoot over a stretch of cactus leaves; women crawl on their knees across the atrium of the church which has a pumice-stone floor one hundred meters wide. The object is to arrive bleeding before the holy image. It is only in this way can one be sure of forgiveness or that the miracle one has prayed for will be granted.

Many attend this fair not out of religious motives but for its commercial activity. A great variety of things are bought and sold: incense, Easter tapers, silver votive offerings, horses, fighting cocks, a team of oxen, a woman.

At the 1950 Ocampo fair, Jovita X, the old woman who sat in the rush-bottom chair looking out to sea in the afternoons, sold a fourteen-year-old girl named Blanca to Arcángela and Serafina Baladro for three hundred pesos.

According to The Skeleton who witnessed the transaction, it took place in one of the sheds in Ocampo in which the pilgrims were put up. The Baladros inspected the child thoroughly and saw no defect other than discoloured teeth – everybody's teeth are discoloured in Ticomán because of the water they drink from the wells in the creek bed. The teeth became a bargaining point. Señora Jovita was asking four hundred pesos.

Something took place that day which, as The Skeleton recalled many years later, had all the ear-marks of a bad omen. What happened was this. A pair of sisters came to the same restaurant where the Baladros had their meals while in Ocampo. They were with their father who was there fulfilling a vow. Serafina, on the lookout for girls for the Molino Street house, noticed that these two were pretty, and, taking advantage of a moment when their father was not there, struck up a conversation. Serafina told them that she owned a shoe-shop in Pedrones and needed sales-girls. She offered them room and board and two hundred pesos a month. The prospect of living in Pedrones apparently appealed to the girls and they promised to give her an answer the next day – that is, the day the Baladros bought Blanca.

After closing the Blanca deal, the Baladros took her to the restaurant. The four of them – The Skeleton was the fourth – were on the second course, the rice, when the man who was keeping the vow arrived accompanied this time not by his two daughters but by two policemen who arrested Serafina. She was held in the municipal jail for twenty-four hours on the charge of attempted corruption of minors. Arcángela had to pay two hundred fifty pesos to get her out. The omen – The Skeleton explains – was that Blanca's first day with them ended in the first night Serafina spent in a jail.

Blanca's character:

Even though she was separated from her family under false pretences, sold for a price, and initiated into prostitution at the age of fourteen, everything seems to indicate that she was happy.

It is not known what Señora Jovita might have promised Blanca – or what she promised the mother and the mother promised Blanca – that induced her to accompany her for four hundred kilometers, the distance between Ticomán and Ocampo. Most likely, however, the promise was not kept. Nevertheless, when the deception was exposed and the Baladros were inspecting Blanca amidst the cots in the pilgrims' shed, the child showed no signs of surprise or embarrassment – The Skeleton says admiringly – and accompanied the Baladros without a word when Señora Jovita told her to 'go along with the Señoras.' Similarly her appetite was unaffected when the policemen took Serafina, Blanca being the only one who went on to eat the dessert. Several days later at the *México Lindo* when Arcángela explained her duties – the moment, according to The Skeleton, when many begin to cry – Blanca answered impassively, 'Whatever you say, Señora.' In all Blanca's years as a prostitute, The Skeleton recalls much praise but not a single word of complaint.

She used various names, being listed in the State of Mezcala Venereal Disease Registry as María de Jesús Gómez, María Elena Lara, Pilar Cardona, Norma Mendoza, and, finally, under the name she kept until her death and by which she is remembered to this day: Blanca Medina.

(The only reason she did not keep changing her name, The Skeleton observes, was not because she wouldn't have liked to, but because Dr Arellano, who was in charge of the Registry, got annoyed and told her quite angrily that this name changing of hers had to stop.)

That she assumed such a variety of names seems to be related to certain aspects of her personality, which, despite its simplicity, had many facets. Those who knew her say that her great talent and the secret of her success lay in her ability to project instantly the qualities that each man expected without himself realizing it. This explains the contradictions in the accounts given by her admirers. She made one of them wait for her at the bar, alone, while she sat at a table, also alone, making believe that she was waiting for 'a suitor' who did not exist and, of course, never arrived. Finally feigning vindictiveness towards this man, she summoned the one at the bar, took him to her room, and delivered herself in a kind of erotic catalepsy that he considered sensational. In contrast, with another man, a lawyer, she tore his necktie in the act of undressing him, pushed him violently back on the bed, and threw herself on top of him. He, likewise, was a satisfied customer.

Some say she was an attentive listener who patiently heard out all the stories she was told no matter how long-winded they were. Others describe her as talkative. The Whoremaster, for example, says that each time he visited her over a period of several months, she related a new episode in a story she had made up. What most impressed The Whoremaster, however, was that simultaneously Blanca was telling a completely different story, also made up, to a friend of his who was frequenting her during this same period. On the other hand, a mining engineer who had been with Blanca just once, relates that they had a memorable tussle lasting a couple of hours during which she did not utter a word.

The other girls she worked with remember her with admiration and affection. Although she earned more than any of them, she aroused no envy. She would recommend the services of her less-favoured companions and if a good opportunity presented itself, she would not hesitate to stand aside. Nobody can recall her ever getting into a hair-pulling match with any of the girls out of jealousy or greed. She gave away clothing that was still in good condition. The Baladros and The Skeleton adored her.

It is known that Blanca felt inhibited about only one thing, her discoloured teeth. This prompted the acquisition of the only luxury she ever permitted herself. After saving for years, she went to the best dentist in Pedrones who replaced her four upper incisors with gold teeth. Although Blanca's appearance must have been changed by this innovation, it does not seem to have disfigured her at all. According to The Whoremaster, who knew her with her discoloured teeth, without them - while she was waiting for the new ones to be put in - and with her gold teeth, he was not sure which way he liked her best. The glitter of gold only accentuated her exotic beauty: Blanca was black.

This is the story Blanca told The Whoremaster:

Blanca said that one day while she was out for a stroll she sat down on a bench in the square. A man she regarded as very handsome walked by. Then, he walked by again, and again, and finally sat down on a bench across from hers. He kept looking at her. Blanca went back to the house without his venturing to speak. The next day, Blanca returned to the square and the same man passed back and forth. He ended by sitting down and looking at her again. On the third day, he approached her, told her he was a professional soccer player, and wanted to know who she was. She told him she was a waitress. He proposed marriage. She told him that would be impossible because she had an invalid mother.

Many episodes followed in which the man, who insisted on pursuing her, was about to discover her true profession. For example, he invited her to an oyster bar where, after having drunk several bottles of beer, she did things she can't remember and was later haunted by the fear that during her mental lapse she may have said, 'What the hell! I'm a whore!.' Or else, the man came to the *México Lindo* with his team-mates and she had to hide under a table, etc.

The story ends on the night The Whoremaster came to the cabaret and found Blanca downcast, asked her why, and she told him that the soccer player was dead. She then described, with a wealth of realistic detail, a bloody highway smash-up. Blanca never mentioned the soccer player again after that night and The Whoremaster could not bring himself to ask about him.

Her illness:

In September, 1962 – when the Plan de Abajo brothels were closed – Blanca discovered she was pregnant. It was not the first time. As on previous occasions, she went to The Skeleton for help, who – according to her own statement – prepared an infusion of rue and wormwood leaves which the patient drank hot, one cupful three times a day. This remedy, prepared many times before by The Skeleton and used with excellent results by the women who worked for the Baladro sisters, was considered infallible for inducing an abortion. Blanca took it for two months without effect; she then decided to consult the Baladros. Serafina advised an operation and told her that she and her sister would pay for it.

Doctor Arellano, whose signature appeared on a number of IOUs held by Arcángela, admits that he performed the operation in exchange for his outstanding debts, but only after considerable urging by the sisters in the face of his warning that the abortion would be dangerous because of the advanced stage of pregnancy. He operated on Blanca one day in November with The Skeleton assisting. The operation was not completely successful because the patient hemorrhaged profusely, which the doctor attributed to a hematological imbalance produced by the large quantity of rue and wormwood she had taken. He had to give her eight vitamin K injections before the bleeding finally stopped at eleven o'clock that night, and everybody thought Blanca was saved. The doctor left the house after Arcángela returned his IOUs. Serafina and Arcángela went down to attend to the cabaret and The Skeleton to supervise the rooms. The patient remained in her room, asleep. The next morning when The Skeleton opened the door and went in, carrying a glass of orange juice, she noted that Blanca's features looked twisted. On closer inspection it was apparent that the entire left side of her body was paralysed.

Doctor Arellano refused to visit the patient. As a consequence, Serafina called in Doctor Abdulio Meneses over the objections of Arcángela who was afraid of the cost and possible complications. He examined Blanca and after asking a number of awkward questions about how the illness started – which must have received even clumsier answers – decided that she should be moved to his private hospital for intensive treatment.

Blanca was admitted on December 4, 1962 to the Sacred Heart Sanatorium which had the reputation of being the best in the region. Serafina Baladro's name appears on the admission record as her closest relative and the person responsible for all bills. Several of the girls came to visit her on the 5th and the 6th and found her much improved. The Whoremaster brought her a bunch of red roses on the 7th and was unable – according to one of the nurses present – to control a grimace of horror at seeing her so deformed. On the 11th, Doctor Meneses, having decided that Blanca's bill would never be paid, ordered treatment to be suspended and the patient discharged.

The record of her discharge from the Sacred Heart Sanatorium gives the impression that the patient was picked up by relatives. There is an illegible signature on the slip. That same day, Blanca was admitted to the San Pedro de las Corrientes Municipal Hospital under the name of María Méndez – the only one she ever bore in her life that she had not invented – with no indication on the admittance slip of next of kin or attending physician.

The Whoremaster went to visit Blanca in January and the receptionist at the Sacred Heart Sanatorium informed him that the patient had been discharged and picked up by relatives. The Whoremaster assumed that Blanca must have recovered and was back with the Baladros and so did not look for her any further. He felt certain that the sisters would soon reappear in a new place either in San Pedro or some other town in the region and that, being one of their steadiest customers, he would be notified whenever that happened.

The Baladros, however, in their distress over the closing down of the houses and the tumult of moving, forgot about Blanca for a time. When they finally remembered her, they assumed that she was still at the Sacred Heart Sanatorium with a huge bill that Serafina had accepted the responsibility of paying. This was the reason they made no attempt to visit her or to check up on how she was doing.

Finally, in March, the Whoremaster had to make a trip to Concepción to collect a bill – he is an automobile salesman. After taking care of his business, in an upsurge of erotic nostalgia he decided to have a look at the outside of the *Casino del Danzón.* He left his car near the square, walked to Independence Street, and was standing before the sealed door when to his surprise, The Skeleton, on her way to buy lard, came out of the adjoining house. They embraced like the old friends they were and The Skeleton told him two lies – that she was coming from a visit to an old acquaintance, Señora Benavides, and that the other girls were all living in Muérdago. When The Whoremaster asked about Blanca, she told him that she was at the Sacred Heart Sanatorium.

That is how it came out that Blanca had disappeared. As they were strolling together towards the butcher shop, The Whoremaster got the idea of notifying the police. The Skeleton begged him not to – in explaining why it was necessary to be so discreet, she was compelled to tell him where the Baladros, she, and the other women were living – and The Whoremaster agreed to hunt for Blanca on his own and if he found her to leave word by telephone at the taxi-stand where Ladder worked.

Three days after this conversation, The Whoremaster found Blanca in the first place he looked: the women's ward of the Municipal Hospital. She did not even remotely resemble the woman he knew. Her mental faculties were impaired and her face so grotesquely distorted that it cost him an effort to believe it was she. The invalid's speech was practically unintelligible because one side of her mouth was paralysed.

The Whoremaster was so upset by the experience that after notifying The Skeleton as he had promised, he wanted to know nothing more of Blanca.

The Skeleton visited Blanca the next day. When the hospital superintendent noticed that the patient Mariá Méndez had a visitor, he called The Skeleton aside, informed her that the woman's condition was hopeless, and asked her to notify her relatives to come and take her away because other patients who could be helped were waiting for a bed.

The day after that, the Baladros arrived at the Municipal Hospital in Ladder's car, signed the necessary papers, and took Blanca to the *Casino del Danzón.*

According to the statements of witnesses, two of the women carried Blanca down from the room in the mornings to the yard where they would leave her to bask in the sun curled up in a galvanized metal bathtub. Later on, they would carry her back up to her room. She was completely emaciated - her only food was the gruel The Skeleton prepared for her - and she gave no sign of understanding what was spoken to her and nobody understood what she herself spoke.

In May, Arcángela, who was constantly complaining of the cost of feeding all those mouths while nothing was coming in, decided that as Blanca was unable to chew anyway, it would be just as well to remove her gold teeth and sell them to compensate in part for all the trouble she was causing. Arcángela entered Blanca's room one morning with that intention and tried to pull out the teeth but the invalid clamped her jaws shut so tightly that after a brief struggle Arcangela gave up.

On July 5th, The Skeleton took a trip to Pedrones to consult a famous healer, Tomasa X, on how to cure paralysis. Tomasa X explained the treatment which is described later and which The Skeleton recommended as being very effective. Back in Concepción, she asked permission from her employers to attempt a cure and it was granted.

(Several days went by when The Skeleton and various of the other women were busy preparing the *mole* that was to be the main dish at the celebration of the blessing of the farm.)

On July 17th, Ticho wired the legs of three tables together and placed them in the middle of the cabaret, chosen by The Skeleton as the most appropriate place for applying the treatment. Ticho then left the house with no idea what was to take place later on. At eleven o'clock, two braziers were lighted and placed on either side of the tables. Marta, Rosa, Evelia, and Feliza, acting as The Skeleton's assistants, placed six irons to heat on the braziers as The Skeleton rubbed the invalid's body with a tincture of the bark of the *casaguate* tree. The assistants tied the patient to the tables with two sheets. The Baladro sisters watched the treatment from the balcony of the cabaret. The assistants covered the patient's body with a light flannel blanket. Marta, a pitcher of water in her hand, was in charge of wetting the blanket to which The Skeleton applied the hot irons; Rosa changed the irons as they cooled; Evelia and Feliza held the patient down when she writhed.

The prescription was the following: apply hot irons to the dampened blanket on the paralyzed side of the patient until the blanket turns dark brown.

In the beginning, it seemed that the treatment was working. Not only were the invalid's screams more coherent than her speech had been in the last few months, but, it was also noted that when the irons were applied, she moved muscles that had been inert for a long time. Afterwards, the invalid fainted. The women tried to bring her around by giving her Coca-Cola but it was impossible to make her swallow it, the liquid dribbling out between her lips. The Skeleton hesitated momentarily about whether or not to continue the treatment. She decided to go on with it and kept applying the irons until the blanket turned dark brown as specified by Señora Tomasa. They tried giving her Coca-Cola again but without success. On lifting the blanket off the patient's body they were surprised to see that her skin was stuck to the cloth.

'Cover her up! Cover her up!' Serafina screamed from the balcony, they say.

One of the women ran for another blanket. The others untied the invalid. After covering her, they carried her to her room and put her to bed. She did not regain consciousness. The girls and the Baladros stayed with her until midnight, the hour when she stopped breathing.

Various Views

María del Carmen Regulez states in regard to that day, that after breakfast The Skeleton told her and three of the other girls: 'Go out for a walk, take your time, stop in at the market, stay a while, and look over the vegetables. Don't come back before five o'clock.'

She gave each of them one peso for food. These orders surprised the girls but they obeyed. As they were walking along Cuauhtemoc Street they went by a garage where three boys who knew them worked. On seeing them pass, the boys followed 'making vulgar remarks'. They kept on walking to the edge of town and then headed toward the reservoir where the boys caught up and 'took advantage of them' behind some bushes. After a bite to eat in the market, they took turns around the square until it got to be five o'clock.

When they returned to the *Casino del Danzón*, they went to the kitchen with the idea of letting The Skeleton know they were back. There was no one there. There was no sign of food. The fire had not been made. And there was no charcoal on the grates.

María del Carmen went out to the yard to take in the clothes she had hung on the line. She noticed that Blanca's tub was not under the lemon tree but next to the cabaret door which was closed.

When she returned to the kitchen she found several of the other girls there who had also just got back. Eleven women went out that day – something that rarely happened.

She says that when she got upstairs she heard voices in Blanca's room and was very curious but did not dare go in because she thought she recognized the voices of the Baladros among them; that she stayed in her room for a while and, then, on hearing a noise in the hall that she opened the door a crack and saw Arcángela and The Skeleton walking towards the stairs: that she heard Arcángela say, 'It was all your fault!'

Ticho states, with reference to the events that took place that night and the day before, that after tying the legs of the tables together and putting them where The Skeleton told him, he asked for permission to go to work. (After the *México Lindo* was closed, the Baladros stopped Ticho's salary and he had to take odd jobs loading and unloading trucks and carrying goods.)

He relates that he went to the Barajas Brothers' warehouse and was shifting crates of tomatoes, baskets of chilli-peppers, and sacks of potatoes from rooms that had leaks to dry ones, that he knocked off at two o'clock and went across the street to the market for a giblets taco, that he returned to the warehouse and was carrying until eight o'clock at night, when the boss called a halt and paid him the twenty pesos he had been promised.

He states that when he returned to the *Casino del Danzón* there was nobody around to notify that he was back – that is to say, neither the Baladros nor The Skeleton – that he went into the kitchen, saw there was no dinner, and then went to the charcoal bin in which he lived. He lay down on the cot and fell asleep.

He states: I couldn't say what time I woke up. The Skeleton was at the door holding an oil lamp. I said, 'My little Skeleton' and started to lift her skirt. But she didn't want to. She just said, 'Come with me' and left. I thought she was going to give me some dinner and so I followed her but instead of going into the kitchen she went out to the yard where she stopped and said to me, 'Get a pick and shovel out of the shed.'

When I came back The Skeleton walked off and I followed. We got as far as the other end of the yard (the northwest corner) where she put the lamp down on the ground and said to me, 'I want you to do a job without making any noise.'

(She ordered him to dig a rectangular hole two paces long by one pace wide and deep enough so that when he stood up in it his armpits would be on a level with the ground. After giving these directions, The Skeleton went back to the house. Ticho dug easily in the soft earth until his pick began hitting stones and Arcángela and The Skeleton came out of the house and told him to stop. The hole was hardly a meter deep. Ticho goes on to say: 'Señora Arcángela said, "Leave it at that. It's better than to risk waking the neighbours."')

The Skeleton took me to the kitchen, made me a fried egg, and gave me a mug of orange-leaf tea with a shot of alcohol in it. I said, 'My little Skeleton' again and she didn't want to again so I went back to sleep.

It was getting light when I woke up. The Skeleton was at the door with the lamp. I said 'My little Skeleton' but she pushed my hand away and again said, 'Come with me.'

We went to the other end of the yard. I saw that somebody had shovelled earth into the hole I made, filling it about half full.

'I want you to finish filling in this hole' – The Skeleton told me – 'and to tamp it down good with the *mezquite* stump. And, now, get this, if there is any dirt left over, I want you to spread it around the yard with the shovel so that nobody will notice that there was ever a hole there.'

I did the job just as I was ordered. By the time The Skeleton saw the hole filled, the earth tamped down, and the left-over spread around the yard, it was broad daylight. She took me to the kitchen and gave me a plate of cracklings she just prepared for breakfast. While I was eating them, one of the girls came into the kitchen and asked The Skeleton how Blanca was doing. The Skeleton answered that she took so sick that they had to sent her to the hospital again. That was when I got the idea of what it was I had been doing all night.

Captain Bedoya states:

July the 17th sticks in my mind because it was a very hectic day. Major Marín, who brought the pay-roll, arrived two days late at the same time as the hay truck which was supposed to have been there by the 20th. I left the camp with barely enough time to rush to the telegraph office before the money-order window closed. (Captain Bedoya bought a fifty-peso draft to the order of Carmelita Bedoya – his little daughter – accompanied by a message that read: 'CONGRATULATIONS FROM DADDY OCCASION YOUR SAINT'S DAY.' It was sent to an address in Mexico City.) From the telegraph office – Captain Bedoya continues – I want to Serafina's.

I found her in the dining room, upset and trembling. I asked what was wrong and she told me that she had had a nerve-wracking day because Blanca took a very bad turn. She looked so jittery that I said good-night to her, had some supper at the Gómez Hotel, and spent the night on the post. The following day, Serafina told me they had to take Blanca to the hospital.

I said, 'The Municipal Hospital, I hope.'

She answered that, as a matter of fact, the Municipal Hospital was exactly where they had taken her.

Captain Bedoya had always considered it insanity for the Baladros to be spending money on Blanca. When they hospitalized her in Doctor Meneses's sanatorium, several witnesses heard him make the following comment: 'It's throwing away money. Maybe that woman will be able to walk again someday but nobody is ever going to fix that face of hers and what good is a whore that gives you the horrors to look at?'

When Blanca was finally brought back to the *Casino del Danzón* from the hospital, Serafina preferred to say nothing to the Captain, until one day he went out to the yard and found the paralysed woman lying in the bathtub under the lemon tree.

'What's this?' they say he asked several of the women who were nearby.

The told him it was Blanca. The Captain then said, 'That woman is no good any more. What they ought to do is have Ticho carry her out to the garbage dump one of these nights and leave her there for the dogs to eat.'

Captain Bedoya says: I woke up in a good mood the next morning, put on my underwear shorts and a *guayabera* shirt, and went out to the back of the house to breathe in some fresh morning air. It was a day without clouds as in the dry season. As I was looking up at the sky I saw the vultures. There were two of them and they were flying in circles around a spot that seemed to be right over my head.

I swear I am an atheist, but I got such an awful feeling I crossed myself.

Extract from the confrontation between Aurora Bautista and Eustiquio Natera, known as Ticho, during the investigation:

Aurora Bautista: Isn't it true that when you were carrying a sack of charcoal into the house one day, Doña Arcángela said to you, 'Cut off a *cazahuate* branch and drive off those goddam birds that are walking around in the yard?'

Ticho: I do not recall that occasion.

Aurora Bautista: And don't you remember that you chopped off a handful of branches from the bush and that you went over to where the vultures were and scared them off and that they flew around for a while and then landed back on the ground in the same place again?

Ticho: I have chased off vultures more than once in my life. Which time is it you want me to remember?

Aurora Bautista: The time that Doña Serafina couldn't stand it any more, went for her pistol, gave it to you, and said, 'Shoot the damn things!' And then Doña Arcángela came out to the back and said to you, 'What are you people trying to do, scare the neighbours?' Do you remember, now?

Ticho: It must have been somebody else who was there at the time.

Aurora Bautista: And I suppose you weren't the one either who was in the kitchen with The Skeleton, Luz María, and me when Captain Bedoya came in and asked for a glass of water and then after he drank it he said, 'I wonder where that stink could be coming from.' And The Skeleton said, 'It must be that dead dog next door.' Weren't you the one who was sitting there then eating a tortilla?

(Ticho gave evasive answers to this question and the following ones Aurora Bautista put to him.)

Isn't it true that you came in one day with a can and Doña Arcángela asked you how much the gasoline cost?

Don't you remember the night you took the pick and shovel and dug a hole in the rear of the yard?... and later that night you made a fire that burned for a long time and the next morning the air smelled foul?

Ticho: I think you must have dreamed what you are saying. It never happened.

Martial Law

Every year on the 24th September, one of the girls, María del Carmen Régulez, visited her mother, whose name was Mercedes.

Every year, two evenings before that date, María del Carmen would ask Serafina for permission to miss work on the night of the 24th and Arcángela for money from her account or, if the balance was low, as an advance. María del Carmen states that she had never had any problems. She always got permission from Serafina and money from Arcángela. On the 23rd, María del Carmen would go to the market where she would buy a bunch of flowers – gladiolas, preferably – which always withered by the time they reached her mother's outstretched arms. The trip always started at dawn because María del Carmen had to change buses three times to reach the *rancho* where her family lived. She would get off the third bus at a point half-way up a bleak hill and walk along a barely distinguishable foot-path until she came to a *pitayo* tree. The houses and the cactus patch of the settlement could be seen from there.

The dogs would forget María del Carmen from one visit to the next and every year her mother and sisters-in-law would come out of the kitchen to quiet them; every year on finding themselves together again, the women would cry; every year they would go into the kitchen, sit around the brazier, and talk – someone had died, a baby had been born, the crops had been lost. The men would return from the fields in mid-afternoon, the family would sit down at the table, María del Carmen helped wait on them. Only her mother knew about her daughter's profession – she was the one who had sold her – the rest of the family thought she was a servant. At night they would drink orange-leaf tea spiked with alcohol and get drunk. The next day at dawn, María del Carmen started back to the whorehouse.

On September 22nd of that year, María del Carmen asked Serafina for permission to go to the *rancho* and, for the first time, it was refused.

'My sister has decided,' she told her, 'that nobody can go out except the girls The Skeleton takes with her to bring the food from the market.'

She did not explain the reason for this prohibition, nor did she tell her how long it would last. María del Carmen did not dare ask questions on either point because like all the Baladros' employees she was afraid of them. She did, however, tell the other women that Serafina had forbidden her to go to the *rancho* and that only the girls who went to market with The Skeleton – they were always the same two – could leave the house. These conversations repeated over and over again in the lethargic atmosphere of the inactive brothel made the eleven women, denied the privilege of going out, feel as though they were prisoners. And, what is more significant, they were united.

Rosa X and Marta X were the two girls who went out with The Skeleton to buy the food.

Rosa's name appears in the San Pedro de las Corrientes Anti-venereal Register, successively, as Margarita Rosa, Rosa de las Nieves, and Maria del Rosal. At the whorehouse she was called just Rosa. She had a reputation for being meek and servile. When the whorehouse opened in the evening – those who worked with her say – she was always the first girl down from her room to pass inspection by the madam – either Serafina or Arcángela, she worked for them both. If any fault was found – flaking nail polish or a hair bow that did not go with the colour of her dress – Rosa would go back to her room without grumbling – something no other girl did – and try to correct it. In the closed-down whorehouse, it was known that Rosa could be counted on to do the hardest, the most disagreeable, or the most unnecessary jobs, such as cleaning the caked outside of greasy pots or carrying the heaviest basket from the market.

She also had the reputation for being two-faced and an informer. This reputation had its basis in two incidents. On one occasion, a drunken customer took his wrist-watch off and left it on the table, and the woman sitting with him picked it up and hid it away. Rosa was the only person who saw her do this. Arcángela intervened and before the evening was over compelled the girl to return the watch and slapped a fine on her that took months to pay off. On another occasion, Carmelo X, a waiter in the Molino Street house, worked out a system for cheating Serafina which consisted of giving out tokens for fictitious drinks to various of the girls who were in with him; they handed in the tokens to Serafina, collected their commissions, and split with Carmelo. This lasted until he made the mistake of inviting Rosa into his organization. The next day he was fired.

Aside from being servile and two-faced, Rosa had no other virtues. Her complexion was sallow and she suffered from a permanent cold – The Skeleton said that every time she blew her nose it sounded like a bugle – and she wore an unending expression of martyrdom. Any man who approached her was either very drunk or unable to see clearly in the dim light of the cabaret. Those who knew her say that her favourite topic of conversation at the tables was her bad luck – 'life gave me a raw deal' being one of her frequent remarks. Not many customers ventured to go up to Rosa's room and even fewer did so a second time.

The Baladros put up with Rosa for ten and a half years, partly because of her servility and partly because she was an informer, but mainly because they were unable to get rid of her. First, they passed her from one house to the other; then, they tried several times to sell her; but, after seeing her, any potential purchaser would back out. Finally, the Baladros gave up and used her to get rid of troublesome or insolvent customers.

Rosa's earnings were meagre and she piled up the biggest debt that appears in Arcángela's book over the ten years – forty-five thousand, four hundred pesos. It is possible that Arcángela, with an irrationality characteristic of the greedy, cultivated the belief that Rosa might suddenly become attractive one day and begin to pay off all the money she owed the family.

It was Rosa's misfortune that she walked through the hall between the rooms at the wrong hour.

On learning from María del Carmen that nobody was going to be allowed to go out except the two who accompanied The Skeleton, one of the girls, Aurora Bautista, decided to escape from the whorehouse.

She mentioned the idea to three of the other girls and they agreed to go along. They met several times in the room of one of them to make plans. It was decided that the break should be made when everybody was asleep between eleven o'clock and midnight – the time of the last bus to Pedrones. It was impossible to leave the house by the same route as the Baladros because they would therefore need the key to the dining room that hung in Serafina's bosom; to climb over one of the walls meant landing in a strange yard amid unfriendly dogs; the only solution, then, was to use a ladder to reach the roof of the *Casino* and to jump across to the roof of the neighbouring house of Señora Benavide from where they could easily get down to the street level and leave through the front gate which was bolted on the inside.

The house had a ladder that was kept in the shed where Ticho slept. Ticho was known for sleeping like the dead.

On the afternoon the four women were planning their escape from the whorehouse by means of the ladder, they heard a noise in the hall as though somebody might be eavesdropping, and fell silent. Luz María, whose room it was, got up and cautiously opened the door. Nobody was just outside it, but Rosa was several meters away walking down the hall.

For a while, the women weighed the possibility that Rosa had overheard, but reached the conclusion that it was unlikely. However, to be on the safe side, it was decided not to delay and to make the move that same night.

One can imagine their baggage: the string-bags, the cartons tied up with rope. Each made a selection of her prized possessions – the orange-coloured evening dress, the patent leather slippers – taking into consideration the jump that had to be made and the possibility that it might be necessary to run through the streets. They say that they scraped together enough among the four of them to cover the fare to

Pedrones and forty-five pesos extra which they planned to use to keep on travelling as far as possible in a direction away from Concepción.

At night, when everything was quiet, the women, bare-footed, met in the hall, went downstairs, and across the patio. One of them, Luz María, confesses that she picked up a round stone so big she had to carry it in both arms to drop on Ticho's head in case he woke up. They went into the shed which had no door. Ticho did not wake up, but the women, feeling around in the dark, realized that the ladder was not there.

They came out of the shed dismayed and met in the kitchen in the dark, where they held a whispered conference and concluded that Rosa had squealed. They were infuriated.

The subsequent scene must have been as follows: a woman is asleep in a large bed in a dark room; the door opens silently – the Baladros had all bolts removed from the rooms after the whorehouse was closed so that the girls could not lock themselves in; silhouettes cross the threshold against the penumbra; the door closes.

It is not known if Rosa woke up when the others turned on the light, when they pulled the covers back, or when they began to beat her. Nor is it known if the beating took place in the dark or with the light on. Nor if Rosa was struck dumb with fear, if the attackers prevented her from crying out, or if she shouted at the top of her lungs without anybody hearing.

'They gave her the shoe treatment,' says The Skeleton in describing this revenge.

Rosa's wounds were produced by the high heels of the shoes with which the girls beat her.

The following day, when all the women were having breakfast in the kitchen and Rosa did not appear, The Skeleton went up to her room to see if anything was wrong. She heard a groan as she approached her room. Rosa was in bed, semi-conscious, a blanket over her. There were no marks on her face, but her body, particularly the buttocks, were covered with black-and-blue welts and wounds which later became infected and developed into running sores because of lack of attention.

Rosa did not know, or did not want to say, who attacked her. The Baladros had made up their minds to punish this 'disorderly conduct' severely but did not know to whom to attribute it – which indicates that Rosa had not divulged the escape plan and that the ladder was missing from its usual place only by chance.

The woman who served the madams their dinner that afternoon asserts that Captain Bedoya was the one who advised them how to discover who had been involved.

The woman saw the Captain walking around the yard, his head down, stooping every little while to pick up a stone, weighing it in his hand, and making a pile of those that were spherical and neither very light nor very heavy. Then, he went around examining the floors of the house until he found one that seemed most appropriate for the purpose he had in mind. It was a small patio next to the kitchen which was part of the original construction and paved with broken stone embedded in concrete.

The Baladros called the women together in this place and Arcángela said to them, 'Who beat up Rosa?'

There was no answer.

Arcángela ordered the women to kneel on the irregular surface and when they had obeyed, the Captain, who was present from the beginning, ordered them to hold their arms stretched out at their sides, shoulder-high, palms up. When they were all in that position, the Captain and The Skeleton took stones from the pile he had got together and put one in each hand.

When a woman dropped a stone Arcángela struck her with a stick. (This was the first instance of corporal punishment in the history of the *Casino del Danzón*.) The stick used and others had been cut off the *cazahuate* bush by the Captain that same afternoon. They say that the guilty ones confessed in less than fifteen minutes, upon which punishment of the others was suspended.

The Skeleton brought Aurora Bautista, Luz María, María de Carmen, and Socorro into the Baghdad Salon where they were subjected to another punishment also devised by the Captain. It consisted of each in turn beating the other three until all four were so bruised that they were unable to move for days after.

Over the twenty-three years that Captain Bedoya served in the army there is no record of his having administered or ordered the administration of any corporal punishment nor does any soldier who served with or under him recall his ever having been involved in any act of cruelty. When questioned during the trial with respect to his participation in the 'penitance' and the blows the women gave one another, the Captain admitted having thought up both practices. He explained: 'I felt that those women were guilty of an act of insubordination and that they had to be found out and punished as an example to the others.'

'Are you satisfied that the way you acted on those occasions was proper?' the judge asked him.

'Yes, sir.'

Instead of things settling down after the 'lesson', another act of insubordination occurred.

Marta Henríquez Dorantes, the other woman who was allowed to leave the house to go to market with The Skeleton, was in the laundry-shed wringing out clothes when she realized that several of her companions had entered and were standing around her, in silence.

She barely had time to become aware of their presence before they were on top of her. Being four, they overcame her easily. They threw her to the floor, gagged her, and tied her arms and legs together with the wet clothes she had been washing, and stood her up. They then tried to kill her in a strange manner. There was an old outhouse in a far corner that had been in disuse for many years. The women dragged Marta to this building, removed the boards covering the hole, and tried to stuff her in. (The description of this deed leads to the conclusion that the attackers intended to bury their victim alive.) Her fatness saved her. Marta is a very broadly built woman and no matter how hard they tried, her assailants were unable to push her through the opening. They were engaged in the attempt when The Skeleton arrived.

This time the women were not punished; they were segregated. The Baladros decided that the four who had attacked Marta were to be taken to *Los Pirules* farm and shut up in the barn and the four who attacked Rosa should be locked in their rooms.

Considering that holding four women in solitary confinement called for vigilance at night, Captain Bedoya assigned a trusted subaltern – Brave Nicolás – to stand guard, armed, and to be at the orders of the Baladros in case anything came up.

What Teófilo Did

Teófilo Pinto, Eulalia Baladro's husband, is a taciturn individual with the morose expression of a man who has worked honestly all his life without a holiday only to lose everything three times and end up in jail.

In explaining his actions, he stated: as a business *Los Pirules* farm was a failure. My sisters-in-law were to blame because they did not turn the money over to me that they said they would.

They would send Ticho out every Saturday with just the exact amount to cover the payroll. I had to put up the money for any additional expenses out of my own pocket and then keep sending messages with Ticho to get them to pay me back.

The situation was bad enough right along but towards the middle of October it got worse. Saturday came around, midday passed, and no sign of Ticho. The *peones* and I sat on the end of the irrigation ditch, watching the buses go by on the road without stopping to let Ticho and his envelope of money off. By the time the sun was going down, I couldn't stand the embarrassment any longer. I walked back to the house, took the emergency money Eulalia had been saving out of the drawer, came back to where the *peones* were and gave them each ten pesos.

'Be patient, boys,' I told them, 'I'll pay you the balance on Monday.'

They went off, their heads bent, putting the money into their pockets.

The *peones* returned on Monday and worked for a while but when midday came and Ticho did not appear with the money they knocked off and left. They came back Monday and again on Tuesday to collect but I couldn't pay them, so that night they played me dirty.

I had covered the irrigation ditch with fourteen sheets of corrugated roofing paper to keep the water from seeping out and flooding the road. Well, when it looked like there was no hope of ever collecting their wages, they came back during the night and carried off all the cardboard sheets.

When I got up the next morning and looked out of the window, the first thing I saw was the reflection off the water that covered the road. It wasn't hard to imagine who was to blame. You've really got to have it in for a person to come and carry off fourteen sheets of cardboard from such an out-of-the-way place.

I think the *peones* did something to the tractor, too, because on Thursday it stopped in the middle of ploughing and there was no way I could get it started.

I was desperate by the time I got back to the house.

'I have a good mind,' I told my wife, 'for us to pack up, go out on the highway, and get on the first bus that comes by and ride to wherever it takes us, so as never to have to see this place of your sisters again.'

That is what we should have done and didn't.

The following Monday, we were in the kitchen eating when we heard a horn blowing as though somebody was calling for help. We went to the door and saw the blue car my sisters-in-law always used stuck in the mud in the middle of the road. It was crammed with people.

I had to carry over stones and put them in the mud so Arcángela could get out of the car without dirtying her shoes. As soon as she stepped onto dry ground, I began complaining about her not sending the money for the *peones* and told her that they had left. She stopped me.

'Wait a minute,' she said, 'I've got something to tell you that's more important.'

She made me walk a few steps with her to where she thought the people in the car wouldn't be able to hear. 'There are four girls in the car who have behaved very badly,' she said. 'I want to separate them from the others before they get any ideas from them, so I am leaving them here for a few days to cool down!'

It was then that I realized there were four women in the back of the car and they were looking at me in a very strange way. They were scared.

Arcángela gave me various instructions: 'Keep them locked up. Give them whatever you want to eat. If you see any one of them trying to get away, take the rifle, and shoot her.'

The barn on *Los Pirules* farm is a long, narrow room with a cement floor, unfinished cinder block walls and a concrete roof. The door is made of *mezquite* wood and is secured from the outside with a hasp and lock. There are iron bars across the transom set too close together for a body to squeeze between them. Little light filters through.

In preparing the barn, Teófilo removed anything that might be useful for escaping: an iron bar, a stool, a shovel. He left it empty except for a pile of straw and some corncobs.

Teófilo gave the women reed-mats which they laid out on the floor. Although they had brought blankets with them, they suffered from the cold because the transom opening could not be closed and it was a very sharp November – there had been four frosts. All the women were ill but recovered after a few days.

The greatest mystery is how two people as proud and as proper as the Pintos allowed themselves to serve as jailers without putting up the slightest resistance. The answer might lie, at least partially, in the two-thousand peso cheque drawn on Arcángela's account and cashed by Teófilo at the Pedrones bank on November 3rd. There is no evidence that he tried to hire other *peones* after that date. A good part of the land that had been ploughed remained unplanted. Whatever farming was done Ticho was responsible for – the Baladros ordered that instead of carrying sacks he was to go out to the farm every morning 'to see what should be attended to.' It was Ticho who picked the ripened ears of corn, put them into sacks, and brought them into the house; and Ticho who put on rubber boots, took a shovel, and spent the day in the mud seeing to it that the recently sown wheat received water. Teófilo, meanwhile, was obsessed with getting the tractor started, and spent hours cranking and puttering with it, to no avail.

The four women spent three weeks in the barn, during which time, apparently, they were not ill-treated by either Teófilo or Eulalia. Their life was as follows: Teófilo would open the door early in the morning and let them out into the field for a while to do their wants and wash, if they wished, in the pond. After that he locked them up again. At around nine o'clock, he would open the door a second time and Eulalia would enter with dishes of food. The prisoners' breakfast consisted of tortillas, beans, chilli-pepper sauce, and a mug of orange-leaf tea. It was not very filling but neither did it leave them too hungry. Eulalia returned for the dishes which she washed herself. The women spent the rest of the day locked in. At six o'clock in the evening, Teófilo let them out into the field for another spell after which they went back into the barn, had their supper consisting of the same food in the same amounts that they had had for breakfast, and after collecting the dishes, Teófilo locked the door and did not open it again until the next day.

The relations between the Pintos and the women were relatively cordial. Teófilo warned the prisoners: 'There's no quarrel between you and us and we are not enemies. You have to stay here for a while because those are Doña Arcángela's orders. Nobody has it in for you and you won't be lacking for anything here, so just behave yourselves and nobody will have any trouble.'

One of them ventured to ask how long they were going to be kept locked up, to which Teófilo replied, 'As long as Doña Arcángela says.'

Ticho gets up before dawn – by choice, since he prefers spending the day out in the country to lugging sacks in a warehouse – and takes the first bus out of Concepción. His way of dressing is between that of a bouncer and a farm-hand – undershirt with holes in it, a suit, rough sandals, and a broad-brimmed straw hat. He reaches the farm as day is breaking, while everybody is asleep except the dog which does not bark at him. He puts on a pair of rubber boots that are under the shed and, shovel in hand, goes to check on the irrigation ditch to see what damage has been done and what progress the water has made during the night.

On the day and hour that concern us, Ticho was standing on the end of the irrigation ditch near the highway. What he saw can be imagined:

The road and the ditch run parallel and next to each other in the direction away from him. The road is boggy with puddles and mud; the ditch is in a bank of earth covered with weeds. They divide the farm in two. On Ticho's right is the planted and watered field – an area of black earth with tiny green dots of wheat – and on his left is the ash grey ploughed but unsown surface, its furrows lumpy crags. At the other end of the ditch and road is the pond, next to it the barn, and, next to the barn, the house. The house is painted white, has a porch and two windows; the barn is the colour of the cinder block and has one closed door. A few meters to the left of the house is the shed and under the shed, the tractor, which is red.

It is early morning, and cold. There is not a cloud in the sky.

A figure comes out on the porch of the house, goes to the barn, and opens the big door. Four figures wrapped in rags come out of the barn, one by one, at unhurried intervals. They stand in the sun for a moment, then go to the fence, lift their skirts, and squat in a line. The figure that opened the door goes to the shed, leans over the front end of the tractor, makes a sudden movement with his arm, and a white puff of smoke appears at the other end above the exhaust pipe. Intermittent explosions are heard, then silence. Another figure appears on the porch of the house and remains there, motionless.

Ticho's attention wanders. He leans over the shovel, moves a chunk of earth aside to let the water run by, reinforces the edge of the ditch. He does not raise his head again until he hears a shout.

The scene he now sees is different. The four women who had been squatting are now running over the ploughed field. Ticho realizes that they are trying to cross diagonally to reach the highway at the point furthest away from where he is standing. The figure that was on the porch has disappeared, the one that was under the shed is moving towards the porch. The four figures crossing the furrows separate. The going is difficult, ankles twist, feet sink into the clumps of earth; they run but make little headway. The other two figures are now together in the portal. The one that went back into the house has come out again and is handing something to the one that has just arrived from the shed who takes it in his two hands. This figure, standing straight, remains motionless a moment. Neither the flash nor the smoke can be seen. The reports take Ticho by surprise and startle him.

'Señor Don Teófilo says that the four women you left him in charge of tried to run away, so, as you ordered, he shot at them with the rifle you gave him for guarding the cows. One is dead already and one is dying. The other two gave up and are locked up in the barn again. That's how it is. Don Teófilo also says he is waiting for orders about what he should do now.'

These, more or less, were the words with which Ticho broke the news to Arcángela scarcely an hour after the event. One can imagine what Arcángela said on hearing them. She did not admit at the time nor does she admit now to having ever mentioned the world 'rifle' in relation to the four women she brought to *Los Pirules* farm.

'I said that he should keep an eye on them, that he should take care of them, that he should not let them get away but not that he should shoot them.'

At the present time, in speaking of Teófilo she invariably refers to him as 'my brother-in-law, that horse's ass'.

It should be pointed out that neither Ladder, who drove the women to the farm, nor Eulalia, who went out to the car with Teófilo when it was stuck in the mud, heard Arcángela mention the rifle.

It all adds up to the same thing: Arcángela gave Teófilo the rifle and brought the women to the farm and Teófilo shot at them in the conviction that he was carrying out Arcángela's orders.

Not long after hearing the news, Arcángela began feeling ill – as she said, she got sick with anger – and had to take to her bed where The Skeleton brought her a mug of passion-flower tea.

On that occasion, according to The Skeleton, Arcángela said to her, 'It looks to me, little Skeleton, that we are really in the fucking soup, now.'

While Arcángela was recovering, Serafina and Ticho drove out to *Los Pirules* farm in Ladder's car. By the time they arrived, the wounded woman was dead.

Nobody recalls that Serafina reproached Teófilo for what he had done. She confined herself to taking the steps she thought advisable. She crossed the field with Ticho following behind balancing a pick and shovel on his shoulder, until she came to what seemed to her to be a suitable spot. It was far from the highway at the foot of a little embankment shielded from indiscreet eyes – actually there was nothing except cactuses. She ordered Ticho to dig.

Serafina returned to the farm-house as this work was being done. Having reached the conclusion that neither Teófilo nor her sister Eulalia was capable of 'minding women', she had him open the barn, ordered the girls to come out, had them get into the car, and drove back to town with them. After seeing to it that they were each locked up in a room, she returned to the farm to supervise the burial.

The dead women's clothing was put in a pile and set on fire. The bodies, wrapped in sacks, were carried from the shed – where they had been laid out – by Ticho, Ladder, and Teófilo who was reluctant, at first, to participate in the grisly task. After Ladder and Ticho had filled in the grave and obliterated the traces as best they could, Serafina was satisfied. Night was falling and it was cold. Eulalia invited them in to have a bite to eat – the men were very hungry – but Serafina declined the invitation saying that it was time to be getting back to town. They all went to the car and said goodbye there: Serafina kissed her sister,

Teófilo opened the car door and, they say, asked his sister-in-law, 'What do you want me to do, now?'

'Nothing,' she answered. 'When Arcángela feels better, she will decide what to do about you.'

With that, they drove off towards Concepción. Teófilo and Eulalia remained alone on the farm with two crimes on their conscience, two bodies buried at the edge of the embankment fifty meters away, and the disturbing feeling that those who had given them work were not satisfied with them.

Enter the Police

After receiving instructions to place Serafina Baladro Juárez at the disposition of the Attorney General's Office of the State of Mezcala, Chief of Police Teódulo Cueto decided first to meet with Captain Bedoya in the Gómez Hotel bar. Chief Cueto denies that such a meeting took place. Captain Bedoya, on the other hand, described what was said during it, as follows: 'He told me that he was notifying me that he had received a warrant of arrest for Serafina and that it would be a good idea for her to have a lawyer on hand. I told him that I could not imagine why there should be a warrant for Serafina and even less why she should need a lawyer. The Chief then told me that there had been a shooting and that her name appeared in the official record. On hearing this, I answered, "Chief, I give you my oath as an officer of the Mexican Army and on the honour of my sainted mother that Serafina knows nothing of any shooting."

'The Chief said that he appreciated my frankness and that he was certain there was no criminal charge against Serafina but that he would have to take her into custody, nonetheless. I thanked him for giving me the tip. He told me that in accordance with the instructions he had received, he would have to break the seals on the *Casino del Danzón* the next day and check over the interior of the premises. He told me he felt sure that he would find everything in order, after which we said goodnight.'

Captain Bedoya got to the *Casino* as fast as he could. The news, naturally, caused consternation. Orders went flying through the house and there was general mobilization. Ticho mixed mortar in the dining room and began to close up the opening in the wall. Ladder was summoned. The women were ordered to pack up blankets and dishes for spending the night at *Los Pirules* farm. Serafina tried to locate *Licenciado* Rendón who disappears from the story at this point. The Baladros tried to get in touch with him over thirty times over the next two weeks without success. Moments of vacillation were not wanting. At one point, Serafina suggested to her sister before witnesses, 'Let's go to the United States.'

But they went to the farm. Ladder made four trips in his car that afternoon. The eleven remaining girls were together once more. They laid down reed-mats in the barn and went to sleep in apparent harmony with The Skeleton on guard. It was cold. In the morning, Rosa was found to have a high fever. The Skeleton diagnosed it as a chill and gave her marjoram tea. Rosa drank it, seemed to improve, and died three hours later. Ticho buried her at the foot of the embankment in a grave that he dug hurriedly next to the other two.

The next day, January 14th, Chief Cueto broke the seals on the Independence Street house and entered with three uniformed officers and a marshal. Apparently, they made a tour of the house and found nothing irregular. The police spent barely fifteen minutes in the building. The official report of the inspection omits any reference to the fact that the tortillas found in the kitchen could not have been there for two years.

Chief Cueto went to *Los Pirules* farm that same afternoon. The water had seeped out of the irrigation ditch, the road was soft and muddy, and his car got stuck. While the three policemen and the marshal were trying to free it, the inspector walked the two hundred meters to the house. Arcángela and Serafina were standing on the porch as though they were expecting him. Chief Cueto states that before he could even say good morning, Arcángela said to him, 'It will be worth ten thousand pesos to you if you report that you couldn't locate my sister.'

What the Chief replied is not known. (The Baladros never said that they had offered or gave him money.) The Chief wrote a report that night which he sent to headquarters stating that he broke the seals on the *Casino del Danzón*, inspected the interior of the premises, and visited *Los Pirules* farm 'without finding the wanted person'. The terms in which the document is couched are definitive. Anybody, unfamiliar with the story, who read his report might assume that the investigation must have ended at that point.

This was not the case. Chief Cueto returned to the *Casino del Danzón* the following day accompanied by the three uniformed policemen and the marshal, as on the previous occasion.

(It should be noted that Chief Cueto's motives for returning to the *Casino del Danzón* are as obscure as those for his having warned Captain Bedoya in their conversation at the Gomez Hotel that he was about to make an arrest. He gives the following explanation for his actions: 'The amount Señora Arcángela offered me was so large that it made me suspect that the Señoras Baladro had something very serious on their consciences. That was the reason I decided to return to the *Casino del Danzón* and make a more thorough inspection.)

On their second visit to the *Casino del Danzón*, Chief Cueto and his men went through the rooms, up and down the stairs, in and out of the cabaret, checked over the kitchen and the charcoal shed, and finally ended up in the yard. Countless traces of recent occupation must have turned up but that was not what interested them. The Chief paced back and forth over the yard.

'All at once,' he states, 'I noticed that my feet sank into the ground in a certain spot. I called one of the officers with me and told him to get a shovel and dig a hole right where I was standing. I wanted to see what was underneath.'

When the officer had dug down about one meter, what was left of one of Blanca's hands appeared.

Chief Cueto's role in the apprehension of the Baladro sisters is one of the obscure parts of this story. The following hypothesis seems reasonable.

At the outset, Chief Teódulo Cueto, whose name appears in the section of Arcángela's notebook marked 'Disbursements' (see Appendix 5), tried to do his duty while at the same time giving the Baladros opportunities to escape: he tips off Captain Bedoya in the Gómez Hotel bar; he enters the *Casino* at a time when nobody is there; when he finds the woman he was ordered to arrest, he does not take her into custody. It is possible that he accepted the ten thousand pesos Arcángela offered him, not to close the case for an indefinite time, but only to give them two days' start. It is also possible that after collecting, the Chief may have changed his mind – when Blanca's hand was uncovered in the yard, for instance – and decided to speed up the proceedings and make the arrest. The Baladros would have needed twenty-four hours to make good their escape.

It must be granted that this hypothesis does not account for the Chief's discovery of Blanca's body on his second visit to the *Casino del Danzón*, which may have come about purely by chance.

When the Baladros reached the Concepción Police Headquarters, they were led along a corridor on to which opened the office where the girls who had been rescued from the barn were making their statements. It is said that when the two women passed by in custody, several of them got to their feet and shouted insults at them, the first the sisters had ever received from their employees.

Captain Bedoya and Serafina had arranged to meet in Nogales. Unaware that the Baladros had been arrested, he slept on the post, got up early, held inspection, had breakfast at the Gómez Hotel, and reached the Plan de Abajo Commercial Bank as it was opening.

The Captain was filling out a withdrawal slip with which to close out his savings account when two detectives entered the bank to arrest him. They went up to him and, in a low voice, so as not to attract the employees' attention, one of them said to him, 'My Captain, you are under arrest.'

The detective states that Captain Bedoya did not blink an eye on hearing this. He tore up the withdrawal slip, put his pen back in his pocket, and held out his wrists to be handcuffed. The detectives carried no handcuffs and the three men left the bank arm in arm like friends pleased to have run into one another.

Brave Nicolás who did not think he was guilty of anything, was arrested in the barracks. Ladder, the taxi-driver, who also considered himself innocent, was arrested two days later while seated on the fence of the San Francisco church atrium discussing the case of the Baladros with the other taxi-drivers. Nobody had denounced Ticho and he was not wanted by the authorities. He gave himself up voluntarily when he learned that the Baladros were in jail. He practically had to insist that the police lock him up. Eulalia and Teófilo Pinto would have escaped, because the police had no photographs of them, had it not occurred to them to cross the border 'to reach safety'. They were detained in Texas for travelling without a passport and turned over to the Mexican authorities to whom they gave their real names.

The Concepción jail, which usually housed only the drunks who were freed in the morning after sweeping the streets for the first time, held nineteen prisoners.

Epilogue

Among the inmates who are now free, Brave Nicolás is currently a shoemaker – a trade he learned in jail; Ticho has a steady job in the Barajas Brothers' warehouse; Ladder went back to his former occupation and now owns a fleet of taxis in San Pedro de las Corrientes – bought, as the gossip goes, with money given him by Arcángela.

Teófilo won a fortune in jail playing Spanish rummy and then lost it. Eulalia, who is free, sells coconut candies on the street. Captain Bedoya is in the Pedrones penitentiary where he is a trusty in charge of a cell-block and highly regarded by both guards and prisoners. The Baladros are still in the women's prison from which they have no expectation of coming out alive. Serafina has a soft-drink business – charging exorbitant prices – and Arcángela sells food prepared by The Skeleton. Both are also money-lenders and have a joint capital estimated by the other prisoners at upwards of a hundred thousand pesos.

Appendices

1. Ticho's life as told by him.

When I was a small boy, the other children were afraid of me. My parents sent me to school but the teacher did not want me. She said I was too big and might set a bad example. They put me to work carrying – stones, bags of cement, bags of sand. One afternoon, I gave a friend of mine a hug and when I let loose of him he fell down on the ground. The people who saw what happened said I killed him. So, they put me in jail. In jail, they had me carrying stones again. Then, the man who carried the dead bodies in the hospital died himself and the doctor came to the jail to look for somebody to take his place. The director of the jail sent for me and said to me: 'Go along with this man.' I carried stiffs back and forth for ten years until one morning the doctor said to me, 'You can go, now,' and he opened the hospital gate. I went out on the street and started walking. I came to the railroad tracks and began to follow them. I walked at night because there was a moon. In the daytime, I lay in a ditch and slept. When I saw a house I would go to the kitchen – dogs never bark at me – and I would peek in and say to the women there, 'I'm hungry,' and they would get scared and give me food. When I came to a town I would beg but nobody gave. One day I was asleep on the sidewalk outside a market and when I opened my eyes Doña Arcángela was looking down at me. There were two girls with her carrying baskets. Doña Arcángela said to me, 'You sure are big, you are homely as sin, and you look like a dunce. I have a job for you you will like.'

The girls laughed.

From that day on I was a bouncer. My duties were to sit in a chair and be ready for whatever came up.

2. The Whoremaster's statement.

He states that it was intellectual curiosity that impelled him to go to the *México Lindo* so often. He describes some of the more noteworthy women he knew in that house. One undressed in great embarrassment four or five times every night saying that no man had ever seen her naked before. Another had sexual relations with the narrator on more than twenty occasions and never once recognized him. Another always told the same story: she had just received a telegram saying that her mother had taken sick and needed money urgently.

The most interesting part of my visits – says the Whoremaster – would be the conversations I had with Doña Arcángela who always had me sit at her table. She was a philosopher. For example, she believed that after you died your soul remained floating in the atmosphere for a length of time that depended on the memory you left behind in the minds of those who knew you. A bad memory made the soul suffer; a good one gave it joy. When everybody has forgotten the dead person or when all those who knew him have died, the soul disappears.

3. What the judo champion said.

I was among those chosen to represent Mexico City in the Pan American Championships which were held in the city of Pedrones in 1958. (He describes the accommodations provided him, his impressions of the city, how the Mexico City team was eliminated in the first round. After that they went to the *México Lindo*.) When the girls found out that we were the Mexico City judo team, they crowded around our table asking for autographs. The madam (Serafina) came over to shake hands with us, had the girls put wreaths of paper flowers around our necks, and gave us a drink on the house.

'Boys, a toast to your victory!' she said to us.

We didn't have the heart to tell her we had already been eliminated. (He describes the place, makes a comparison between Mexico City and Pedrones prostitutes, finding that the latter are less expensive and more sincere than the former, relates his experiences with a girl named Magdalena, and regrets that the Molino Street house was closed before he had a chance to pay it another visit.)

4. Statement of Don Gustavo Hernández.

Ask me: what is a man doing in a whorehouse every Saturday night when he has a wife and several daughters and a happy home life? I wouldn't know what to answer you, but that's how it was – as if I was under a spell. Every Saturday night, as soon as the church clock struck nine, I would close my haberdashery shop and go to the *México Lindo*. The minute I set foot inside the place everything seemed beautiful to me: the decorations, the girls, the music. I didn't miss a thing. I danced, I drank, I talked, and there wasn't a woman who came through there between '57 and '60 that I didn't have.

I would get home with the first rays of the sun. 'Where were you?' my wife would ask. 'At a Catholic Action meeting.' She never believed me. For years she suspected I had a mistress. She doesn't know I deceived her with forty-three women.

Doña Arcángela would say to me 'Don Gustavo, don't deny yourself anything. If you don't have the money on you, just sign. You are as good as the Bank of Mexico for me.'

Those words were my downfall. One morning, *Licenciado* Rendón walked into the haberdashery. He had IOUs signed by me for over fourteen thousand pesos in his briefcase. He wanted to know when I was going to pay up.

Doña Arcángela took the haberdashery away from me but I got a lesson that cured me of the vice and I never feel tempted to go to a whorehouse any more. I live a contented life now with my family.

5. The Photo

1. Arcángela Baladro
2. The Skeleton
3. Serafina Baladro
4. Blanca (died, July 17)
5. Evelia (died, September 14)
6. Feliza (ditto)
7. Rosa (died, January 15)
8. Marta (did not fit into the outhouse hole)
9. Aurora Bautista (received compensation)
10. The women killed by Teófilo Pinto
11. The women killed by Teófilo Pinto

6. Arcángela's notebook

Arcángela's notebook was found in her room in the *Casino del Danzón*. It has three sections. The first contains the weekly balance sheet of the employees which has been described earlier.

The second section is headed *Due from Customers*. It contains the names of the most respectable citizens of San Pedro de las Corrientes, the dates of their IOUs, interest at the rate of ten percent per month, payments on account, etc. All these accounts have been liquidated.

The third section is headed *payments*. This consists of an itemized list of the amounts Arcángela was paying out to the authorities to be at peace with the township. For example, ten pesos daily to the policemen on the block, sixty to the mayor, sixty to the chief of police, and so on.

Russell Hoban
Footplacers, London Transport, Owls, Wincer-Boise

Why do some people take care not to step on the cracks in the paving while others take no notice whatever of the cracks? One says 'cracks' but of course they are not cracks; they are the edges where, apparently, one square of paving ends and another begins. That one calls them cracks is significant; it betokens a recognition of a surface that might be broken through, a surface that keeps separate the overness from an underness in which move creatures of the other in ways not to be understood by us. Who has not at one time or another sensed in that dark otherness, sometimes quaint and solemn, sometimes mad and strangely echoing, the footplacer? Yes, yes, the footplacer: in the concrete underfoot it lives and walks, not in hollow spaces but molecularly in the solid concrete; particularly it is to be found in the concrete station-platforms of the underground; it is upside-down to us and we are upside-down to it as it places its feet softly one by one against our pacing feet. Perhaps it thinks of us as being the reflection or the shadow of its own walking; perhaps footplacers talking amongst themselves call *us* footplacers, think of us as strange beings who walk upside-down aboveground softly placing our feet one by one against theirs. The footplacer is a cumulative creature; as it places its feet against our feet all the footsteps of our lives are added up and gathered into it. Where did we go and when? What did we do there? All those footsteps have been gathered up into the footplacer, all those goings that are gone.

So much walking there is in a great city, so many footsteps! Sometimes from the escalators in the underground there comes a cry like the hooting of an owl, and indeed it is an owl that cries but not a small and feathered one: the owls that one hears in the escalators are the treadmill owls; they are made of steel and nickel, brass and copper; they weigh a ton or more; they are at least eight feet tall and they smell of machine oil. Great dark glistening things they are, all gleaming joints and pistons – one can't imagine them hatching from an egg. No one knows where they came from; it is believed that they were there in the subterranean dark long before the underground was built. When the tunnels were opened they came blinking into the light, indicating by gestures that they were peaceful and wanted to work. They were accordingly set to walking great treadmills that powered the endlessly ascending and descending stairs, and there they have remained ever since, walking their treadmills. No one knows whether they are living creatures or intelligent machines; no one knows how long they live or how long they last. No one knows what they do when the underground is closed. No one knows whether or not they can fly. No one knows if anyone has ever seen them.

Wincer-boise also are creatures of the underground but there is nothing dark about them, nothing heavy. Wincer-boise is a collective name; there are many of them. They are called boise because there is something boyish about them and they make a noise; possibly they *are* a noise, one can't say for certain because they cannot be seen. London Transport does not acknowledge their presence, and whatever their function may be it is entirely unofficial. They live among the rails of the underground and they become greatly excited at the approach of a train; it is then that their strange wincing cry is heard: 'Wheats-yew, wheats-yew!' They spring up onto the rails and race ahead of the train, only turning aside into the tunnel niches just before the next station so that the wincer-boise waiting there can have their sport in turn. Wincer-boise seem to be especially active on dry cold days.

Here we have not the space in which to take up the matter of those variously shaped and patterned iron plates in the pavement, some of which tilt up a little under the pressure of a footstep and fall back with that characteristic sound well known by those who lie awake in the small hours of the night. On some of these plates there appear the raised iron letters LEB or NTGB; some spell out whole words such as POST OFFICE TELEPHONES. When LEB means LONDON ELECTRICITY BOARD and when it means LET ENTROPY BE, when NTGB means NORTH THAMES GAS BOARD and when it means NOTHING TO GO BACK – such aspects of the traffic between the underness and the overness of London cannot be dealt with here.

GRANTA

LEONARD MICHAELS

MY FATHER'S LIFE

Six days a week he rose early, dressed, ate breakfast alone, put on his hat, and walked to his barbershop at 207 Henry Street on the Lower East Side of Manhattan, about half a mile from our apartment. He returned after dark. The family ate dinner together on Sundays and Jewish holidays. Mainly he ate alone. I don't remember him staying home from work because of illness or bad weather. He took few vacations, but once we spent a week in Miami and he tried to enjoy himself, wading into the ocean, being brave, stepping, inch by inch, into the warm blue unpredictable immensity. Then he slipped. In water no higher than his *pupik*, he came up thrashing, struggling back to the beach on skinny white legs. 'I nearly drowned,' he said, very exhilarated. He never went into the water again. I think he preferred his barbershop to the natural world. He retired after thirty-five years, when his hands trembled too much for scissors and razors and angina made it impossible for him to stand up for long periods. Then he took walks in the neighbourhood and carried a vial of whisky in his shirt pocket. When pain stopped him in the street, he'd stand very still and sip his whisky. A few times I stood beside him, as still as he, waiting for the pain to end, both of us speechless and frightened.

He was vice-president of his synagogue society, keeping records, attending to the maintenance of the synagogue's building. He spoke Yiddish, Polish, maybe some Russian, and had the Hebrew necessary for prayers. He spoke to me in Yiddish until I began, at about the age of six, speaking to him mainly in English. Sometimes, when he switched from one language to the other, I'd not even notice. He could play the violin and mandolin. As a youth in Poland, he'd been in a band. When old friends visited our apartment, he'd drink a *schnaps* with them. He smoked cigars and pipes. He read the Yiddish newspaper the *Forward* and the *Daily News*. He voted Democratic but had no faith in politicians, political systems, or 'the people'. Aside from family, work, and synagogue, his passion was friends. My mother reminded me, when I behaved badly, of his friends. She'd say, 'Nobody will like you.' Everybody liked Leon Michaels.

He was slightly more than five feet tall. My mother is barely five feet. Because I'm five-ten, she thinks I'm a giant. She came from Brest Litovsk. He came from Drohiczyn, a town on the river Bug near the Russian border. When I visited Poland in 1979, I asked my hosts about Drohiczyn. They said, 'You'll see new buildings and Russian troops.

No reason to go there.' So I didn't go there. It would have been a sentimental experience, essentially empty. My father never talked about the town, rarely said anything about his past. We also never had any long, deep talks of the father-and-son kind, but when I was fifteen, I fell in love and he said a memorable thing to me.

The girl had many qualities – tall, a blond, a talented musician – but mainly she wasn't Jewish. My father learned about her when we were seen together watching a basketball game at Madison Square Garden, among eighteen thousand people. I'd been foolish to suppose I could go to the Garden with a blond and not be spotted. My father had many friends. You saw them in his barbershop, 'the boys', snazzy dressers jingling coins in their pockets or poor Jews from the neighbourhood who came just to sit, to rest in their passage between miseries. Always a crowd in the barbershop – cab-drivers, bookies, waiters, salesmen. One of them spotted me and phoned my father. When I returned that night, he was waiting up for me with the fact. He said we would discuss it in the morning.

I lay awake in anguish. No way to deny that the girl I loved killed Jews because she wasn't one. I'd been seeing her secretly for months. Her parents knew about the secrecy. I was so ashamed of it that when I called for her, I'd ring the bell and then wait for her in the street. She pleaded with me to come upstairs, meet her parents. After a while, I did so. Maybe they understood. Her previous boyfriend was the son of a rabbi.

In the morning my father said, 'Let's take a walk.' We walked around the block, then around the block again, in silence. It took a long time to walk twice around the block, but the silence was so dense, it felt like one infinitely heavy immobilized minute. Then, as if he'd rehearsed a speech and dismissed it, he sighed. 'I'll dance at your wedding,' he said.

Thus we spent a minute together, just he and I, father and son, and he said a memorable thing. The sentence speaks for itself. It is concise, its burden huge. If witty, it is so in the manner of Hieronymus Bosch, making a picture of demonic gaiety. My wedding takes place in the middle of the night. My father is a small figure among dancing Jews, frenzied, hysterical with joy.

For a fifteen-year-old insanely in love, this sentence was a sentence – judgement, punishment – and, at the same time, a release from brutal sanctions. He didn't order me not to see her. I could do as I pleased. As it happened, she met someone else. I was very shocked and hurt. I was also relieved. The light of her hair returned to me in dreams.

My father did dance at my wedding, twelve years later, when I married a black-haired, dark-skinned German Jew. Because her parents were dead, the traditional ceremony was held in our apartment. Her aunts and uncles sat along one wall, mine along another. The living room was small. Conversation, forced by closeness, was lively and nervous. The rabbi, delayed by traffic, arrived late, and then the ceremony was hurried. Everyone seemed to shout instructions. Did she circle me or I her? My father was satisfied, maybe delighted. The marriage lasted five years, and when we fought, which was every day, she'd threaten to tell my father the truth about me. 'It will kill him,' she said. After we separated, she had a series of love affairs, then killed herself. At her funeral, the only person I noticed crying was my father. What he felt exactly I don't know, but somebody in her family or mine had to cry. He cried alone. Before the wedding, he didn't say, 'Let's take a walk,' then tell me this marriage would lead to horror. I had tried to talk to him about her psychotic violence, but he was unable to assimilate the details; he couldn't hear what I was saying. He said, 'She's an orphan. You cannot abandon her.'

If he ever hit me, I don't remember it, but I remember being malicious. A bad boy. My brother, three years younger than I, was practising scales on my father's violin one afternoon. When he finished, he started to carry the violin across the room. I put out my foot. He tripped, fell. We heard the violin hit the floor and crack. Instantly – quicker than instantly – I wanted to undo the act, not trip my brother. But it was done. I was stuck with myself. I think I smiled. My father looked at the violin and said, 'I had it over twenty years.'

Maybe I tripped my brother because I'm tone-deaf and could never learn to play any musical instrument. Nothing forgives me. I wish my father had become enraged, knocked off my head, so I could forget the incident. I never, never, never felt insufficiently loved, and yet I think, *When Abraham raised the knife to Isaac, the kid had it good.*

In all photos of my father, however badly lit or ill-focused, he looks like himself, whereas I almost never look like myself, despite the competence of the photographer. I see perversions of musculature about the eyes and mouth, lids weirdly, sickishly drooping, lips stiffening through a sneer toward a smile that will never be natural. This isn't me, I think. Like a baby, my father appears, inevitably, like himself. Perhaps in our similarities it is guaranteed I'll always be other than myself, whatever that is. When someone admires me, I think there's been a mistake; when someone disapproves of me, I want revenge. Like my father, I have a lot of friends, but when I wake up alone in a strange motel and I can't remember what city I'm in and there's nobody to phone, I feel unbearably happy.

My father never owned a car or flew in an airplane. He could imagine no alternatives to being himself. He had only his neighbourhood, the hectic variety in human traffic, the barbershop. Looking out my window, I can see San Francisco Bay and how the world bends toward China.

I was in London, returning from three months in Paris, when he died. My flight to New York had been cancelled. I was stranded, waiting for another flight. Nobody in New York knew where I was. I couldn't be phoned. At last, the day after the funeral, I arrived. My brother met me at the door of the apartment, where my mother still lives, and told me the news. I went alone to my parents' bedroom and sat on the bed. I didn't want to be seen crying.

Day after day, people visited the apartment to offer condolences and to reminisce. Then a rabbi came, a tiny, fragile man dressed all in black, with a white beard twice the length of his face. He asked my mother to give him some of my father's clothes, particularly things he'd worn next to his skin. As the rabbi started to leave, a bundle of clothes in his arms, he noticed me sitting at the kitchen table. He said in Yiddish, 'Sit lower.' I didn't know what he was getting at. Did he want me to crouch? I was doing nothing, sitting there alone, but I was somehow susceptible to criticism. My mother interceded. 'He feels,' she said. 'He feels plenty.'

The rabbi said, 'I didn't ask how he feels. Tell him to sit lower.'

I got up and left the kitchen, looking for a lower place to sit. I was very angry but not enough to start yelling at a fanatical midget. Besides, he was correct.

One Friday night, I was walking to the subway on Madison Street. My winter coat was open, flying with my stride. I wore a white shirt and a sharp red tie. I'd combed my hair in the style of the day, a gorgeous pompadour fixed and sealed with Vaseline. I was nineteen-years-old terrific. The night was cold, but I was hot. The wind was strong. My hair was stronger, imperturbable in its rigid gleam. As I entered the darkness below the Manhattan Bridge, where it strikes across Madison Street and makes a high, gloomy, mysterious vault, I met my father. He was returning from the barbershop, following his usual route. His coat was buttoned to the neck, his hat pulled down to protect his eyes. He stopped. As I approached, I saw him study me, his creation. We stood for a moment beneath the bridge, facing each other in the darkness and wind. An American giant, five feet ten inches tall. A short Polish Jew. He said, 'Button your coat. Everyone doesn't have to see your tie.'

I buttoned my coat.

'Why don't you wear a hat?'

I shrugged. 'I'm all right.'

'You need a haircut. You look like a bum.'

'I'll come to the barbershop tomorrow.'

He nodded, as if to say 'Goodnight' and 'What's the use'. He was on his way home to dinner, to sleep. He'd worked all day. I was on my way to sexual adventure. Then he asked, 'Do you need money?'

'No.'

'Here,' he said, pulling change from his coat pocket. 'For the subway. Take.'

He gave.

I took.

GRANTA

Jonathan Schell
Nuclear Arms and the Fate of the Earth

Since July 16, 1945, when the first atomic bomb was detonated at the Trinity test site near Alamogordo, New Mexico, mankind has lived with nuclear weapons. Each year, the number of bombs has grown, until now there are some fifty thousand warheads in the world, possessing the explosive yield of roughly twenty billion tons of TNT, or one million six hundred thousand times the yield of the bomb that was dropped by the United States on the city of Hiroshima after the Trinity explosion. These bombs were built as 'weapons' for 'war', but their significance greatly transcends war and all its causes and outcomes. They grew out of history, yet they threaten to end history. They were made by men, yet they threaten to annihilate man. They are a pit into which the whole world can fall – a nemesis of all human intentions, actions, and hopes. Only life itself, which they threaten to swallow up, can give the measure of their significance. Yet in spite of the immeasurable importance of nuclear weapons, the world has declined, on the whole, to think about them very much. We have thus far failed to fashion, or to discover within ourselves, an emotional or intellectual or political response to them. This peculiar failure of response, in which hundreds of millions of people acknowledge the presence of an immediate, unremitting threat to their existence and to the existence of the world they live in but do nothing about it – a failure in which both self-interest and fellow-feeling seem to have died – has itself been such a striking phenomenon that it has to be regarded as an extremely important part of the nuclear predicament itself. It is only very recently in Europe and the United States that public opinion has been stirred, and that ordinary people may be beginning to ask themselves how they should respond to the nuclear peril.

In what follows, I shall offer some thoughts on the origins and the significance of this predicament, on why we have so long resisted attempts to think about it (we even call a nuclear holocaust 'unthinkable') or deal with it, and on the shape and magnitude of the choice that it forces upon us. But first I wish to describe the consequences for the world, insofar as these can be known, of a full-scale nuclear holocaust at the current level of global armament. We have lived in the shadow of nuclear arms for more than thirty-six years, so it does not seem too soon for us to familiarize ourselves with them – to acquaint ourselves with such matters as the 'thermal pulse', the 'blast wave', and the 'three stages of radiation sickness'. A description of a full-scale holocaust seems to be made necessary by the simple but basic rule that in order to discuss something one should first know what it is. A considerable number of excellent studies concentrating on various aspects of the damage that can be done by nuclear arms do exist, many of them written only in the last few years. Drawing on them and other printed sources, and also on interviews that I conducted recently with a number of scientists, I have attempted to piece together an account of the principal consequences of a full-scale holocaust. Such an account, which in its nature must be both technical and gruesome, cannot be other than hateful to dwell on, but it may be only by now descending into this hell in imagination that we can hope to escape descending into it in reality at some later time.

Whereas most conventional bombs produce only one destructive effect – the shock wave – nuclear weapons produce many destructive effects. At the moment of the explosion, when the temperature of the weapon material, instantly gasified, is at the superstellar level, the pressure is millions of times the normal atmospheric pressure. Immediately, radiation, consisting mainly of gamma rays, which are a very high-energy form of electromagnetic radiation, begins to stream outward into the environment. This is called the 'initial nuclear radiation', and is the first of the destructive effects of a nuclear explosion. In an air burst of a one-megaton bomb – a bomb with the explosive yield of a million tons of TNT, which is a medium-sized weapon in present-day nuclear arsenals – the initial nuclear radiation can kill unprotected human beings in an area of some six square miles.

Virtually simultaneously with the initial nuclear radiation, an electro-magnetic pulse is generated by the intense gamma radiation acting on the air. This is the second destructive effect of the explosion. In a high-altitude detonation, this pulse can knock out electrical equipment over a wide area by inducing a powerful surge of voltage through various conductors, such as antennas, overhead power lines, pipes, and railroad tracks. The United States Defense Department's Civil Preparedness Agency reported in 1977 that a single multi-kiloton nuclear weapon detonated one hundred and twenty-five miles over Omaha, Nebraska, could generate an electromagnetic pulse strong enough to damage solid-state electrical circuits throughout the entire continental United States and in parts of Canada and Mexico, and thus threaten to bring the economies of these countries to a halt.

When the fusion and fission reactions have blown themselves out, a fireball takes shape. As it expands, energy is absorbed in the form of X rays by the surrounding air, and then the air re-radiates a portion of that energy into the environment in the form of the thermal pulse – a wave of blinding light and intense heat – which is the third of the destructive effects of a nuclear explosion. The thermal pulse of a one-megaton bomb lasts for about ten seconds and can cause second-degree burns in exposed human beings at a distance of nine and a half miles, or in an area of more than two hundred and eighty square miles, and that of a twenty-megaton bomb (a large weapon by modern standards) lasts for about twenty seconds and can produce the same consequences at a distance of twenty-eight miles, or in an area of two thousand four hundred and sixty square miles.

As the fireball expands, it also sends out a blast wave in all directions, and this is the fourth destructive effect of the explosion. The blast wave of an air-burst one-megaton bomb can flatten or severely damage all but the strongest buildings within a radius of four and a half miles, and that of a twenty-megaton bomb can do the same within a radius of twelve miles. As the fireball burns, it rises, condensing water from the surrounding atmosphere to form the characteristic mushroom cloud. If the bomb has been set off on the ground or close enough to it so that the fireball touches the surface, in a so-called ground burst a crater will be formed, and tons of dust and debris will be fused with the intensely radioactive fission products and sucked up into the mushroom cloud.

This mixture will return to earth as radioactive fallout, most of it in the form of fine ash, in the fifth destructive effect of the explosion. Depending upon the composition of the surface, from forty to seventy per cent of this fallout – often called the 'early' or 'local' fallout – descends to earth within about a day of the explosion, in the vicinity of the blast and downwind from it, exposing human beings to radiation disease, an illness that is fatal when exposure is intense. Air bursts may also produce local fallout, but in much smaller quantities. The lethal range of the local fallout depends on a number of circumstances, including the weather, but under average conditions a one-megaton ground blast would, according to the report 'The Effects of Nuclear

War' published in 1979 by the American Congressional Office of Technology Assessment, lethally contaminate over a thousand square miles.

The initial nuclear radiation, the electromagnetic pulse, the thermal pulse, the blast wave, and the local fallout may be described as the local primary effects of nuclear weapons. Naturally, when many bombs are exploded the scope of these effects is increased accordingly. But in addition these primary effects produce innumerable secondary effects on societies and natural environments, some of which may be even more harmful than the primary ones. For example, nuclear weapons, by force and heat, generate mass fires, and in some cases these may kill more people than the original thermal pulses and blast waves. Moreover, there are global primary effects, which become significant if thousands of bombs are detonated all around the earth. And these global primary effects produce innumerable secondary effects of their own throughout the earth as a whole. For a full-scale holocaust is more than the sum of its local parts; it is also a powerful direct blow to the ecosphere. In that sense, a holocaust is to the earth what a single bomb is to a city.

Three grave direct global effects have been discovered so far. The first is the 'delayed' or 'worldwide' fallout. In detonations greater than one hundred kilotons, part of the fallout does not fall to the ground in the vicinity of the explosion but rises high into the troposphere and into the stratosphere, circulates the earth, and then, over months or years, descends, contaminating the whole surface of the globe – although with doses of radiation far weaker than those delivered by the local fallout. Nuclear-fission products comprise some three hundred radioactive isotopes, and though some decay to relatively harmless levels of radioactivity within a few hours, minutes, or even seconds, others persist to emit radiation for up to millions of years. The short-lived isotopes are the ones most responsible for the lethal effects of the local fallout, and the long-lived ones are responsible for the contamination of the earth by stratospheric fallout. By convention, the energy released by fallout is not calculated in the stated yield of a weapon, yet in a ten-thousand-megaton attack the equivalent of forty thousand times the yield of the Hiroshima bomb would be released in the form of radioactivity alone. This release may be considered a protracted afterburst, which is dispersed into the land, air, and sea, and into the tissues, bones, roots, stems, and leaves of living things, and goes on detonating there almost indefinitely after the explosion.

The second of the global effects that have been discovered so far is the lofting, from ground bursts, of millions of tons of dust into the stratosphere; this is likely to produce general cooling of the earth's surface.

The third of the global effects is a predicted partial destruction of the layer of ozone that surrounds the entire earth in the stratosphere. A nuclear fireball, by burning nitrogen in the air, produces large quantities of oxides of nitrogen. These are carried by the heat of the blast into the stratosphere, where, through a series of chemical reactions, they bring about a depletion of the ozone layer. Such a depletion may persist for years. In its 1975 report, 'Long-Term Worldwide Effects of Multiple Nuclear-Weapons Detonations', the National Academy of Sciences estimated that in a holocaust in which ten thousand megatons were detonated in the Northern Hemisphere the reduction of ozone in this hemisphere could be as high as seventy per cent and in the Southern Hemisphere as high as forty per cent, and that it could take as long as thirty years for the ozone level to return to normal. The ozone layer is crucial to life on earth, because it shields the surface of the earth from lethal levels of ultraviolet radiation, which is present in sunlight. In *The Effects of Nuclear Weapons*, Samuel Glasstone remarks simply, 'If it were not for the absorption of much of the solar ultraviolet radiation by the ozone, life as currently known could not exist except possibly in the ocean.' Without the ozone shield, sunlight, the life-giver, would become a life-extinguisher. In judging the global effects of a holocaust, therefore, the primary question is not how many people would be irradiated, burned, or crushed to death by the immediate effects of the bombs but how well the ecosphere, regarded as a single living entity, on which all forms of life depend for their continued existence, would hold up. The issue is the habitability of the earth, and it is in this context, not in the context of the direct slaughter of hundreds of millions of people by the local effects of nuclear weapons, that the question of human survival arises.

Our knowledge of the local primary effects of the bombs is quite solid. And our knowledge of the extent of the local primary effects of many weapons used together, obtained simply by using the multiplication table, is also solid. Nevertheless, our knowledge of even the primary effects may still be incomplete, as new ones keep being discovered. One example is the electromagnetic pulse, whose importance was not recognized until around 1960, when, after more than a decade of tests, scientists realized that this effect accounted for unexpected electrical failures that had been occurring all along in equipment around the test sites. And it is only in recent years that the American Defense Department has been trying to take account strategically of this startling capacity of just one bomb to put the technical equipment of a whole continent out of action.

When we proceed from the local effects of single explosions to the effects of thousands of them on societies and environments, the picture clouds considerably, because then we go beyond both the certainties of physics and our slender base of experience. In its entirety, a nuclear holocaust can be said to assail human life at three levels: those of individual life, human society, and the natural environment. At no level can the destructiveness of nuclear weapons be measured in terms of firepower alone. At each level, life has both considerable recuperative powers, which might restore it even after devastating injury, and points of exceptional vulnerability, which leave it open to sudden and permanent collapse, even when exposed to comparatively little violence. A modern technological society may stop if its fuel supply is cut off, and an ecosystem may collapse if its ozone shield is depleted. Nuclear weapons thus do not only kill directly, with their tremendous violence, but also kill indirectly, by breaking down the man-made and the natural systems on which individual lives collectively depend. Human beings require constant provision and care, supplied by their societies and the natural environment, and if these are suddenly removed people will die just as surely as if struck by a bullet. The destructive consequences of a nuclear attack are immeasurably compounded by the likelihood that all or most of the bombs will be detonated within the space of a few hours, in a single huge concussion. Normally, a locality devastated by a catastrophe will sooner or later receive help from untouched outside areas, as Hiroshima and Nagasaki did after they were bombed; but a nuclear holocaust would devastate the 'outside' areas as well, leaving the victims to fend for themselves in a shattered society and natural environment. And what is true for each city is also true for the earth as a whole: a devastated earth can hardly expect 'outside' help.

The incredible complexity of all these effects precludes confident detailed representation of the events in a holocaust. However, it is important to point out that our uncertainty pertains not to *whether* the effects will interact, multiplying their destructive power as they do so, but only to *how*. It follows that our almost built-in bias, determined by the limitations of the human mind in judging future events, is to underestimate the harm. To fear interactive consequences that we cannot predict, or even imagine, may not be impossible, but it is very difficult.

Let us consider, for example, some of the possible ways in which a person in a targeted country might die. He might be incinerated by the fireball or the thermal pulse. He might be lethally irradiated by the initial nuclear radiation. He might be crushed to death or hurled to his death by the blast wave or its debris. He might be lethally irradiated by the local fallout. He might be burned to death in a firestorm. He might be injured by one or another of these effects and then die of his wounds before he was able to make his way out of the devastated zone in which he found himself. He might die of starvation, because the economy had collapsed and no food was being grown or delivered, or because existing local crops had been killed by radiation, or because the local ecosystem had been ruined, or because the ecosphere of the earth as a whole was collapsing. He might die of cold, for lack of heat and clothing, or of exposure, for lack of shelter. He might be killed by people seeking food or shelter that he had obtained. He might die of an illness spread in an epidemic. He might be killed by exposure to the sun if he stayed outside too long following serious ozone depletion. Or he might be killed by any combination of these perils.

A nuclear holocaust is an event that is obscure because it is future, and uncertainty, while it has to be recognized in all calculations of future events, has a special place in calculations of a nuclear holocaust, because a holocaust is something that we aspire to keep in the future forever, and never to permit into the present. You might say that uncertainty, like the thermal pulses or the blast waves, is one of the features of a holocaust. We must not, then, insist on a precision that is beyond our grasp but inquire into the rough probabilities insofar as we can judge them, and then ask ourselves what our political responsibilities are in the light of these probabilities.

There are two further aspects of a holocaust which, though they do not further obscure the factual picture, nevertheless vex our understanding of this event. The first is that although we can imaginatively survey the whole prospective scene of destruction, no one experiencing a holocaust would have any such overview. The news necessary to put together that picture would be one of the things immediately lost, and each surviving person, his vision drastically foreshortened by the collapse of his world, and his impressions clouded by his pain, shock, bewilderment, and grief, would see only as far as whatever scene of chaos and agony happened to lie at hand. For it would not be only such abstractions as 'industry' and 'society' and 'the environment' that would be destroyed in a nuclear holocaust; it would also be, over and over again, the small collections of cherished things, known landscapes, and beloved people that made up the immediate contents of individual lives.

The other obstacle to our understanding is that when we strain to picture what the scene would be like after a holocaust we tend to forget that for most people, and perhaps for all, it wouldn't be *like* anything, because they would be dead. To depict the scene as it would appear to the living is to that extent a falsification, and the greater the number killed, the greater the falsification. The right vantage point from which to view a holocaust is that of a corpse, but from that vantage point, of course, there is nothing to report.

The specific train of events that might lead up to an attack is, obviously, among the unpredictables, but a few general possibilities can be outlined. One would be a wholly accidental attack, triggered by human error or mechanical failure. On three occasions in the last couple years, American nuclear forces were placed on the early stages of alert: twice because of the malfunctioning of a computer chip in the North American Air Defense Command's warning system, and once when a test tape depicting a missile attack was inadvertently inserted in the system. The greatest danger in computer-generated misinformation and other mechanical errors may be that one error might start a chain reaction of escalating responses between command centres, leading, eventually, to an attack. If in the midst of a crisis Country A was misled by its computers into thinking that Country B was getting ready to attack, and went on alert, Country B might notice this and go on alert in response, and so on, until either the mistake was straightened out or an attack was launched. A holocaust might also be touched off by conventional or nuclear hostilities between smaller powers, which could draw in the superpowers. It could be deliberate, unprovoked pre-emptive strike by one side against the other. Most observers regard an attack of this kind as exceedingly unlikely but the logic of present nuclear strategy drives both sides to prepare to respond to one, for the central tenet of nuclear strategy is that each side will refrain from launching an all-out first strike against the other only if it knows that even after it has done so the other side will retain forces sufficient to launch an utterly devastating counterblow. More likely is a pre-emptive strike launched in the midst of an international crisis. Neither quite planned (in the sense of being a cold-blooded, premeditated strike) nor quite accidental (in the sense of being caused by technical failure), such an attack would be precipitated by a combination of belligerency, reckless actions, miscalculation, and fear of a first strike by the other side. Each side's fear of a possible first strike by the other has become an element of increasing danger in recent years. Modern weapons, such as the Soviet SS-18 and SS-19 and the improved American Minuteman III missile and planned MX missile, have a greatly increased ability to destroy enemy missiles in their silos, thus adding to the incentive to strike first. The peril is that in a crisis either side, fearful of losing the advantage, would order a first strike.

It was during an international crisis – the Cuban missile crisis in 1962 – that the world apparently came as close as it has yet come to a nuclear holocaust. On that occasion, a dread of nuclear doom became palpable not only in the councils of power but among ordinary people around the world. At the height of the crisis, it is reported, President John Kennedy believed that the odds of a holocaust were between one out of three and even. In the memoir *Thirteen Days*, Robert Kennedy, Attorney General at the time, offered a recollection of the moments of greatest peril. President Kennedy had ordered a blockade of all shipping to Cuba, where, American intelligence had found, the Soviet Union was emplacing missiles capable of carrying nuclear warheads. Missile crews in the United Stated had been placed on maximum alert. Now, at a few minutes after ten o'clock on the morning of October

24th, two Russian ships, accompanied by a Russian submarine, had approached to within a few miles of the blockade. Robert Kennedy wrote:

> I think these few minutes were the time of gravest concern for the President. Was the world on the brink of a holocaust? Was it our error? A mistake? Was there something further that should have been done? Or not done? His hand went up to his face and covered his mouth. He opened and closed his fist. His face seemed drawn, his eyes pained, almost grey. We stared at each other across the table. For a few fleeting seconds, it was almost as though no one else was there and he was no longer the President.... We had come to the time of final decision.... I felt we were on the edge of a precipice with no way off. This time, the moment was now – not next week – not tomorrow, 'so we can have another meeting and decide;' not in eight hours, 'so we can send another message to Khrushchev and perhaps he will finally understand.' No, none of that was possible. One thousand miles away in the vast expanse of the Atlantic Ocean the final decisions were going to be made in the next few minutes. President Kennedy had initiated the course of events, but he no longer had control over them.

Any number of future crises that would lead to an attack can be pictured, but I would like to mention one possible category that seems particularly dangerous. In the theory of nuclear deterrence, each side would ideally deter attacks at every level of violence with a deterrent force at the same level. Thus, conventional attacks would be deterred with conventional forces, tactical attacks would be deterred with tactical forces, and strategic attacks would be deterred with strategic forces. The theoretical advantage of matching forces in this fashion would be that the opening moves in hypothetical hostilities would not necessarily lead to escalation – for example, by leading the side weaker in conventional forces to respond to a conventional attack with nuclear weapons. However, the facts of geography make such ideal deterrent symmetry impracticable. The Soviet Union's proximity both to Western Europe and to the Middle East gives it a heavy conventional preponderance in those parts of the world. Therefore, throughout the postwar period it has been American policy to deter a Soviet conventional attack in Europe with tactical nuclear arms. And in January of 1980 President Carter, in effect, extended the policy to include protection of the nations around the Persian Gulf. In his State of the Union address for 1980, Carter said, 'An attempt by any outside force to gain control of the Persian Gulf region will be regarded as an assault on the vital interests of the United States of America. And such an assault will be repelled by any means necessary, including military force.' Since the United States clearly lacked the conventional power to repel a Soviet attack in a region near the borders of the Soviet Union, 'any means' could refer to nothing but nuclear arms. The threat was spelled out explicitly shortly after the speech, in a story in the New York *Times* – thought to be a leak from the Administration – about a 1979 Defence Department 'study', which, according to the *Times*, said that American conventional forces could not stop a Soviet thrust into northern Iran, and that 'to prevail in an Iranian scenario, we might have to threaten or make use of tactical nuclear weapons.' The words of this study put the world on notice that the use of nuclear arms not only was contemplated in past crises but will continue to be contemplated in future ones.

Not surprisingly, predictions of the course of an attack are subject to intellectual fashion (there being nothing in the way of experience to guide them). In the 1960s, for example, it was widely believed that the most important attack to deter was an all-out one, but in the last few years the idea that a 'limited nuclear war' might be fought has come into vogue. The premise of the limited-war theory is that nuclear hostilities can be halted at some new equilibrium in the balance of forces, before all-out attacks have been launched. In particular, it has been argued recently by nuclear theorists that the Soviet Union is now able to launch a devastating first strike at American bombers and land-based missiles, leaving the United States in the unfavourable position of having to choose between using its less accurate submarine-based missiles to attack Soviet society directly – and thus risk a direct attack on its own society in return – and doing nothing. Rather than initiate the annihilation of both societies, it is argued, American leaders might acquiesce in the Soviet first strike.

But there is something dreamlike and fantastic in this concept of a wholly one-way nuclear strike, which, while leaving intact the power of the assaulted country to devastate the society of the aggressor, would somehow allow the aggressor to dictate terms. What seems to have been forgotten is that, unless one assumes that the adversary has gone insane (in which case not even the most fool-proof scenarios can save us), military actions are taken with some aim in mind – for example, the aim of conquering a particular territory. This imagined first strike would in itself achieve nothing, and the moment the Soviet Union might try to achieve some actual advantage – for example, by marching into the Middle East to seize its oil fields – two or three nuclear weapons from among the thousands remaining in American arsenals would suffice to put a quick end to the undertaking. Or if the United States retaliated with only ten bombs on Soviet cities, holding back the rest, the Soviet Union would suffer unprecedented losses while gaining nothing. In other words, in this scenario – and, indeed, in any number of other scenarios for 'limited nuclear war' which could be mentioned – strategic theory seems to have taken on a weird life of its own, in which the weapons are pictured as having their own quarrel to settle, irrespective of mere human purposes. In general, in the theoretically sophisticated but often humanly deficient world of nuclear strategic theory it is likely to be overlooked that the outbreak of nuclear hostilities in itself assumes the collapse of every usual restraint of reason and humanity. Once the mass killing of a nuclear holocaust had begun, the scruples, and even the reckonings of self-interest, that normally keep the actions of nations within certain bounds will by definition have been trampled down, and will probably offer little further protection for anybody. In the unimaginable mental and spiritual climate of the world at that point it is hard to imagine what force could be counted on to hold the world back from all-out destruction.

However, it would be misleading to suggest that once one nuclear weapon had been used it would be inevitable for all of them to be used. Rather, the point is that once a catastrophe that we now find 'unthinkable' actually commenced, people would act in ways that are unforeseeable by theorists – or, for that matter, by the future actors themselves. Predictions about the size and form of a nuclear holocaust are really predictions about human decisions, and these are notoriously incalculable in advance – especially when the decisions in question are going to be made in the midst of unimaginable mayhem. The United States Secretary of Defense Robert McNamara probably said the last word on this subject when he remarked before the House Armed Services Committee in 1963, in regard to a possible defence of Europe, that once the first tactical nuclear weapon had been used the world would have been launched into 'a vast unknown'. In picturing a Soviet attack on the United States I shall not venture any predictions concerning the shape and size of the attack, since to do so, it seems to me, would be to pretend to a kind of knowledge that we are incapable of. Instead, I shall simply choose two basic assumptions – not as predictions but postulates. The first is that most of the Soviet strategic forces are used in the attack, and the second is that the attack is aimed at military facilities, industry, and the population centres of the United States. I have chosen these assumptions because, in the absence of any basis for confident prediction, and, in particular, of any reliable assurance that an attack would remain 'limited', they are the only assumptions that represent the full measure of our peril. The first assumption is supported by many statements by leaders on both sides. The Soviet government, which, of course, is one of the actors concerned, has frequently stated the view that nuclear hostilities cannot be limited, and Defense Secretary Harold Brown also said, in 1977, that a nuclear conflict probably could not be limited. Concerning the second assumption, the significant point is that the fundamental logic of the strategy of both sides is, in McNamara's words, to hold not just the military forces of the other side hostage but also its 'society as a whole'. Just how the strategists on both sides achieve this is unknown, but it seems unwarranted to suppose that there will be much relief for either population in the merciful sentiments of targeters.

A further set of assumptions that influence one's judgement of the consequences of a holocaust concerns the possibility of civil defence, since shelters, even if they existed, would be of no use. It is now commonly acknowledged that economically feasible shelters cannot provide protection against the blast, heat, intense radiation, and mass fires that would probably occur in densely populated regions of the country – that such shelters could save lives only in places that were subjected to nothing worse than modest amounts of fallout. It is also worth mentioning that, whatever the potential value of shelters might be, most existing ones either are situated in places where they are useless (in large cities, for example) or lack some or all of the following necessary equipment for an effective shelter: adequate shielding from radiation; air filters that would screen out radioactive particles; food and water to last as long as several months; an independent heating system, in places where winters are severe; medical supplies for the injured, sick, and dying, who might be in the majority in the shelters; radiation counters to measure levels of radiation outdoors, so that people could know when it was safe to leave the shelter and could determine whether food and drink were contaminated; and a burial system wholly contained within the shelter, in which to bury those who died of their injuries or illness during the shelter period.

Systems setting up evacuation procedures and shelters are often presented as humanitarian measures that would save lives in the event of a nuclear attack. In the last analysis, however, the civil-defence issue is a strategic, not a humanitarian, question. It is fundamental to the nuclear strategy of both the Soviet Union and the United States that each preserve the capacity to devastate the population of the other after itself absorbing the largest first strike that is within the other's capacity. Therefore, any serious attempt by either side to make its population safe from nuclear attack – assuming for the moment that this could be done – would be extremely likely to call forth a strategic countermove by the other side, probably taking the form of increased armament. Since the extraordinary power of modern weapons makes such compensation quite easy, it is safe to assume that for the foreseeable future the population of each side is going to remain exactly as vulnerable as the other side wants it to be.

The yardsticks by which one can measure the destruction that will be caused by weapons of different sizes are provided by the bombings of Hiroshima and Nagasaki and American nuclear tests in which the effects of hydrogen bombs with up to sixteen hundred times the explosive yield of the Hiroshima bomb were determined. The data gathered from these experiences make it a straightforward matter to work out the distances from the explosion at which different intensities of the various effects of a bomb are likely to occur. In the back of Samuel Glasstone's book, for instance, the reader will find a small dial computer that places all this information at his fingertips. Thus, if one would like to know how deep a crater a twenty-megaton ground burst will leave in wet soil one has only to set a pointer at twenty megatons and look in a small window showing crater size to find that the depth would be six hundred feet – a hole deep enough to bury a fair-sized skyscraper. Yet part of the horror of thinking about a holocaust lies in the fact that it leads us to supplant the human world with a statistical world; we seek a human truth and come up with a handful of figures. The only source that gives us a glimpse of that human truth is the testimony of the survivors of the Hiroshima and Nagasaki bombings.

On August 6, 1945, at 8.16 a.m., a fission bomb with a yield of twelve and a half kilotons was detonated about nineteen hundred feet above the central section of Hiroshima. By present-day standards, the bomb was a small one, and in today's arsenals it would be classed among the merely tactical weapons. Nevertheless, it was large enough to transform a city of some three hundred and forty thousand people into hell in the space of a few seconds. 'It is no exaggeration,' the authors of *Hiroshima and Nagaski* tell us, 'to say that the whole city was ruined instantaneously.' In that instant, tens of thousands of people were burned, blasted, and crushed to death. Other tens of thousands suffered injuries of every description or were doomed to die of radiation sickness. The centre of the city was flattened, and every part of the city was damaged. The trunks of bamboo trees as far away as five miles from ground zero – the point on the ground directly under the centre of the explosion – were charred. Almost half the trees within a mile and a quarter were knocked down. Windows nearly seventeen miles away were broken. Half an hour after the blast, fires set by the thermal pulse and by the collapse of the buildings began to coalesce into a firestorm, which lasted for six hours. Starting about 9 a.m. and lasting until late afternoon, a 'black rain' generated by the bomb (otherwise, the day was fair) fell on the western portions of the city, carrying radioactive fallout from the blast to the ground. For four hours at midday, a violent whirlwind, born of the strange meteorological conditions produced by the explosion, further devastated the city. The number of people who were killed outright or who died of their injuries over the next three months is estimated to be a hundred and thirty thousand. Sixty-eight per cent of the buildings in the city were either completely destroyed or damaged beyond repair, and the centre of the city was turned into a flat, rubble-strewn plain dotted with the ruins of a few of the sturdier buildings.

In the minutes after the detonation, the day grew dark, as heavy clouds of dust and smoke filled the air. A whole city had fallen in a moment, and in and under its ruins were its people. Among those still living, most were injured, and of these most were burned or had in some way been battered or had suffered both kinds of injury. Those within a mile and a quarter of ground zero had also been subjected to intense nuclear radiation, often in lethal doses. When people revived enough from their unconsciousness or shock to see what was happening around them, they found that where a second before there had been a city getting ready to go about its daily business on a peaceful, warm August morning, now there was a heap of debris and corpses and a stunned mass of injured humanity. But at first, as they awakened and tried to find their bearings in the gathering darkness, many felt cut off and alone. In a recent volume of recollections by survivors called *Unforgettable Fire*, in which the effects of the bombing are rendered in drawings as well as in words, Haruko Ogasawara, a young girl on that August morning, recalls that she was at first knocked unconscious. She goes on to write:

> How many seconds or minutes had passed I could not tell, but, regaining consciousness, I found myself lying on the ground covered with pieces of wood. When I stood up in a frantic effort to look around, there was darkness. Terribly frightened, I thought I was alone in a world of death, and groped for any light. My fear was so great I did not think anyone would truly understand. When I came to my senses, I found my clothes in shreds, and I was without my wooden sandals.

Soon cries of pain and cries for help from the wounded filled the air. Survivors heard the voices of their families and their friends calling out in the gloom. Ogasawara writes:

> Suddenly, I wondered what had happened to my mother and sister. My mother was then forty-five, and my sister five years old. When the darkness began to fade, I found that there was nothing around me. My house, the next door neighbour's house, and the next had all vanished. I was standing amid the ruins of my house. No one was

> around. It was quiet, very quiet – an eerie moment. I discovered my mother in a water tank. She had fainted. Crying out, 'Mama, Mama,' I shook her to bring her back to her senses. After coming to, my mother began to shout madly for my sister: 'Eiko! Eiko!'
>
> I wonder how much time had passed when there were cries of searches. Children were calling their parents' names, and parents were calling the names of their children. We were calling desperately for my sister and listening for her voice and looking to see her. Suddenly, Mother cried 'Oh Eiko!' Four or five meters away, my sister's head was sticking out and was calling my mother. ...Mother and I worked desperately to remove the plaster and pillars and pulled her out with great effort. Her body had turned purple from the bruises, and her arm was so badly wounded that we could have placed two fingers in the wound.

Others were less fortunate in their searches and rescue attempts. In *Unforgettable Fire*, a housewife describes a scene she saw:

> A mother, driven half-mad while looking for her child, was calling his name. At last she found him. His head looked like a boiled octopus. His eyes were half-closed, and his mouth was white, pursed, and swollen.

Throughout the city, parents were discovering their wounded or dead children, and children were discovering their wounded or dead parents. Kikuno Segawa recalls seeing a little girl with her dead mother:

> A woman who looked like an expectant mother was dead. At her side, a girl of about three years of age brought some water in an empty can she had found. She was trying to let her mother drink from it.

The sight of people in extremities of suffering was ubiquitous. Kinzo Nishida recalls:

> While taking my severely wounded wife out to the river-bank by the side of the hill of Nakahiro-machi, I was horrified, indeed, at the sight of a stark naked man standing in the rain with his eyeball in his palm. He looked to be in great pain, but there was nothing that I could do for him.

Many people were astonished by the sheer sudden absence of the known world. The writer Yoko Ota later wrote:

> I just could not understand why our surroundings had changed so greatly in one instant.... I thought it might have been something which had nothing to do with the war – the collapse of the earth, which it was said would take place at the end of the world, and which I had read about as a child.

And a history professor who looked back at the city after the explosion remarked later, 'I saw that Hiroshima had disappeared.'

As the fires sprang up in the ruins, many people, having found injured family members and friends, were now forced to abandon them to the flames or to lose their own lives in the firestorm. Those who left children, husbands, wives, friends, and strangers to burn often found these experiences the most awful of the entire ordeal. Mikio Inoue describes how one man, a professor, came to abandon his wife:

> It was when I crossed Miyuki Bridge that I saw Professor Takenaka, standing at the foot of the bridge. He was almost naked, wearing nothing but shorts, and he had a ball of rice in his right hand. Beyond the streetcar line, the northern area was covered by red fire burning against the sky. Far away from the line, Ote-machi was also a sea of fire.
>
> That day, Professor Takenaka had not gone to Hiroshima University, and the A-bomb exploded when he was at home. He tried to rescue his wife, who was trapped under a roof-beam, but all his efforts were in vain. The fire was threatening him also. His wife pleaded, 'Run away dear!' He was forced to desert his wife and escape from the fire. He was now at the foot of Miyuki Bridge.
>
> But I wonder how he came to hold that ball of rice in his hand. His naked figure, standing there before the flames with that ball of rice, looked to me as a symbol of the modest hopes of human beings.

In *Hiroshima*, John Hersey describes the flight of a group of German priests and their Japanese colleagues through a burning section of the city:

> The street was cluttered with parts of houses that had slid

> into it, and with fallen telephone poles and wires. From every second or third house came the voices of people buried and abandoned, who invariably screamed, with formal politeness, '*Tasukete kure!* Help, if you please!' The priests recognized several ruins from which these cries came as the homes of friends, but because of the fire it was too late to help.

And thus it happened that throughout Hiroshima all the ties of affection and respect that join human beings to one another were being pulled and rent by the spreading firestorm. Soon processions of the injured – processions of a kind that had never been seen before in history – began to file away from the centre of the city toward its outskirts. Most of the people suffered from burns, which had often blackened their skin or caused it to sag off them. A grocer who joined one of these processions has described them in an interview with Robert Jay Lifton which appears in his book *Death in Life*:

> They held their arms bent [forward] ... and their skin – not only on their hands but on their faces and bodies, too – hung down .... If there had been only one or two such people ... perhaps I would not have had such a strong impression. But wherever I walked, I met these people.... Many of them died along the road. I can still picture them in my mind – like walking ghosts. They didn't look like people of this world.

The grocer also recalls that because of people's injuries 'you couldn't tell whether you were looking at them from in front or in back.' People found it impossible to recognize one another. A woman who at the time was a girl of thirteen, and suffered disfiguring burns on her face, has recalled, 'My face was so distorted and changed that people couldn't tell who I was. After a while I could call others' names but they couldn't recognize me.' In addition to being injured, many people were vomiting – an early symptom of radiation sickness. For many, horrifying and unreal events occurred in a chaotic jumble. In *Unforgettable Fire*, Torako Hironaka enumerates some of the things that she remembers:

1. Some burned work-clothes.
2. People crying for help with their heads, shoulders, or the soles of their feet injured by fragments of broken window

glass. Glass fragments were scattered everywhere.

3. [A woman] crying, saying 'Aigo! Aigo!' (a Korean expression of sorrow).
4. A burning pine tree.
5. A naked woman.
6. Naked girls crying, 'Stupid America!'
7. I was crouching in a puddle, for fear of being shot by a machine gun. My breasts were torn.
8. Burned down electric power lines.
9. A telephone pole had burned and fallen down.
10. A field of watermelons.
11. A dead horse.
12. What with dead cats, pigs, and people, it was just a hell on earth.

Physical collapse brought emotional and spiritual collapse with it. The survivors were, on the whole, listless and stupefied. After the escapes, and the failures to escape, from the firestorm, a silence fell over the city and its remaining population. People suffered and died without speaking or otherwise making a sound. The processions of the injured, too, were soundless. Dr Michihiko Hachiya has written in his book *Hiroshima Diary*:

> Those who were able walked silently toward the suburbs in the distant hills, their spirits broken, their initiative gone. When asked whence they had come, they pointed to the city and said, 'That way,' and when asked where they were going, pointed away from the city and said, 'This way.' They were so broken and confused that they moved and behaved like automatons.
>
> Their reactions had astonished outsiders, who reported with amazement the spectacle of long files of people holding stolidly to a narrow, rough path when close by was a smooth, easy road going in the same direction. The outsiders could not grasp the fact that they were witnessing the exodus of a people who walked in the realm of dreams.

Those who were still capable of action often acted in an absurd or an insane way. Some of them energetically pursued tasks that had made sense in the intact Hiroshima of a few minutes before but were now utterly inappropriate. Hersey relates that the German priests were bent on bringing to safety a suitcase, containing diocesan accounts and a sum of money, that they had rescued from the fire and were carrying around with them through the burning city. And Dr Lifton describes a young soldier's punctilious efforts to find and preserve the ashes of a burned military code book while people around him were screaming for help. Other people simply lost their minds. For example, when the German priests were escaping from the firestorm, one of them, Father Wilhelm Kleinsorge, carried on his back a Mr Fukai, who kept saying that he wanted to remain where he was. When Father Kleinsorge finally put Mr Fukai down, he started running. Hersey writes:

> Father Kleinsorge shouted to a dozen soldiers, who were standing by the bridge, to stop him. As Father Kleinsorge started back to get Mr Fukai, Father LaSalle called out, 'Hurry! Don't waste time!' So Father Kleinsorge just requested the soldiers to take care of Mr Fukai. They said they would, but the little, broken man got away from them, and the last the priests could see of him, he was running back toward the fire.

In the weeks after the bombing, many survivors began to notice the appearance of petechiae – small spots caused by hemorrhages – on their skin. These usually signalled the onset of the critical stage of radiation sickness. In the first stage, the victims characteristically vomited repeatedly, ran a fever, and developed an abnormal thirst. (The cry 'Water! Water!' was one of the few sounds often heard in Hiroshima on the day of the bombing.) Then, after a few hours or days, there was a deceptively hopeful period of remission of symptoms, called the latency period, which lasted from about a week to about four weeks. Radiation attacks the reproductive function of cells, and those that reproduce most frequently are therefore the most vulnerable. Among these are the bone-marrow cells, which are responsible for the production of blood cells. During the latency period, the count of white blood cells, which are instrumental in fighting infections, and the count of platelets, which are instrumental in clotting, drop precipitously, so the body is poorly defended against infection and is liable to hemorrhaging. In the third, and final, stage, which may last for several weeks, the victim's hair may fall out and he may suffer from diarrhea and may bleed from the intestines, the mouth, or other parts of the body, and in the end he will either recover or die. Because the fireball of the Hiroshima bomb did not touch the ground, very little ground material was mixed with the fission products of the bomb, and therefore very little local fallout was generated. (What fallout there was descended in the black rain.) Therefore, the fatalities from radiation sickness were probably all caused by the initial nuclear radiation, and since this affected only people within a radius of a mile and a quarter of ground zero, most of the people who received lethal doses were killed more quickly by the thermal pulse and the blast wave. Thus, Hiroshima did not experience the mass radiation sickness that can be expected if a weapon is ground-burst. Since the Nagasaki bomb was also burst in the air, the effect of widespread lethal fallout on large areas, causing the death by radiation sickness of whole populations in the hours, days, and weeks after the blast, is a form of nuclear horror that the world has not experienced.

What happened at Hiroshima was less than a millionth part of a holocaust at present levels of world nuclear armament. The more than millionfold difference amounts to more than a difference in magnitude; it is also a difference in kind. The authors of *Hiroshima and Nagasaki* observe that 'an atomic bomb's massive destruction and indiscriminate slaughter involves the sweeping breakdown of all order and existence – in a word, the collapse of society itself,' and that therefore 'the essence of atomic destruction lies in the totality of its impact on man and society.' This is true also of a holocaust, of course, except that the totalities in question are now not single cities but nations, ecosystems, and the earth's ecosphere. Yet with the exception of fallout, which was relatively light at Hiroshima and Nagasaki, the immediate devastation caused by today's bombs would be of a sort similar to the devastation in those cities. The immediate effects of a twenty-megaton bomb are not different in kind from those of a twelve-and-a-half-kiloton bomb; they are only more extensive. In bursts of both weapons, for instance, there is a radius within which the thermal pulse can ignite newspapers: for the twelve-and-a-half-kiloton weapon, it is a little over two miles; for the twenty-megaton weapon, it is twenty-five miles. (Since there is no inherent limit on the size of a nuclear weapon, these figures can be increased indefinitely, subject only to the limitations imposed by the technical capacities of the bomb builder – and of the earth's capacity to absorb the blast. The Soviet Union, which has shown a liking for sheer size in so many of its undertakings, once detonated a sixty-megaton bomb.)

The Hiroshima people's experience, accordingly, is of much more than historical interest. It is a picture of what our whole world is always poised to become – a backdrop of scarcely imaginable horror lying just behind the surface of our normal life, and capable of breaking through into that normal life at any second. Whether we choose to think about it or not, it is an omnipresent, inescapable truth about our lives today that at every single moment each one of us may suddenly become the deranged mother looking for her burned child; the professor with the ball of rice in his hand whose wife has just died in the fires; Mr Fukai running back into the firestorm; the naked man standing on the blasted plain that was his city, holding his eyeball in his hand; or, more likely, one of millions of corpses. For whatever our 'modest hopes' as human beings may be, every one of them can be nullified by a nuclear holocaust.

One way to begin to grasp the destructive power of present-day nuclear weapons is to describe the consequences of the detonation of a one-megaton bomb, which possesses eighty times the explosive power of the Hiroshima bomb, on a large city, such as New York. Burst some eighty-five hundred feet above the Empire State Building, a one-megaton bomb would gut or flatten almost every building between Battery Park and 125th Street, or within a radius of four and four-tenths miles, or in an area of sixty-one square miles, and would heavily damage buildings between the northern tip of Staten Island and the George Washington Bridge, or within a radius of about eight miles, or in an area of about two hundred square miles. A conventional explosive delivers a swift shock, like a slap, to whatever it hits, but the blast wave of a sizable nuclear weapon endures for several seconds and 'can surround and destroy whole buildings' (Glasstone). People, of course, would be picked up and hurled away from the blast along with the rest of the debris. Within the sixty-one square miles, the walls, roofs, and floors of any buildings that had not been flattened would be collapsed, and the people and furniture inside would be swept down onto the street. In New York, where the buildings are tall and are constructed of heavy materials, the physical collapse of the city would certainly kill millions of people. The streets of New York are narrow ravines running between the high walls of the city's buildings. In a nuclear attack, the walls would fall and the ravines would fill up. The people in the buildings would fall with the debris of the buildings, and the people in the street would be crushed by this avalanche of people and buildings. At a distance of two miles or so from ground zero, winds would reach four hundred miles an hour, and another two miles away they would reach a hundred and eighty miles an hour. Meanwhile, the fireball would be growing, until it was more than a mile wide, and rocketing upward, to a height of over six miles. For ten seconds, it would broil the city below. Anyone caught in the open within nine miles of ground zero would receive third-degree burns and would probably be killed; closer to the explosion, people would be charred and killed instantly. From Greenwich Village up to Central Park, the heat would be great enough to melt metal and glass. Readily inflammable materials, such as newspapers and dry leaves, would ignite in all five boroughs (though in only a small part of Staten Island) and west to the Passaic River, in New Jersey, within a radius of about nine and a half miles from ground zero, thereby creating an area of more than two hundred and eighty square miles in which mass fires were likely to break out.

If it were possible (as it would not be) for someone to stand at Fifth Avenue and Seventy-second Street (about two miles from ground zero) without being instantly killed, he would see the following sequence of events. A dazzling white light from the fireball would illumine the scene, continuing for perhaps thirty seconds. Simultaneously, searing heat would ignite everything flammable and start to melt windows, cars, buses, lamp-posts, and anything else made of metal or glass. People in the street would immediately catch fire, and would shortly be reduced to heavily charred corpses. About five seconds after the light appeared, the blast wave would strike, laden with the debris of a now non-existent midtown. Some buildings might be crushed, as though a giant fist had squeezed them on all sides, and others might be picked up off their foundations and whirled uptown with the other debris. On the far side of Central Park, the West Side skyline would fall from south to north. The four-hundred-mile-an-hour wind would blow from south to north, die down after a few seconds, and then blow in the reverse direction with diminished intensity. At the same time, the fireball would be burning in the sky for the ten seconds of the thermal pulse. Soon huge, thick clouds of dust and smoke would envelop the scene, and as the mushroom cloud rushed overhead (it would have a diameter of about twelve miles) the light from the sun would be blotted out, and day would turn to night. Within minutes, fires, ignited both by the thermal pulse and by broken gas mains, tanks of gas and oil, and the like, would begin to spread in the darkness, and a strong, steady wind would begin to blow in the direction of the blast. As at Hiroshima, a whirlwind might be produced, which would sweep through the ruins, and radioactive rain, generated under the meteorological conditions created by the blast, might fall. Before long, the individual fires would coalesce into a mass fire, which, depending largely on the winds, would become either a conflagration or a firestorm. In a conflagration, prevailing winds spread a wall of fire as far as there is any combustible material to sustain it; in a firestorm, a vertical updraft caused by the fire itself sucks the surrounding air in toward a central point, and the fires therefore converge in a single fire of extreme heat. A mass fire of either kind renders shelters useless by burning up all the oxygen in the air and creating toxic gases, so that anyone inside the shelters is asphyxiated, and also by heating the ground to such high temperatures that the shelters turn, in effect, into ovens, cremating the people inside them. In Dresden, several days after the firestorm raised there by Allied conventional bombing, the interiors of some bomb shelters were still so hot that when they were opened the inrushing air caused the contents to burst into flame. Only those who had fled their shelters when the bombing started had any chance of surviving. (It is difficult to predict in a particular situation which form the fires will take. Hiroshima suffered a firestorm and Nagasaki suffered a conflagration).

In this vast theatre, all the scenes of agony and death that took place at Hiroshima would again take place, but now involving millions of people rather than hundreds of thousands. Like the people of Hiroshima, the people of New York would be burned, battered, crushed, and irradiated in every conceivable way. The city and its people would be mingled in a smouldering heap. And then, as the fires started, the survivors (most of whom would be on the periphery of the explosion) would be driven to abandon to the flames those family members and other people who were unable to flee, or else to die with them. Before long, while the ruins burned, the processions of injured, mute people would begin their slow progress out of the outskirts of the devastated zone. However, this time a much smaller proportion of the population than at Hiroshima would have a chance of escaping. In general, as the size of the area of devastation increases, the possibilities for escape decrease. When the devastated area is relatively small, as it was at Hiroshima, people who are not incapacitated will have a good chance of escaping to safety before the fires coalesce into a mass fire. But when the devastated area is great, as it would be after the detonation of a megaton bomb, and fires are springing up at a distance of nine and a half miles from ground zero, and when what used to be the streets are piled high with burning rubble, and the day (if the attack occurs in the daytime) has grown impenetrably dark, there is little chance that anyone who is not on the very edge of the devastated area will be able to make his way to safety. In New York, most people would die wherever the blast found them, or not very far from there.

If instead of being burst in the air the bomb was burst on or near the ground in the vicinity of the Empire State Building, the overpressure would be very much greater near the centre of the blast area but the range hit by a minimum of five pounds per square inch of overpressure would be less. The range of the thermal pulse would be about the same as that of the air burst. The fireball would be almost two miles across, and would engulf midtown Manhattan from Greenwich Village nearly to Central Park. Very little is known about what would happen to a city that was inside a fireball, but one would expect a good deal of what was there to be first pulverized and then melted or vaporized. Any human beings in the area would be reduced to smoke and ashes; they would simply disappear. A crater roughly three blocks in diameter and two hundred feet deep would open up. In addition, heavy radioactive fallout would be created as dust and debris from the city rose with the mushroom cloud and then fell back to the ground. Fallout would begin to drop almost immediately, contaminating the ground beneath the cloud with levels of radiation many times lethal doses, and quickly killing anyone who might have survived the blast wave and the thermal pulse and might now be attempting an escape; it is difficult to believe that there would be appreciable survival of the people of the city after a megaton ground burst. And for the next twenty-four hours or so more fallout would descend downwind from the blast, in a plume whose direction and length would depend on the speed and the direction of the wind that happened to be blowing at the time of the attack. If the wind was blowing at fifteen miles an hour, fallout of lethal intensity would descend in a plume about a hundred and fifty miles long and as much as fifteen miles wide. Fallout that was sub-lethal but could still cause serious illness would extend another hundred and fifty miles downwind. Exposure to radioactivity in human beings is measured in units called *rems* – an acronym for 'roentgen equivalent in man'. The roentgen is a standard measurement of gamma- and X-ray radiation, and the expression 'equivalent in man' indicates that an adjustment has been made to take into account the differences in the degree of biological damage that is caused by radiation of different types. Many of the kinds of harm done to human beings by radiation – for example, the incidence of cancer and of genetic damage – depend on the dose accumulated over many years; but radiation sickness, capable of causing death, results from an 'acute' dose, received in a period of anything from a few seconds to several days. Doses in the thousands of rems, which could be expected throughout the city, would attack the central nervous system and would bring about death within a few hours. Doses of around a thousand rems, which would be delivered some tens of miles downwind from the blast, would kill within two weeks everyone who was exposed to them. Doses of around five hundred rems, which would be delivered as far as a hundred and fifty miles downwind (given a wind speed of fifteen miles per hour), would kill half of all exposed able-bodied young adults.

At this level of exposure, radiation sickness proceeds in the three stages observed at Hiroshima. The plume of lethal fallout could descend, depending on the direction of the wind, on other parts of New York State and parts of New Jersey, Pennsylvania, Delaware, Maryland, Connecticut, Massachusetts, Rhode Island, Vermont, and New Hampshire, killing additional millions of people. The circumstances in heavily contaminated areas, in which millions of people werc all declining together, over a period of weeks, toward painful deaths, are ones that, like so many of the consequences of nuclear explosions, have never been experienced.

A description of the effects of a one-megaton bomb on New York City gives some notion of the meaning in human terms of a megaton of nuclear explosive power, but a weapon that is more likely to be used against New York is the twenty-megaton bomb, which has one thousand six hundred times the yield of the Hiroshima bomb. The Soviet Union is estimated to have at least a hundred and thirteen twenty-megaton bombs in its nuclear arsenal, carried by Bear intercontinental bombers. In addition, some of the Soviet SS-18 missiles are capable of carrying bombs of this size, although the actual yields are not known. Since the explosive power of the twenty-megaton bombs greatly exceeds the amount necessary to destroy most military targets, it is reasonable to suppose that they are meant for use against large cities. If a twenty-megaton bomb were air-burst over the Empire State Building at an altitude of thirty thousand feet, the zone of heavy damage from the blast wave (the zone hit by a minimum of two pounds of overpressure per square inch) would have a radius of twenty-one and a half miles, or an area of one thousand four hundred and fifty square miles, reaching to the southernmost tip of Staten Island, north as far as southern Rockland County, east into Nassau County, and west to Morris County, New Jersey. The fireball would be about four and a half miles in diameter and would radiate the thermal pulse for some twenty seconds. People caught in the open twenty-three miles away from ground zero, in Long Island, New Jersey, and southern New York State, would be burned to death. People hundreds of miles away who looked at the burst would be temporarily blinded and would risk permanent eye injury. (After the test of a fifteen-megaton bomb on Bikini Atoll, in the South Pacific, in March of 1954, small animals were found to have suffered retinal burns at a distance of three hundred and forty five miles.) The mushroom cloud would be seventy miles in diameter. New York City and its suburbs would be transformed into a lifeless, flat, scorched desert in a few seconds.

If a twenty-megaton bomb were ground-burst on the Empire State Building, the range of severe blast damage would, as with the one-megaton ground blast, be reduced, but the fireball, which would be almost six miles in diameter, would cover Manhattan from Wall Street to northern Central Park and also parts of New Jersey, Brooklyn, and Queens, and everyone within it would be instantly killed, with most of them physically disappearing. Fallout would again be generated, this time covering thousands of square miles with lethal intensities of radiation. A fair portion of New York City and its incinerated population, now radioactive dust, would have risen into the mushroom cloud and would now be descending on the surrounding territory. On one of the few occasions when local fallout was generated by a test explosion in the multi-megaton range, the fifteen-megaton bomb tested on Bikini Atoll, which was exploded seven feet above the surface of a coral reef, 'caused substantial contamination over an area of more than seven thousand square miles.' If, as seems likely, a twenty-megaton bomb ground-burst on New York would produce at least a comparable amount of fallout, and if the wind carried the fallout onto populated areas, then this one bomb would probably doom upward of twenty million people, or almost ten per cent of the population of the United States.

The 'strategic' forces of the Soviet Union are so far capable of carrying seven thousand warheads with an estimated maximum yield of more than seventeen thousand megatons of explosive power, and, barring unexpected developments in arms-control talks, the number of warheads is expected to rise in the coming years. The actual megatonnage of the Soviet strategic forces is not known; however, it is reasonable to suppose that the actual megatonnage is as much as two-thirds of the maximum, which would be about eleven and a half thousand megatons. If we assume that in a first strike the Soviets held back about a thousand megatons (itself an immense force), then the attack would amount to about ten thousand megatons, or the equivalent of eight hundred thousand Hiroshima bombs. I asked Dr Kendall, who has done considerable research on the consequences of nuclear attacks, to sketch out in rough terms what the actual distribution of bombs might be in a ten-thousand-megaton Soviet attack in the early 1980s on all targets in the United States, military and civilian.

'Without serious distortion,' he said, 'we can begin by imagining that we would be dealing with ten thousand weapons of one megaton each, although in fact the yields would, of course, vary considerably. Let us also make the assumption, based on common knowledge of weapons design, that on average the yield would be one-half fission and one-half fusion. This proportion is important, because it is the fission products – a virtual museum of about three hundred radioactive isotopes, decaying at different rates – that give off radioactivity in fallout. Targets can be divided into two categories – hard and soft. Hard targets, of which there are about a thousand in the United Stated, are mostly missile silos. The majority of them can be destroyed only by huge, blunt overpressures, ranging anywhere from many hundreds to a few thousand pounds per square inch, and we can expect that two weapons might be devoted to each one to assure destruction. That would use up two thousand megatons. Because other strategic military targets – such as Strategic Air Command bases – are near centres of population, an attack on them as well, perhaps using another couple hundred megatons, could cause a total of more than twenty million casualties. If the nearly eight thousand weapons remaining were then devoted to the cities and towns of the United States in order of population, every community down to the level of fifteen hundred inhabitants would be hit with a megaton bomb – which is, of course, many, many times what would be necessary to annihilate a town that size. For obvious reasons, industry is highly correlated with population density, so an attack on the one necessarily hits the other, especially when an attack of this magnitude is considered. Ten thousand targets would include everything worth hitting in the country and much more; it would simply *be* the United States. The targeters would run out of targets and victims long before they ran out of bombs. If you imagine that the bombs were distributed according to population, then, allowing for the fact that the attack on the military installations would have already killed about twenty million people, you would have about forty megatons to devote to each remaining million people in the country. For the seven and a half million people in New York City, that would come to three hundred megatons. Bearing in mind what one megaton can do, you can see that this would be preposterous overkill. In practice, one might expect the New York metropolitan area to be hit with some dozens of one-megaton weapons.'

In the first moments of a ten-thousand-megaton attack on the United States, flashes of white light would suddenly illumine large areas of the country. In those same moments, when the first wave of missiles arrived, the vast majority of the people in the regions first targeted would be irradiated, crushed, or burned to death. The thermal pulses would subject more than six hundred thousand square miles, or one-sixth of the total land mass of the nation, to a minimum level of forty calories per centimeter squared – a level of heat that chars human beings. (At Hiroshima, charred remains in the rough shape of human beings were a common sight.) Tens of millions of people would go up in smoke. As the attack proceeded, as much as three-quarters of the country could be subjected to incendiary levels of heat, and so, wherever there was inflammable material, could be set ablaze. In the ten seconds or so after each bomb hit, as blast waves swept outward from thousands of ground zeros, the physical plant of the United States would be swept away like leaves in a gust of wind. The six hundred thousand square miles already scorched by the forty or more calories of heat per centimeter squared would now be hit by blast waves of a minimum of five pounds per square inch, and virtually all the habitations, places of work, and other man-made things there – substantially the whole human construct in the United States – would be vaporized, blasted, or otherwise pulverized out of existence. Then, as clouds of dust rose from the earth, and mushroom clouds spread overhead, often linking to form vast canopies, day would turn to night. (These clouds could blanket as much as a third of the nation.) Shortly, fires would spring up in the debris of the cities and in every forest dry enough to burn. These fires would simply burn down the United States.

When one pictures a full-scale attack on the United States, or on any other country, therefore, the picture of a single city being flattened by a single bomb – an image firmly engraved in the public imagination, probably because of the bombings of Hiroshima and Nagasaki – must give way to a picture of substantial sections of the country being turned by a sort of nuclear carpet-bombing into immense infernal regions, literally tens of thousands of square miles in area, from which escape is impossible. In Hiroshima and Nagasaki, those who had not been killed or injured so severely that they could not move were able to flee to the undevastated world around them, where they found help, but in any city where three or four bombs had been used – not to mention fifty, or a hundred – flight from one blast would only be flight toward another, and no one could escape alive. Within these regions, each of three of the immediate effects of nuclear weapons – initial radiation, thermal pulse, and blast wave – would alone be enough to kill most people: the initial nuclear radiation would subject tens of thousands of square miles to lethal doses; the blast waves, coming from all sides, would nowhere fall below the overpressure necessary to destroy almost all buildings; and the thermal pulses, also coming from all sides, would always be great enough to kill exposed people and, in addition, to set on fire everything that would burn. The ease with which virtually the whole population of the country could be trapped in these zones of universal death is suggested by the fact that the sixty per cent of the population that lives in an area of eighteen thousand square miles could be annihilated with only three hundred one-megaton bombs. That would leave nine thousand seven hundred megatons, or ninety-seven per cent of the megatonnage in the attacking force, available for other targets. (It is hard to imagine what a targeter would do with all his bombs in these circumstances. Above several thousand megatons, it would almost become a matter of trying to hunt down individual people with nuclear warheads.

Nevertheless, while the immediate nuclear effects are great enough in a ten-thousand-megaton attack to destroy the country many times over, they are not the most powerfully lethal of the local effects of nuclear weapons. The killing power of the local fallout is far greater. Therefore, if the Soviet Union was bent on producing the maximum overkill – if, that is, its surviving leaders, whether out of calculation, rage, or madness, decided to eliminate the United States not merely as a political and social entity but as a biological one – they would burst their bombs on the ground rather than in the air. Although the scope of severe blast damage would then be reduced, the blast waves, fireballs, and thermal pulses would still be far more than enough to destroy the country, and, in addition, provided only that the bombs were dispersed widely enough, lethal fallout would spread throughout the nation. The amount of radiation delivered by the fallout from a ground burst of a given size is still uncertain – not least because, as Glasstone notes, there has never been a 'true land surface burst' of a bomb with a yield of over one kiloton (the Bikini burst was in part over the ocean). However, calculations on the basis of figures for a one-megaton ground burst which are given in the United States Congressional Office of Technology Assessment's report show that ten thousand megatons would yield one-week doses around the country averaging more than ten thousand rems. In actuality, of course, the bombs would almost certainly not be evenly spaced around the country but, rather, would be concentrated in populated areas and in missile fields; and the likelihood is that in most places where people lived or worked the doses would be many times the average, commonly reaching several tens of thousands of rems for the first week, while in remote areas they would be less, or, conceivably, even non-existent.

These figures provide a context for judging the question of civil defence. With overwhelming immediate local effects striking the vast majority of the population, and with one-week doses of radiation then rising into the tens of thousands of rems, evacuation and shelters are a vain hope. Needless to say, in these circumstances evacuation before an attack would be an exercise in transporting people from one death to another. In some depictions of a holocaust, various rescue operations are described, with unafflicted survivors bringing food, clothes, and medical care to the afflicted, and the afflicted making their way to thriving, untouched communities, where churches, school auditoriums, and the like would have been set up for their care – as often happens after a bad snowstorm, say. Obviously, none of this could come about. In the first place, in a full-scale attack there would in all likelihood *be* no surviving communities, and, in the second place, everyone who failed to seal himself off from the outside environment for as long as several months would soon die of radiation sickness. Hence, in the months after a holocaust there would be no activity of any sort, as, in a reversal of the normal state of things, the dead would lie on the surface and the living, if there were any, would be buried underground.

If anyone hid himself deep enough under the earth and stayed there long enough to survive, he would emerge into a dying natural environment. The vulnerability of the environment is the last word in the argument against the usefulness of shelters: there is no hole big enough to hide all of nature in. Radioactivity penetrates the environment in many ways. The two most important components of radiation from fallout are gamma rays, which are electromagnetic radiation of the highest intensity, and beta particles, which are electrons fired at high speed from decaying nuclei. Gamma rays subject organisms to penetrating whole-body doses, and are responsible for most of the ill effects of radiation from fallout. Beta particles, which are less penetrating than gamma rays, act at short range, doing harm when they collect on the skin, or on the surface of a leaf. Two of the most harmful radioactive isotopes present in fallout are strontium-90 (with a half-life of twenty-eight years) and cesium-137 (with a half-life of thirty years). They are taken up into the food chain through the roots of plants or through direct ingestion by animals, and contaminate the environment from within. Strontium-90 happens to resemble calcium in its chemical composition, and therefore finds its way into the human diet through dairy products and is eventually deposited by the body in the bones, where it is thought to cause bone cancer. (Every person in the world now has in his bones a measurable deposit of strontium-90 traceable to the fallout from atmospheric nuclear testing.)

Plants in general have a higher tolerance to radioactivity than animals do. Nevertheless, according to Dr George M. Woodwell, who supervised the irradiation with gamma rays of a small forest at Brookhaven National Laboratory, a gamma-ray dose of ten thousand rads 'would devastate most vegetation' in the United States, and, as in the case of the pastured animals, when one figures in the beta radiation that would also be delivered by fallout the estimates for the lethal doses of gamma rays must be reduced – in this case, cut in half. As a general rule, Dr Woodwell and his colleagues at Brookhaven discovered, large plants are more vulnerable to radiation than small ones. Trees are among the first to die, grasses among the last. The most sensitive trees are pines and the other conifers, for which lethal doses are in roughly the same range as those for mammals. Any survivors coming out of their shelters a few months after the attack would find that all the pine trees that were still standing were already dead. Then, after the trees had died, forest fires would break out. Lethal doses for grasses on which tests have been done range between six thousand and thirty-three thousand rads, and a good deal of grass would therefore survive, except where the attacks had been heaviest. Most crops, on the other hand, are killed by doses below five thousand rads, and would be eliminated.

When vegetation is killed off, the land on which it grew is degraded. And as the land eroded after an attack life in lakes, rivers, and estuaries, already hard hit by radiation directly, would be further damaged by minerals flowing into the watercourses, causing eutrophication – a process in which an oversupply of nutrients in the water encourages the growth of algae and microscopic organisms, which, in turn, deplete the oxygen content of the water. When the soil loses its nutrients, it loses its ability to 'sustain a mature community' (in Dr Woodwell's words), and 'gross simplification' of the environment occurs, in which 'hardy species', such as moss and grass, replace vulnerable ones, such as trees; and 'succession' – the process by which ecosystems recover lost diversity – is then 'delayed or even arrested'. In sum, a full-scale nuclear attack would devastate the natural environment on a scale unknown since early geological times, when, in response to natural catastrophes whose nature has not been determined, sudden mass extinctions of species and whole ecosystems occurred all over the earth. How far this 'gross simplification' of the environment would go once virtually all animal life and the greater part of plant life had been destroyed and what patterns the surviving remnants of life would arrange themselves into over the long run are imponderables; but it appears that at the outset the United States would be a republic of insects and grass.

It has sometimes been claimed that the United States could survive a nuclear attack by the Soviet Union, but the bare figures on the extent of the blast waves, the thermal pulses, and the accumulated local fallout dash this hope irrevocably. They spell the doom of the United States. And if one imagines the reverse attack on the Soviet Union, its doom is spelled out in similar figures. Likewise, any country subjected to an attack of more than a few hundred megatons would be doomed. Japan, China, and the countries of Europe, where population densities are high, are especially vulnerable to damage, even at 'low' levels of attack. There is no country in Europe in which survival of the population would be appreciable after the detonation of several hundred megatons; most European countries would be annihilated by tens of megatons. And these conclusions emerge even before one takes into account the global ecological consequences of a holocaust, which would be superimposed on the local consequences. As human life and the structure of human existence are seen in the light of each person's daily life and experience, they look impressively extensive and solid, but when human things are seen in the light of the universal power unleashed onto the earth by nuclear weapons they prove to be limited and fragile, as though they were nothing more than a mould or a lichen that appears in certain crevices of the landscape and can be burned off with relative ease by nuclear fire.

Since the notion of 'limited nuclear war' has recently become attractive to the American leadership, it may not be digressive to discuss what the consequences of smaller attacks would be. Our knowledge of nuclear effects is too imprecise to permit us to know at exactly what level of attack a given percentage of the population would survive, but the fact that sixty per cent of the population lives in eighteen thousand square miles and could be eliminated by the thermal pulses, blast waves, and mass fires produced by about three hundred one-megaton bombs suggests some rough magnitudes. The fallout that would be produced by the bombs if they were ground burst would very likely kill ten or fifteen percent of the remaining population (it could lethally contaminate some three hundred thousand square miles), and if several hundred additional megatons were used the percentage of the entire populaton killed in the short term might rise to something like eighty-five. Or, to put it differently, if the level of attack on civilian targets did not rise above the low hundreds of megatons tens of millions of people might survive in the short term. But that same level of attack would destroy so much of the physical plant of the economy, and, of course, so many of the labourers and managers who make it work, that in effect the economy would be nearly one hundred percent destroyed.

Strategists of nuclear conflict often speak of a period of 'recovery' after a limited attack, but a likelier prospect is a long-term radical deterioration in the conditions of life. For a while, some supplies of food and clothing would be found in the rubble, but then these would give out. For a people, the economy – any kind of economy, primitive or modern – is the means of survival from day to day. So if you ruin the economy – if you suspend its functioning, even for a few months – you take away the means of survival. Eventually, if enough people do live, the economy will revive in one form or another, but in the meantime people will die: they will starve, because the supply of food has been cut off; they will freeze, because they have no fuel or shelter; they will perish of illness, because they have no medical care. If the economy in question is a modern technological one, the consequences will be particularly severe, for then the obstacles to restoring it will be greatest. Because a modern economy, like an ecosystem, is a single, interdependent whole, in which each part requires many other parts to keep functioning, its wholesale breakdown will leave people unable to perform the simplest, most essential tasks. Even agriculture – the immediate means of subsistence – is caught up in the operations of the interdependent machine, and breaks down when that machine breaks down. Modern agriculture depends on fertilizers to make crops grow, on machines to cultivate the crops, on transportation to carry the produce thousands of miles to the consumers, on fuel to run the means of transportation and the agricultural machinery, and on pesticides and drugs to increase production. If fertilizers, machines, transportation, fuel, pesticides, and drugs are taken away, agriculture will come to a halt, and people will starve. Also, because of the interdependence of the system, no sector of the economy can be repaired unless many of the other sectors are in good order.

Lastly, over the decades not only would the survivors of a limited attack face a contaminated and degraded environment but they themselves – their flesh, bones, and genetic endowment – would be contaminated: the generations that would be trying to rebuild a human life would be sick and possibly deformed. The actual doses received by particular survivors would, of course, depend on their circumstances, but some notion of the extent of the contamination can perhaps be gathered from the fact that if people came out of shelters after three months into an area in which the fallout would in the long run deliver a dose of ten thousand rems they would still receive about three per cent of the total, or three hundred rems, over their lifetimes, with two hundred of those rems being received in the first year.

In considering the global consequences of a holocaust, the first question to be asked is how widespread the hostilities would be. It is often assumed that a holocaust, even if it were full-scale, would be restricted to the Northern Hemisphere, destroying the United States, the Soviet Union, Europe, China, and Japan, but in fact there is no assurance that hostilities would not spread to other parts of the world. Both Soviet and American leaders believe that the rivalry between their countries has worldwide ideological significance, and in the name of their causes they might well extend their attacks almost anywhere. It is easy to see that once the superpowers had absorbed several thousand megatons of nuclear explosives they no longer would *be* superpowers; indeed, they no longer would exist as nations at all. At that point, any sizable nation that had been spared – for example,

Vietnam, Mexico, Nigeria, Australia, or South Africa – becomes a potential target. Mere survival would be the stuff of global might, and either or both of the ex-superpowers might then set about destroying the surviving middle-ranking powers that seemed closest to sharing the ideology of the enemy. Again, it is impossible to know what thoughts would go through the minds of men in caves, or perhaps in airborne command posts, who had just carried out the slaughter of hundreds of millions of people and whose nations had been annihilated in a similar slaughter (and it should always be borne in mind that sheer insanity is one of the possibilities), but it could be that in some confused attempt to shape the political future of the post-holocaust world (if there is one) they would carry their struggle into the would-be-neutral world. It could be that even now the United States has a few dozen megatons reserved in one contingency plan or another for, say, Cuba, Vietnam, and North Korea, while the Soviet Union may have a similar fate in mind for, among others, Israel, South Africa, and Australia. We also have to ask ourselves what the Chinese, the French, and the British, who all possess nuclear arms, and the Israelis, the South Africans, and the Indians, who are all suspected of possessing them, would attempt once the mayhem began. And this list of nuclear-armed and possibly nuclear-armed countries shows every sign of being a growing one.

Although it may seem inappropriate to mention 'civilization' in the same breath as the death of hundreds of millions of people, it should at least be pointed out that a full-scale holocaust would, if it extended throughout the Northern Hemisphere, eliminate the civilizations of Europe, China, Japan, Russia, and the United States from the earth.

It would be a misrepresentation to say that human extinction is a certainty – just as it would be a misrepresentation to say that extinction can be ruled out. We know that a holocaust may not occur at all. If one does occur, the adversaries may not use all their weapons. If they do use all their weapons, the global effects, in the ozone and elsewhere, may be moderate. And if the effects are not moderate but extreme, the ecosphere may prove resilient enough to withstand them without breaking down catastrophically. These are all substantial reasons for supposing that mankind will not be extinguished in a nuclear holocaust, or even that extinction in a holocaust is unlikely, and they tend to calm our fear and to reduce our sense of urgency. Yet at the same time we are compelled to admit that there *may* be a holocaust, that the adversaries *may* use all their weapons, that the global effects, including effects of which we are as yet unaware, *may* be severe, that the ecosphere *may* suffer catastrophic breakdown, and that our species *may* be extinguished. We are left with uncertainty, and are forced to make our decisions in a state of uncertainty. If we wish to act to save our species, we have to muster our resolve in spite of our awareness that the life of the species may not now in fact be jeopardized. On the other hand, if we wish to ignore the peril, we have to admit that we do so in the knowledge that the species may be in danger of imminent self-destruction.

When the existence of nuclear weapons was made known, thoughtful people everywhere in the world realized that if the great powers entered into a nuclear-arms race the human species would sooner or later face the possibility of extinction. They also realized that in the absence of international agreements preventing it an arms race would probably occur. They knew that the path of nuclear armament was a dead end for mankind. The discovery of the energy in mass – of 'the basic power of the universe' – and of a means by which man could release that energy altered the relationship between man and the source of his life, the earth. In the shadow of this power, the earth became small and the life of the human species doubtful. In that sense, the question of human extinction has been on the political agenda of the world ever since the first nuclear weapon was detonated, and there was no need for the world to build up its present tremendous arsenals before starting to worry about it. At just what point the species crossed, or will have crossed, the boundary between merely having the technical knowledge to destroy itself and actually having the arsenals at hand, ready to be used at any second, is not precisely knowable. But it is clear that at present, with some twenty thousand megatons of nuclear explosive power in existence, and with more being added every day, we have entered into the zone of uncertainty, which is to say the zone of risk of extinction. But the mere risk of extinction has a significance that is categorically different from, and immeasurably greater than, that of any other risk, and as we make our decisions we have to take that significance into account. Up to now, every risk has been contained within the frame of life; extinction would shatter the frame. It represents not the defeat of some purpose but an abyss in which all human purposes would be drowned for all time. We have no right to place the possibility of this limitless, eternal defeat on the same footing as risks that we run in the ordinary conduct of our affairs in our particular transient moment of human history. To employ a mathematical analogy, we can say that although the risk of extinction may be fractional, the stake is, humanly speaking, infinite, and a fraction of infinity is still infinity. In other words, once we learn that a holocaust *might* lead to extinction we have no right to gamble, because if we lose, the game will be over, and neither we nor anyone else will ever get another chance. Therefore, although, scientifically speaking, there is all the difference in the world between the mere possibility that a holocaust will bring about extinction and the certainty of it, morally they are the same, and we have no choice but to address the issue of nuclear weapons as though we knew for a certainty that their use would put an end to our species. In weighing the fate of the earth and, with it, our own fate, we stand before a mystery, and in tampering with the earth we tamper with a mystery. We are in deep ignorance. Our ignorance should dispose us to wonder, our wonder should make us humble, our humility should inspire us to reverence and caution, and our reverence and caution should lead us to act without delay to withdraw the threat we now pose to the earth and to ourselves.

In trying to describe possible consequences of a nuclear holocaust, I have mentioned the limitless complexity of its effects on human society and on the ecosphere – a complexity that sometimes seems to be as great as that of life itself. But if these effects should lead to human extinction, then all the complexity will give way to the utmost simplicity – the simplicity of nothingness. We – the human race – shall cease to be.

NOTES ON CONTRIBUTORS

'The Modern Common Wind' is from a novel of the same title that **Don Bloch** is currently completing. Bloch spent a year in western Kenya working with anthropologists on a study of the treatment of leprosy. He has just returned from Indonesia and is now living in Amsterdam. Parts of **Russell Hoban**'s *Riddley Walker* originally appeared in *Granta*. He is the author of over forty books for children, and has just completed a new novel, *Pilgermann*. Russell Hoban lives near the District Line, and spends much of his time playing with computers and radios. **Susan Sontag** contributed to the first issue of the new series of *Granta*. **T. Coraghessan Boyle** has worked as a professional tennis player, an estuarine ecologist, a bartender, a rock and roll musician, and is currently a professor of English literature. His first collection of stories, *Descent of Man*, was published by Victor Gollancz Ltd, who also publish *Water Music*, in which 'Mungo among the Moors' appears. *Water Music* is available at £8.95. **Lisa St Aubin de Terán** was born in London in 1953, left England at the age of sixteen, and, with her Venezuelan husband, travelled for two years in Italy before settling at her husband's family home in the Andes. After seven years, during which time she managed a sugar plantation and an avocado farm, she returned to England with her daughter. 'Keepers of the House' is her first published work and is from the novel of the same title that Jonathan Cape publishes this summer. **John L'Heureux** is the author of eight books of fiction. He lives in California. **Ted Mooney** is an editor at *Art in America*. His first novel, *Easy Travel to other Planets*, will be published in Britain later this summer. **Jorge Ibarguengoitia** is from the Basque countries in Spain and is currently living in Paris. 'The Dead Girls' is his first work to appear in English. Parts of Leonard Michaels' first novel, *The Men's Club*, originally appeared in *Granta*. Jonathan Schell was born in 1944 and has been a staff writer for the *New Yorker* for several years. He is the author of *The Village of Ben Suc*, *The Military Half*, and *The Time of Illusion*. His article is from *The Fate of the Earth* which Jonathan Cape and Pan Books co-publish in June.

www.ingramcontent.com/pod-product-compliance
Lightning Source LLC
La Vergne TN
LVHW010605100826
845148LV00014B/2861